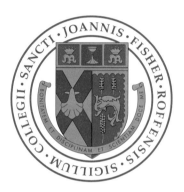

Lavery Library

St. John Fisher

College

Rochester, New York

ORGANIZING
SILENCE

SUNY Series in Communication Studies
Dudley D. Cahn, Editor

ORGANIZING SILENCE

A World of Possibilities

ROBIN PATRIC CLAIR

State University
of New York
Press

Chapter 4 was previously published in "The Use of Framing Devices to Sequester Organizational Narratives: Hegemony and Harassment," *Communication Monographs, 60,* 113–136. © 1993 by Speech Communication Association (SCA). Reprinted by Permission of SCA.

Chapter 5 was previously published in "The Bureaucratization, Commodification, and Privatization of Sexual Harassment through Institutional Discourse: A Study of the Big Ten Universities," *Management Communication Quarterly, 7,* 123–157. © 1993 Sage Publications, Inc. Reprinted by Permission of Sage Publications, Inc.

Chapter 6 was previously published in "Resistance and Oppression as a Self-Contained Opposite: An Organizational Communication Analysis of One Man's Story of Sexual Harassment," *Western Journal of Communication, 58,* 235–262. © 1994 Western States Communication Association (WSCA). Reprinted by permission of WSCA.

Cover photos by Jim Clair. All rights reserved.
Cover design by Robin Clair. All rights reserved.
Name index by Pamela Chapman Sanger.
Subject index by Robin Clair.

Published by
State University of New York Press, Albany

© 1998 State University of New York

Production by Susan Geraghty
Marketing by Anne Valentine

Printed in the United States of America

For information, address State University of New York
Press, State University Plaza, Albany, N.Y., 12246

Library of Congress Cataloging-in-Publication Data

Clair, Robin Patric.
    Organizing silence : a world of possibilities / by Robin Patric
Clair.
        p.   cm. — (SUNY series in speech communication)
    Includes bibliographical references (p.   ) and index.
    ISBN 0-7914-3941-0 (alk. paper). — ISBN 0-7914-3942-9 (pbk. :
alk. paper)
        1. Silence. 2. Communication. 3. Sexual harassment.
    4. Communication in organizations. 5. Resistance (Psychoanalysis)
    6. Aesthetics. I. Title. II. Series.
    P95.53.C58   1998
    302.2—dc21   97-47048
                                                                              CIP

10 9 8 7 6 5 4 3 2 1

LET YOUR WORDS FLY

—Cory Hack, 1993

CONTENTS

ACKNOWLEDGMENTS

Organizing Silence: A World of Possibilities is a book that has been several years in the making. Specifically, it has unfolded over the last decade. During that time, I was influenced by a number scholars and introduced to exciting theoretical perspectives from a variety of academic disciplines. Reflecting on what made this book possible, I realize that what influenced me extends well beyond the ivy-covered brick walls of the academic world. This book has matured as I have listened to the voices of others—in and out of academe. It draws from my own day-to-day exchanges as well as the lived experiences of others. As such, it is beyond my ability to acknowledge everyone who made this book possible, but I can highlight some of those people who were most directly influential in helping me to create and shape this book.

An earlier version of the first chapter of this book, "The First Word Was Silence," appeared as a conference paper in 1986 under the title of "Sound Tools: The Nurturing Source of Language." It was presented at the International Communication Association's (ICA) annual meeting in Chicago, Illinois. Jo Liska's guidance was essential to this early conference paper. This same paper may not have had its debut at ICA without the careful editing of my best and toughest critic, my husband, Tim Hack. Later, Dennis Mumby introduced me to the works of Michel Foucault, whose insights were included in the revisions of the conference paper into its current form. Chapter 1, and all of the following chapters in this book, received the careful editing attention of Pamela Chapman Sanger and Diane Witmer. Their insights were invaluable.

The second chapter in this book, "Silencing Communication," is original and has not appeared elsewhere. My main concern about chapter 2, which is intended to act as an overview of different treatments on the topic of silence, is that because volumes upon volumes have been written on the subject of silence, it was obvious that my review had to be somewhat exclusive. I hope that the works I selected to represent the numerous philosophical positions on silence provide at least an introduction to the reader.

Chapter 3, "Organizing Silence," first appeared as a conference paper under a different title. I presented the paper at the Speech Communication Association's (SCA) annual meeting in Miami, Florida in

1993. The paper received a Top Paper Award. I am indebted to Kathy Miller, who acted as respondent to this paper at the SCA conference and provided both compliments and constructive criticism.

In part II, I present three chapters, each of which has been previously published. All three chapters were presented as conference papers prior to their current form.

Chapter 4, "The Use of Framing Devices to Sequester Organizational Narratives: Hegemony and Harassment," received a Top Paper award from SCA as a conference paper and was recognized by the Organization for the Study of Communication, Gender, and Language as an outstanding conference paper. Once published as an article in 1993 in *Communication Monographs* (volume 60), this article received the Article of Year Award from the Organizational Communication division of SCA as well as the Golden Anniversary Award. These honors are greatly appreciated, but I cannot take full credit. The project could not have been completed without the assistance of many individuals and institutions. First, I must thank Cleveland State University for supplying a research grant that funded the study. Second, I would like to thank Betsy Campbell, Katie Namen, Cindy Rauser, Annie Streepy, Kelly Thompson, and Mike McGoun for their outstanding work on this project. Furthermore, Dennis Mumby, Ed Schiappa, and the *Communication Monograph* reviewers and editor, Chuck Bantz, offered valuable advice and criticisms along the way. Finally, Tim Hack and Jill Rudd offered support as I struggled with the sensitive issue of sexual harassment.

Chapter 5, "The Bureaucratization, Commodification, and Privatization of Sexual Harassment through Institutional Discourse: A Study of the 'Big Ten' Universities," began as a small project that Cynthia Stohl encouraged me to expand. An earlier version of this manuscript was presented as a conference paper at the Speech Communication Association's 1992 annual meeting which was held in Chicago. That version of the manuscript highlighted the rhetorical aspects, while a second manuscript presented at the International Communication Association's 1993 conference focused on the interpretation of the data collected. As the project developed, Linda Putnam and Ed Schiappa both provided critical comments that helped me to shape the work into a completed manuscript for publication. The article was published in 1993, in *Management Communication Quarterly* (volume 7). I would like to thank the reviewers and the editor of *MCQ*, Kathy Miller, for their insights.

Chapter 6, "Resistance and Oppression as a Self-Contained Opposite: An Organizational Communication Analysis of One Man's Story of Sexual Harassment," was first presented as a conference paper at the 1994 ICA annual meeting in Sydney, Australia. It was published later that year in the *Western Journal of Communication* (volume 58). Darla Williams, Diane Grimes, and Monya Emery provided me with illuminating conversations that taught me the critical importance of race in any and all discussions of power. Finally, I would like to thank the *WJC* reviewers and editor, Sandra Petronio, for their insightful comments. In addition, Purdue University generously provided me with a one-semester research leave that allowed me to focus on my research.

In part III, I present three original chapters. An earlier version of chapter 7, "When Silence Speaks: A Discussion of Self-Contained Opposites" was presented at the 1997 annual meeting of the National Communication Association (NCA) and received a Top Paper Award. The current chapter has benefited from the advice of Connie Bullis. Chapter 8, "Artful Practices and the Aesthetic Perspective" benefited from a variety of readings that were suggested by several of my colleagues, including Heidi Gottfried, Dennis Mumby, Cynthia Stohl, Paaige Turner, and Darla Williams. The final chapter of this book, "From Whispers to . . . ," includes a reprint of portions of various speeches that were presented at a special event hosted by the Speech Communication Association in 1996, in San Diego, California. Specifically, this event was sponsored by Judith Trent, the First Vice President of the Speech Communication Association. Judith Trent plans to publish all of the speeches presented at this event in their entirety. I look forward to seeing this collection in press and wish to thank her and the individual contributors. In addition, I would like to thank Rachel Pokora for attending this event with me. The purpose of the final chapter is to remind us that our organizational practices are not isolated. Organization, silence, and aesthetics are part of a wider political picture.

I would like to reiterate my thanks to all who have helped make this book a reality. This includes those people whose names must remain pseudonymous to protect their privacy. It also includes the undergraduate students I have taught who have, over the years, often opened my eyes to issues I had not noticed. Likewise, it includes the professors who guided me through my undergraduate and graduate career. It further includes past and current graduate students whom I have had the privilege to work with, and who have frequently introduced me to readings that I might have missed. For example, Stephanie Baron, Jennifer Birch Szolwinski, Pamela Chapman Sanger, Len Cox, Mariane Dorris, Mary Keehner, Adrianne Kunkel, Ramsey Eric Ramsey, Angela Tretheway, Paaige Turner, Ron Wendt, and Darla Williams (to name a few) each introduced me to a variety of articles, books, or ideas that helped me to frame my thoughts for this book. I would like to thank Beverly Robinson, who assisted me in the preparation of this manuscript in terms of typing, and Kelly Douds, who worked on the final revisions. Once again, I thank Diane Witmer and Pamela Chapman Sanger for their editorial work. And I would like to thank Priscilla Ross at SUNY Press who saw potential in the proposal for this undertaking. Further, I wish to thank Patricia Geist, Gail Fairhurst, and Patrice Buzzanell, as well as my "blind" reviewers.

At this point, I will apologize to those whom I have neglected in these acknowledgments. Many people over the years have influenced my thoughts and provided me with advice and direction. Traces of their influence can be seen in this book.

Finally, I would like to thank my family, specifically, my husband, Timothy Hack, and my children, Cory, Calle, and Shea, who patiently lived through this project.

INTRODUCTION

The title of this book, *Organizing Silence*, can be interpreted in at least two ways. My intention is that it should capture two distinctly unique and yet overlapping meanings simultaneously. Specifically, it refers to the ways in which the interests, issues, and identities of marginalized people are silenced *and* how those silenced voices can be organized in ways to be heard. Furthermore, *Organizing Silence*, as an expression, is intended to represent the complex, dialectical, and sometimes paradoxical aspects of silence and voice. They should be thought of less as bifurcated concepts and more as self-contained opposites. But the image of a self-contained opposite is not intended to make one feel trapped. I do not intend to position the reader in a theoretical claustrophobic conundrum. The circular aspect does not mandate closure or an infinite regress.

In the subtitle of this book, *A World of Possibilities*, it is my intention to provide a theoretical view of the world that provides for creative expressions, creative explorations, and creative solutions to some of the problems we face today. The guiding perspective employed here is an *aesthetic perspective*. Not to get too far ahead of myself here, but in chapters 8 and 9 you will read the following quotes:

> Aesthetic theory provides a unique philosophy as it is grounded in paradox, defies closure, acts as resistance, and intensifies plurality and confusion. (Clair & Kunkel, in press; also cited in chapter 8)

> Simultaneously, an aesthetic perspective calls for a poetic interpretation, an ability to see the spirit or soul of a phenomenon, a rendering that is both rich and veracious, and an expression of the phenomenon that recognizes and recapitulates obscure relationships. Aesthetic perspective provides for the juxtaposition of unexpected insights. It playfully captures the chiaroscuro of the life experience in both its vibrancy and its shadows without dismissing a sensuous and serious portrayal of the depths, the curves, the intricacies and the interstices of life. (see chapter 9)

Although my choice of words to describe the aesthetic perspective are *drawn* primarily from a visual art vocabulary, aesthetic theorists are not constrained by these metaphoric images. My bachelor's degree was in art education. Creating art, enjoying art, and reading about art continues to be one of my passions. My choice is more the result of my artistic background in the visual arts than any restriction placed on the conceptualization of the term *aesthetics*. Art comes in many forms. An aesthetic perspective could include more linguistic choices to highlight other creative forms like orchestration and choreography, poetics and prose, rap and performance, to name but a few. As the discussion of an aesthetic perspective unfolds within this book, I hope the readers will apply whatever metaphors they find most useful in order to connect with the aesthetic perspective being presented in *Organizing Silence*.

This is a scholarly book that approaches the topic of silence as having a rich historical past, an institutional grounding, a vicious means of oppressing marginalized groups, and the possibility to emancipate. This book situates silence as an expressive activity by looking at how certain means of expression have silenced particular groups and how silence can be appropriated into resistance. For example, women have been silenced through a variety of means including physical coercion (Jaimeson, 1988) as well as through linguistic practices (Daly, 1973; Jaimeson, 1988; Penelope, 1990; Spender, 1980). With respect to language, Spender asserts that:

> It is a mark of the sexism of linguistics as a discipline that in all the research which has been done on the history of the language the question of the role played by women in its production and development has received virtually no attention: indeed such a question has not even been asked! (Spender, 1980, p. 32)

Instead, in chapter 1, "The First Word Was Silence," I ask the question that Spender (1980) asserts "has received virtually no attention." I begin my search for the origin of language as well as the origin of silence based on the assumption that marginalized members of society have been excluded as participants in theories that seek the origin of language. This failure to be inclusive has provided theories that fail to speak to the diversity of humanity and to the relationship of language and silence. I explore the possibilities that women and children and men were involved in the creation and development of language. As I explore the origins of language, I find with it, in the same shared space, the origin of silence.

In chapter 2, "Silencing Communication," I review select treatises on the topic of silence, beginning with the early work of Charles Courtenay, whose book is entitled *Empire of Silence*, through to contemporary perspectives that draw from feminist, critical, and postmodern approaches. I then suggest that four themes might be useful in guiding further discussion of silence: (1) subjectivity, (2) the dynamic, dialectical, and self-contained aspects of silence/\language, (3) the interplay and coexistence of micro/\macro level episodes, and (4) the self-contained aspects of resistance/\oppression. The symbol "/\" is used throughout *Organizing Silence: A World of Possibilities* as an indicator that the phenomena coexist and often give impetus to each other. I first used this symbol in 1986 when I envisioned the mother/\infant relationship as giving rise to each other. This symbol, "/\," and the meaning it conveys should become clearer in the following chapters.

In chapter 3, "Organizing Silence," I briefly review a select aspect of Antonio Gramsci's work, in order to establish a framework for discussing coercion and hegemony as means to silence certain groups of people. I also mention the strengths and weaknesses of Gramsci's conceptualization of these issues to explain contemporary forms of silencing or marginalizing certain members of society, especially women and minorities. In addition, I discuss how the labeling of people into groups, such as "women" and "minorities," fails to capture the dynamic plurality of identities. Furthermore, the notion of a plurality of subject positions (a concept most thoroughly developed by Laclau and Mouffe) suggests that marginalized members could be silencing each other. I explore the ways in which these marginalized groups privilege and abandon themselves and each other, respectively, and I use sexual harassment to illustrate these concepts.

In part II, I present three chapters: chapter 4—"The Use of Framing Devices to Sequester Organizational Narrative: Hegemony and Harassment," chapter 5—"The Bureaucratization, Commodification, and Privatization of Sexual Harassment through Institutional Discourse: A Study of the 'Big Ten' Universities," and chapter 6—"Resistance and Oppression as a Self-Contained Opposite: An Organizational Communication Analysis of One Man's Story of Sexual Harassment." Each of these chapters uses sexual harassment experiences as the focal point to discuss the organizing of the silencing of marginalized members of society.

In chapter 4, I focus on the stories of sexual harassment that have been sequestered in organizations. Specifically, I present the stories of women who report having been sexually harassed. I explore their stories in terms of how they *frame* their discourse in ways that might perpetuate their own silence, which creates a hegemonic form of control. It does not escape me that some of their framing techniques might also provide a form of resistance or strategy for survival, but I discuss that in more detail later.

In chapter 5, I focus on how institutional discourse is framed so that it organizes silence in a subtle way. Specifically, I explore the university communiqués concerning sexual harassment. I collected the brochures and other formal materials concerning how people should respond to sexual harassment from the "Big Ten" universities. In this chapter, I offer a critique of how these institutional discourses that are intended to provide a recourse for the victims of sexual harassment, in many ways, only perpetuate the situation and complicate the silencing of the victims of sexual harassment.

In chapter 6, I focus on exploring not the victims' discourse nor the organization's discourse individually, rather I attempt to explore how the victims may be the oppressors and how discourses of resistance can become entangled with discourses of oppression. In this chapter, I attempt to complicate what I have previously attempted to isolate. Here, the idea of the plurality of subject positions is discussed. The notion that communication can be silencing is spotlighted. The idea that the micro-level gives definition to the macro-level—so that each seems to be contained in the other—is exposed. Finally, the idea that resistance and oppression exist in a complicated tension, in a self-contained opposite, is highlighted. All of these issues take form based on one man's story of sexual harassment.

In part III of this book, I attempt to provide a perspective that allows us to reach beyond the somewhat nihilist and defeatist discourses that are sometimes attached to a postmodern perspective. However, I also believe that the postmodern perspective provides tremendous possibilities. I, therefore, draw from the postmodern reservoir of ideas to develop a perspective that accepts the ironies of life, and, at the same time, allows us to challenge those ironies. I draw from feminist perspectives as I simultaneously illustrate feminist perspectives in a new light. It seems to me that most feminist perspectives are laudably engaged in dealing with the oppression and domination of marginalized people, to the point of forgetting to applaud themselves for just how creative and vital they are. I envision feminist forms of expression as art, as the pièce de résistance because their works not only speak of resistance, but also achieve a unique artistic expression that exceeds much of the scholarly work that discusses resistance. In short, the phrase—pièce de résistance—can be applied to feminist works both literally and figuratively. But before exploring these thoughts, I provide additional discussion of the self-contained opposite of resistance/\oppression in chapter 7.

In chapter 7, "When Silence Speaks: A Discussion of Self-Contained Opposites," I review the arguments concerning an antihegemonic versus a counterhegemonic approach to organizing and explain the silences of select groups of people. I then review contemporary work that relies on self-contained opposites to explain sustained silence, especially in the workplace. Finally, I suggest that the value of these articles has yet to be awarded their due. The richness of these works that focus on the self-contained opposite of resistance and oppression should certainly give pause to the reader and may even give inspiration as to how we can explore these issues in the future.

In chapter 8, "Artful Practices and the Aesthetic Perspective," I discuss the artful practices of resistance. Michel de Certeau's concept of *bricolage* and *la perruque* set the stage for a discussion of silent forms of resistance. How silenced or marginalized groups find creative ways to resist the dominant discourses and material practices of oppression is discussed. I advance an aesthetic perspective as useful for exploring social relations. After briefly reviewing traditional discussions on the ontology of aesthetics, I introduce a contemporary view of aesthetics that has been influenced by several feminist scholars. This is followed by a review of how organizational scholars are using aesthetic theories to unravel the mysteries of organizational life and how they might continue to use aesthetic theories to address the organization of silence.

In the final chapter of this book, "From Whispers to . . . ," I summarize the themes of organizing silence, especially as it relates to a variety of organizations. I then discuss how our organizational realities might be explored from an aesthetic perspective. Aesthetics are discussed in terms of ontology, epistemology, methodology, and expressiveness. I then present a few examples of different ways that we might begin to listen to the silences. I add that we should not think that an aesthetic perspective marginalizes discursive or rhetorical approaches to the study of power and social relations. For example, rhetoric can be explored for its aesthetic characteristics, aesthetics can be explored for its persuasion, and together they might provide a unique outlook on the topic of organizing silence. I conclude the book by providing an example of an organization that takes upon itself the task of organizing silence so that we can hear the voices speak.

PART I

CHAPTER 1

The First Word Was Silence

I can hear the silence,
and through it individual sounds.
—Eva Figes, 1987

Origins have piqued the curiosity of philosophers throughout the ages. From the origin of the universe to the origin of the human species, scientists, scholars, sages, and poets have set forth propositions to explain the birth of particular phenomena. Possibly, the most sought-after origin is the quest to understand how language began. Although theories of the origin of language abound, few mention or develop the role of silence. In 1948, Picard provided a notable and early exception when he wrote:

> Speech came out of silence, out of the fullness of silence. The fullness of silence would have exploded if it had not been able to flow out into speech. . . . There is something silent in every word, as an abiding token of the origin of speech. And in every silence there is something of the spoken word, as an abiding token of the power of silence to create speech. (Picard, 1948/1952, p. 24)

Picard was unable to fathom an origin of language that did not rely on the hand of God, but he did recognize that, "Speech and silence belong together" (p. 36).

The expressive qualities of speech and the silencing aspects of communication permeate our everyday presence as well as our rich historical past. Understanding the philosophical underpinnings of the relationship between silence and communication can contribute to our understanding "of the limits and power of language" (van Manen, 1990, p. 112). For example, we are told that "our ancestors constitute a living legacy for life in the 20th century" (Mortensen, 1991, p. 273) and that knowledge of language development or at least the "ecological conditions that made it possible" (p. 274) will help us "to understand elements of stress, strain, struggle, and strife in the social fabric" (p. 273). To seek the relationship of "communication, conflict, and culture" (Mortensen, 1991, p. 273) through exploring early linguistic development is a laudable goal. As Aarsleff (1982) points out, it is a goal that can eventually contribute to the development of knowledge concerning human nature.

3

It is equally important that our theories of the origin of language pursue questions concerning the origin of silence. Seeking the source of silence may provide sketches of the past that reflect the present and may have bearing on the future. Exploring silence as a fundamental part of communication, culture, and conflict may illuminate the complex nature of social relations. It is time to develop theories about the origin of silence and explore its continuing presence in our everyday lives.

Feminist theories provide uniquely promising advantages for exploring the origin, meanings, and functions of silence. These theories demand the inclusion of individuals who have been erased from historical accounts concerning the origin of language. In addition, feminist theories call for an uncovering or recovering of historical interpretations. Furthermore, feminist theories address bifurcations that are discursively created and artificially dissect phenomena like language and silence. I will briefly address each of these theoretical advantages for studying the origin of silence.

First, early theories of the origin of language not only marginalized silence, but also marginalized women and, to a lesser extent, children. Focusing on the invisibility of women in language origin theories, Spender (1980) writes:

> It is a mark of the sexism of linguistics as a discipline that in all the research which has been done on the history of language the question of the role played by women in its production and development has received virtually no attention; indeed such a question has not even been asked! (p. 32)

Thus, the inclusionary aspect of feminist theories should provide a place for women and children and other marginalized individuals within a discussion of silence and language.

Second, feminist theories encourage disrupting old theories in order to uncover their connections with a patriarchal politics. By doing so, the complacency with which women and silence have been marginalized in theories cannot sit comfortably in the corner. Daly (1973) argues that emancipation for women is dependent on uncovering "the silence about women's historical existence since the dawn of patriarchy" (p. 93). Thus, the goal of historical recovery held by a feminist perspective should provide a means to explore historical doctrines on silence as discourses rather than as dogma.

Finally, feminist researchers encourage the reversal of "figure-and-ground relationships" in order to break through constraints imposed by "taken for granted assumptions" (Putnam, 1982, p. 6; also see Dervin, 1993). The terms, *figure* and *ground* are artistic metaphors that are used to explain what is privileged, emphasized, or accented as opposed to what is marginalized, or reduced to being a supportive background. The reversal of figure and ground, for feminist theorists, is designed to uncover patriarchal implications. For example, feminists suggest that males have been privileged or positioned as *figure*, while women are marginalized and positioned as the *background*. With respect to communication, we can think of verbal language as *figure* in relation to nonverbal language as *ground*. Overcoming this general division can be achieved by acknowledging verbal and nonverbal communication as one system of symbolic expression (Langer, 1942; Liska, 1984). Yet this system of communication may still privilege itself in relation to silence by viewing symbolic expression or discursive practices as the vital and sparkling stars set against a vast black space of silence.

Reversing figure and ground, however beneficial, results in the privileging of one construct over another, which fails to release us from the bifurcation of two terms (e.g., silence and language). Derrida (1967/1973, 1967/1976) proposes that after the figure/ground reversal is achieved, researchers should extend beyond the reversal and attempt to escape the dichotomy altogether by creating a third term that both contains and escapes the present dichotomy.

Daly (1973) advises women to rely on the verb "being" in an effort to overcome the marginalization of nonbeing. Moving toward a third term, Dervin (1993) extends Daly's advice by suggesting that "being" can be achieved by addressing "the elusive moments of human communicatings" (p. 53). In particular, Dervin tells us to focus on the verbs, "the in between, the doing, the making, the experiencing" (p. 52), where the artificial dichotomies become one. Thus, we need to explore the silencing aspects of communication and the expressive aspects of silence. This kind of exploration is in agreement with the sort of synthesis that Glennon (1983) and numerous other feminist theorists call for, where "all of life will be a continual, becoming, unfolding dialectical process" (p. 271).

The quintessential example of the privileging of one term over another is apparent in the obsessive search for the origin of language to the neglect of the search for an origin of silence. Over and over again, scholars have attempted to pinpoint the specific situation or conditions that gave rise to the words and gestures we employ today. Bickerton (1981) points out that early theories of the origin of language suffer from their reliance on a Cartesian mind-set. Subsequently, most language-origin theories split verbal from nonverbal communication (Condillac offers an exception—see Aarsleff, 1982; Peaden, 1993). Even if the theories overcome this initial bifurcation (i.e., verbal/nonverbal distinction), they often fall victim to the practice of conceptualizing silence in a *literal* sense, without addressing the *epistemological* and *ontological* aspects of silence (van Manen, 1990).

APPROACHES TO SILENCE

Van Manen (1990) organizes approaches to silence into three categories; literal, epistemological, and ontological. Literal approaches to
the understanding of silence view the phenomenon as the space between
the words. These silences can be awkward or poetic, chilling or rebel-
lious. They function in a variety of ways (e.g., as the silent treatment,
tender concern, forceful condemnation, comfortable intimacy, shared
understanding). The literal approach to silence may be the most prevalent in communication scholarship (see Jaworski, 1993, for a review of
literal approaches to silence).

The epistemological approach to conceptualizing silence is
grounded in Polanyi's (1958, 1969) philosophy of tacit knowledge.
Tacit knowledge is the phenomenon of knowing without being able to
articulate what we know. At times, we may discover that we are unable
to articulate an experience, but others are capable of expressing it for us.
At other times, the experience simply cannot not be described in everyday language and only the talents of an artist can render it visible.
Finally, van Manen (1990) suggests that the unspeakable aspects may
only be temporary and as time passes we may be able to express the
experience or knowledge. It is also possible that we choose not to
express certain experiences.

The third approach to silence, the ontological approach, is "the
silence of Being or Life itself" (van Manen, 1990, p. 114). Here van
Manen draws from Bollnow (1982, as cited in van Manen, 1990), who
describes the silence of life as instilling a sense of awe and inspiration
"that fulfills and yet craves fulfillment" (van Manen, 1990, p. 114).

In addition to these three approaches to understanding silence, one
more perspective must be added. An *ideological perspective*, which is
distinct from the previous three approaches, is necessary to illumine the
silencing of marginalized groups of people. Scholars from the critical
school, the postmodern school, and a variety of feminist schools of
thought recognize the complex and oppressive aspects of ideological
silence. The scholars and activists holding these perspectives have been
most vocal in recognizing the power of silence to also act as resistance.
In the search for a moment where language and silence coincide giving
rise to each other, it is necessary to draw upon the rich body of feminist
scholarship that views silence as ideological, as a powerful aspect of
oppression and possible means to emancipation (e.g., Ardener, 1975;
Daly, 1973; Jamieson, 1988; MacKinnon, 1979, 1989; Penelope, 1990;
Rich, 1984). Other discussions of the silencing nature of certain forms
of communication can be found in the works of critical and postmodern
scholars (e.g., de Certeau, 1986; Deetz, 1992; Habermas, 1979; Fou-

cault, 1966/1973, 1976/1990, 1978). In addition, many scholars combine perspectives in order to address the power of silence (e.g., Jaworski,
1993; Weedon, 1987). The struggle for people to be heard over oppressive governments or patriarchal practices must not be overlooked in this
review of the origin of language theories and the subsequent discussion
of silence and expression.

BACK TO ORIGINS

It is true that many scholars suggest that it is a futile endeavor to expend
energy on the search for origins, as the result can always be challenged
and the answer may be elusive (Derrida, 1967/1976; Foucault,
1966/1973, Kristeva, 1981/1989; Mortensen, 1991; Raffler-Engel,
1988).[1] Yet I do not seek out a definitive truth about a specific origin;
rather, I seek out any possible foundational situation that might express
how silence and linguistic/gestural communication coincide—how
silence may be expressive and how expressive activity can be silencing.
Furthermore, it has been argued that to seek alternative origins is to provide a sense of hope that possibilities for changing and ameliorating the
current social order can and do exist (Lerner, 1986).

Hekman (1990) suggests that both feminist and postmodernist discourses "challenge the modern episteme at its roots" (p. 190). Yet the
"roots" of language (i.e., the origin of language) have not been challenged from a feminist perspective. Before searching for the origins of
expressive silence and the silencing of expression, it is necessary to
review what has been privileged in this theoretical quest.

ORIGIN OF LANGUAGE THEORIES

Origin of language theories are numerous and varied. Past explanations
range from the Divine to the genetic, from physiological to neurological,
from emotional cries to infant babbling (Hewes, 1973). Some theories
rest on the serendipitous discovery of words; others are grounded in
elaborate theories of survival and economics. Various linguistic theories
suggest that language originated with interjections, songs, imitation of
natural sounds, or imitation of tool sounds (Stross, 1976). One theory
even suggests that primitive people needed language to facilitate hunting
and therefore language was born. Theories of the origin of language
were so numerous that by 1866 the Société de Linguistiques de Paris
refused to accept any additional papers dealing with the topic (Aarsleff,
1982; Gans, 1982; Hewes, 1973; Hockett, 1960).

Major scientific and philosophical advances of the mid-1900s spurred researchers toward new attempts at explaining the enigmatic origin of language.[2] In spite of this flurry of theoretical activity, no scholars explored the origins of silence. Perhaps scholars assumed that before there were words and symbolic gestures there was a void—silence—and that the development of language would not affect that silence. Silence was and generally is perceived as a passive background to the noisy activity of communication.

Mortensen's (1991) recent contribution to the field of language origin studies makes room for silence as a phenomenon that reaches beyond the pauses between words. He writes:

> the selection of those who speak is at the expense of nonspeakers. What matters in the long run is not simply the survival of the expressively most fit but also the disappearance of the least articulate. From an evolutionary standpoint, the most basic principle of communicative competence involves nothing less inclusive than the total magnitude of what is lost or gained from what is expressed or left unexpressed. (p. 287)

It is also important to note that communication competence may play a lesser role in the silencing of groups of people than some scholars might imply. Articulate individuals have been literally silenced (e.g., through executions) and virtually silenced (e.g., through imprisonment or exile) merely due to their affiliation with marginalized groups; and communicatively incompetent people have been privileged due in large part to their affiliation with a privileged group. Nevertheless, the sentiment that the unexpressed is equally important to the expressed is worthy of note and has not escaped the attention of postmodern scholars.

Philosophical moves toward a postmodern understanding of the world led Foucault (1966/1973) to explore not only the origin of language, but its ironic conclusion that to seek the origin of the species is to reveal its end. Nevertheless, Foucault provides a detailed account of the origin and development of language (as understood by Classical scholars of the seventeenth and eighteenth centuries), which is grounded in the concepts of *proposition, articulation, designation, and derivation.*

The *theory of proposition,* also called the *theory of the verb,* argues that words do not become language until they contain a statement of proposition. Drawing from the work of Destutt, Foucault (1966/1973) suggests that:

> The yell of the primitive man [sic] in a struggle becomes a true word only when it is no longer the lateral expression of his [sic] pain, and when it has validity as a judgment or as the statement of the type "I am choking." . . . It is in fact the proposition that detaches the vocal sign from its immediate expressive values and establishes its supreme linguistic possibility. (p. 92)

Drawing from Hobbes, Foucault explains that it is the verb that establishes the proposition.[3] Subject and object can both be contained within the verb. The verb, acting as *language activity*, moves beyond the simple primitive expression. Relying on the work of Condillac and Destutt, famous linguists of the Port Royal, Foucault explains that all verbs can be reduced to the verb *to be*.

The *theory of articulation* suggests that the naming of things (i.e., the noun) is certainly important to the development of language, but is secondary to the verb *to be*. Without statements of proposition or affirmation the noun would be virtually useless or at least terribly difficult to develop into language. Thus, the first stage of articulation rests on the notion that verbs represent both process and relationship, which allow for displacement. Language is equated with the articulation of sounds or cries of expression. But what phonemes may have designated the verb *to be*? What phonemes might have designated *language activity*?

The *theory of designation* resulted in a proliferation of etymological activity and a search for the universal or root phoneme(s) that capture(s) the essence of language. Foucault (1966/1973) suggests that

> the theory of roots in no way contradicts the analysis of the language of action, but is to be found within it. . . . Roots are those rudimentary words that are to be found, always identical, in a great number of languages—perhaps in all; they have been imposed upon language by nature in the form of involuntary cries spontaneously employed by the language of action. (p. 107)[4]

Foucault (1966/1973) argues that the general theme of the Port Royal theorists collapses into a needs orientation.[5] For Foucault, the story of two hungry men, who articulate their needs before they are so overcome by hunger as to cry out, represents a possible origin of language as understood from a Classical perspective. The linguistic question then is how this meaningful representation of hunger develops into a rich and complex form of discursive activity. The critical question is why Foucault relies on two men to exemplify his position at the expense of women. I will deal with each question in turn.

The *theory of derivation*, as developed by Condillac, suggests that the representation can be recalled and attached to some other element that is similar in some fashion to the first thing or process named. Thus, the Classical theorists advanced the notion of resemblance through rhetorical devices. Three forms of rhetoric were considered especially pertinent to the derivation of language. They are "synecdoche, metonymy, and catachresis (or metaphor, if the analogy is less immediately perceptible)" (Foucault, 1966/1973, pp. 113–114). For example, "it is no longer a particular oak that is called a *tree*, but anything that includes at least a trunk and branches . . . *night* came to designate, not the end of this particular day, but the period of darkness separating all sunsets from all dawns. Finally, . . . everything was called a *leaf* that was as thin and flexible as the leaf of a tree" (p. 113).

Thus, the Classical School of thought and specifically the theorists of the Port Royal generally perceived the origin of language as a leap from the primitive expression to an articulation of the *language of activity* (i.e., the proposition, the verb), to naming (although some theorists posited that naming preceded the verb), to a designation of meaning, and finally, to a derivation of the term to represent other distinct, yet similar elements and processes. An important aspect of this Classical understanding of the origin of language is *naming* (Foucault, 1966/1973; Langer, 1942/1951). And in this naming came an ontological presence over that which was named.

It is ironic that women have not been *named* as contributors to the creation and development of language. They are virtually invisible in the past and current hypotheses of language origin. Their lives are silenced as if they did not and do not exist. It is time to ask the question that Spender (1980) claims has not yet been asked: What role did women play in the production and development of language?

The following rendering of the origin of language draws in part from the Classical School's criteria of conditions for the origin of language as well as evolutionary, etymological, and ecological models. Further, it advances a feminist position, which rejects the general Classical School of thought that views language solely as the representation of reality and embraces the position that communication both *reflects* and *creates* our realities and that women did indeed participate in the creation of language/\silence. The expressions *language/\silence* or *silence/\language* are ways of denoting that the two phenomena exist simultaneously in a shared space, influencing each other.

A FEMINIST RENDERING OF THE
ORIGINS OF SILENCE/\LANGUAGE

The present rendering of the origin of language, and with it silence, follows the Classical tradition by first establishing the basis for the *expression of the proposition*. In order to do that, it is important to situate prelinguistic people in an evolutionary frame. An evolutionary model is well supported by primate studies (Berstein, 1970; Chevalier-Skolnikoff, 1982; Ettinger, 1977; Gardner & Gardner, 1969; Gerswind, 1970; Hockett, 1960; Jay, 1965; Lieberman, Philip, Crelin & Klatt, 1972; Osman-Hill, 1972; Tanner, 1981; Tanner & Zihlman, 1976). I will take the lib-

erty of highlighting primate studies that emphasize the mother/infant relationship, which may contribute to the development of expressive activity.
This choice is justified in the following sections.

MOTHER/INFANT RELATIONSHIP:
A MODEL FOR LANGUAGE DEVELOPMENT

There are several close relationships within any human society, including maternal/filial, paternal/filial, sibling relationships, mate relationships (be they heterosexual or homosexual relationships), and friend-
ships, just to name a few. However, I will argue here that the most likely
candidate to support the development of the *expression of the proposition* is the maternal/filial relationship. Before proceeding, I must make
two points quite clear. First, my use of the mother/infant relationship in
no way supports that women are "naturally" maternal. Nor do I intend
any reverse chauvinism. Instead, I base this choice on several premises
drawn primarily from evolutionary propositions and primate studies.[6]
   The mother/infant relationship as a model for language development is conducive with several origin of language theories. In 1942,
Langer suggested that the infant's ability to prattle and chatter is a key
component in the development of language. The bubbleluck or babbling
theory of 1943 proposed by Thorndike suggests that baby babbling
leads to vocalization, which in turn leads to word formation. An explanation for this process is not provided in Thorndike's theory (Hewes,
1977). Neither is the process fully developed by Langer. Nevertheless,
Langer offers an intriguing theory that both draws from and extends
Classical arguments on the topic. I will return to her criteria for language development later.
   More recently, Carini (1970) extends the baby babble theory and
attempts an explanation for the development of language. First, he suggests that it was necessary for an infant with the neurological and physical capabilities of babbling to mature and have an offspring with the
same linguistic potential. A healthy mother/infant relationship then provides an environment conducive to vocal play. The infant babbles and
the adult mimics the babbling in association with whatever the child
might be doing. Carini provides an example of his own child using nonsensical words while rocking in a certain fashion. The sound is imitated
by the parents and comes to mean "rocking a certain way."
   This theory can be criticized on several counts, yet it also provides
insight into the early relationships that were most conducive to developing and learning language. It can be criticized from the Classical perspective in that the nonsensical word fails to move beyond the stage of

articulation. It can be criticized from environmentalist and ecological viewpoints in that it does not afford a substantial need or motive for language to develop. It can be criticized from an etymological standpoint in that there are no traces of the specific nonsensical play word provided by Carini in modern language. However, it does provide support for the notion that language originated and developed within the nurturing relationship. This lends support to Revesz's (1946/1956) contact theory, which suggests that social contact is a necessary condition in the development of language. Thus, a nurturing and close relationship is crucial to understanding the development of language, yet in a very different way from Thorndike's or Carini's hypotheses.

IN THE BEGINNING THERE WAS SILENCE

Human infants have the capacity of expressing their biological needs through crying. This crying triggers a physiological reaction in adult human beings. The heart rate and blood pressure of the adult human increases and is accompanied by persistent feelings of annoyance and irritability (Frodi, 1985). A less than loving care-taker might escape this unpleasant situation by leaving. However, if the crying is affecting the entire community, as Frodi's (1985) work indicates, then something must be done. For example, a mother may have discovered that as she picked up the child and walked or rocked the infant the crying ceased. This phenomenon could be related to soothing intrauterine motion. It may be that walking or rocking a baby dates back to prelinguistic times. Most modern parents can attest to attempts to silence an infant through walking or rocking motions.

Expression of the Proposition

Imagine a mother with the neurological and physiological requirements for language. She might begin adding sounds to the rocking motion or they may have developed concomitantly. Had an early hominid mother made the sound 'sh' when the child cried and discovered it had a soothing affect she may have repeated it. The expression *sh* represents the *expression of the proposition* "to be quiet." It is important to note that the rocking motion equally expresses the proposition "to be quiet."

Sh is a logical choice for the linguistic representation of silence for several reasons. First, according to the work of Lieberman (1975) early hominids may have had less difficulty articulating voiceless fricatives or affricates (i.e., consonants sounds that do not depend on a vowel sound for articulation—e.g., *ch*, *sh*, *j*).[7]

Second, linguistic etymologists argue primordial roots rarely disappear from a language because they have been transmitted, transferred, or blended into so many other derivations. Thus, the root becomes frozen in time, a linguistic fossil of sorts (this notion is credited to Mary Foster as cited in Stross, 1976). Without a doubt, *sh* is apparent in modern languages in vocables from *hush* to *Shalom*. The *sh* sound calls for quiet and tranquillity and has been derived into numerous other meanings. Furthermore, the sound produced by the noise *sh* is linked to soothing sounds (whether one imagines wind or water) resulting in a natural sound symbolism, as discussed by Swadesh (1951, 1959).

In addition, the classic works of Susanne Langer (1942) and Kenneth Burke (1966) place the significance of humanity in symbol-making, symbol-using, and symbol-abusing activities. Specifically, Burke states that "Man [sic] is a symbol-using (symbol-making, symbol-misusing) animal . . . inventor of the negative or moralized by the negative" (p. 16). "To be silent" is also consistent with Burke's (1966) notion that language originated in the negative, especially the hortatory negative. That is, the expression "be silent" (e.g., *sh*) is to command that one shall not cry out.

In addition, Liska (1984) draws from Burke's notion of the negative and argues that the first symbol must certainly have been that of the negative of absence. The notion that the first *abstract* symbol required a nonreferential concept is consistent with the proposition *sh*. Silence is not something that early humans could point to.

Finally, *sh* meets the criteria set forth by Gans (1981) who claims that the first word of significance must have had the characteristics of an ostensive (i.e., a word that can both represent itself as well as command itself). Gans provides the example of "Run!"—*run* may indicate the act of running as well as the command that one should "Run!". His examples are self-admittedly weak since they are already established arbitrary symbols within a well-developed language. In other words, Gans asks himself and leaves us wondering where "Run!" came from; it seems to materialize from nowhere.

Although the root (i.e., *sh*) itself is common to several modern languages, I do not suggest that *sh* is the only term to be associated with this activity of calming an infant. For example, the clicking sounds that comprise the language of the Sandawe and Hadza nations of Northern Tanzania (Clarke, 1982) as well as the !Kung nation of the Kalahari (Marshall, 1958) may have been used to quiet the cries of a discontented infant. The purpose instead is to establish the *expression of the proposition* that is "to be silent."

However, neither the mother/\infant relationship, nor the production of the sound *sh* or other equivalent sounds or nonverbal substitutes (taken in isolation), secures the development of language (verbal or nonverbal). Nor do these hypotheses suggest the ecological or environmental impetus for the development of language. Although, as Langer (1942) suggests, the "need" may be the unique human desire to "express" oneself. Nevertheless, in order for an expression of proposition to move toward a symbolic state, the Classical scholars argue that it must establish *articulation, designation,* and *derivation.*

Articulation

If a sibling or any other member of the community showed interest in and an understanding of the expression of proposition, (e.g., *sh*), articulation could be achieved. As stated earlier, it is quite common for siblings to show intense interest in the mother/\infant exchanges among chimpanzees (Goodall, 1971; Jampel, 1984; Jay, 1965; Rumbaugh, 1977). We would expect no less of human children. If the human children imitated the sound with the same reference point, that is, if they said "sh" to quiet the same infant, then the proposition has been articulated, its meaning carried to another member of the community. Yet language is still not complete.

Designation

To extend beyond the initial articulation, the same expression of proposition must be extended to other reference points. For example, if the interested siblings of other caregivers in the community took up the use of *sh* to quiet other infants, then the meaning of the articulation would be sedimented. *Sh* is designated as the sign for silencing infants. This designation still fails to complete the level of symbolicity needed for language. It needs to be derived from the original referent to a similar yet distinct situation. In other words, it must maintain its meaning while developing to a more intense level of abstraction.

Derivation

Derivation may have occurred due to ecological and environmental conditions. As Mortensen (1991) suggests, our ancestors lived in a time of struggle with constant life-and-death situations. This premise has led numerous authors to discuss the cultural imperatives of language development (see, e.g., de Laguna, 1927/1963; Revesz, 1946/1956). One of those situations comes with the meeting and avoidance of predatory animals. It would not have been so bizarre for one member of the community to warn others that a predator was near by. Nor would it have been strange to call for silence as women, children, and men hunted for small game. Lerner (1986) points out that large game hunting was probably a very rare activity and an unlikely candidate as the impetus to language or silence. Nevertheless, a nonverbal counterpart to *sh* could have existed (for example placing the index finger over one's lips) and could have been viewed at a distance during hunting. *Sh*, in its linguistic or nonverbal form, may also have been extended as a warning to noisy siblings in order to protect the sleep of infants or adults. This warning may well have taken the form of the proposition for them "to be silent." Thus, the proposition is moved along the continuum of arbitrariness (see Liska, 1984). *Sh* is extended well beyond its original referent (i.e., the crying infant) to a new referent (i.e., a dangerous situation for the whole community). Grace de Laguna's (1927/1963) cooperation theory is grounded in the notion that environmental and ecological conditions of both conflict and cooperation led early hominids to encapsulate a predicative form of communication or a sentence-word. Furthermore, she argues that this form of cooperation increased the survival rate of early hominids.

Thus, language (i.e., both gestural and verbal) is born in the expression of silence and silence is heard through language. This ironic rendering provides the feminist insight so crucial to understanding the world as a "dialectical unfolding process" (Glennon, 1983) as constant "be-ing" (Daly, 1973). It disturbs the complacent acceptance of dualisms in the study of language origin theories. However, this feminist rendering of the origin of language/\silence, as explained thus far, can be challenged for its failure to deal with the more violent aspects of human life. Mortensen (1991) censures theories that do not deal with the violent aspects of life as "largely watered down, domesticated, or overly pacifistic explanations of human communication" (p. 274). The challenge to address the violent aspects of life and language is dealt with in the following section, not so much because I believe that all societies are like islands developed from violent volcanic eruptions, but because violence is an issue that we cannot afford to ignore.

VIOLENCE

As suggested in the previous section, Mortensen (1991) challenged scholars to deal with the violent aspects of the origin of language. Yet, before this call was issued, a theory of the origin of language as grounded in violence had already been published. This particular theory makes Mortensen's attempts at revealing the relation between language and violence pale in comparison. The theory under discussion was developed by Girard (1972/1977). It is a postmodern piece of writing that might make Stephen King cower. Girard's theory, without a doubt, would not be described as a "water-downed pacifistic" explanation of the origin of language/\silence.

Girard (1972/1977) argues that violence is an inherent human condition. It is violence, he tells us, that gave rise to the origin of language, the origin of silence, and the origin of institutions. He believes that humans do not have an instinctual ability to organize through hierarchies. Subsequently, he believes conflict and strife are commonplace. As rivalries increase, individuals are polarized within the group. Certain members are perceived as the cause of the crisis. These individuals are usually the weakest members of society. They may be "diseased, crippled, of strange appearance or origin—apt to arouse the suspicions of the group" (Gans, 1981, p. 11). In other words, Girard relies on the concept of *other*. The *other* heightens the hostility of the group, whose aggression results in a collective murder. Following the murder, the community witnesses the results of their actions in silence. Girard perceives the lifeless body as a signifier, an articulation of the fear, the hatred, the frustration, and the loathing that culminated in the group murder. The silence that follows is described as "sacred." Girard envisions these early prelinguistic people as so moved by their own actions that they establish a ritual that reenacts the scenario. The ritual reenactment relies on a substitute for the human victim (i.e., the sacrificial animal). This, Girard argues, is the origin of institutions. As the first organization, religion is established based on the reenactment of the first murder. "It is in this context as well that Girard situates his brief remarks on the origin of language, which he sees as emerging from ritual reproduction of the cries accompanying the crisis and murder" (Gans, 1981, p. 12). In short, this theoretical position suggests that the ritual sacrifice is the foundation of organized religion (the first institution) and the ritualized cries are the origin of language while the ritualized pauses between the cries are the origin of "sacred" (i.e., meaningful) silences.

It is possible that the first communal murder was that of the incessantly crying infant by less than empathetic individuals (see Frodi's 1985 work for a full discussion of aggression and nurturance related to infant cries). The image of a child's skull crushed against a cave wall or battered by a flurry of hurled rocks would indeed have given greater impetus for protectors to quiet the cries of an infant. It is also possible that the cries of the infant could have been muffled by the mother's hand until neither cries nor breath emanated from the child. It is also not beyond imagination to picture a caretaker shaking the child in order to command silence, which all too often results in permanent silence due to brain damage or death. The moment of silence that follows this murderous act may indeed represent Girard's collective silence, a silence moved to the realm of the sacred by future ritualistic murders (i.e., sacrifices).[8]

Girard's theory is enhanced and challenged by Gans (1981) who argues that the origin of language, silence, and institutions is found in nonviolence, not violence. Gans (1981) suggests that the aggressive act is not consensual and evokes conflict among members, who are caught in a state of both attraction and repulsion. He argues the following hypothesis: "At a moment when all are about to carry out such a gesture, the fear of conflict is such that the gesture is aborted. This abortive gesture, which *designates* its object without attempting to possess it, is then the first *linguistic* act" (p. 35). It is the abortive act that leads to sacred substitutions, not the original murder. It is *intentional* nonviolence, which is achieved through fear of violence (i.e., members fear they will become the object of aggression), that leads to the institutionalization of the sacred silence.

Gans (1981) argues that the first linguistic symbol needed to be an ostensive that "retains the nonviolent symmetry of the original gesture designating the *sacred* object" (p. 102). Yet he is unable to provide us with any other example than the word *run*, which I suppose demonstrates a nonviolent symmetry, but as suggested earlier fails to provide a coherent background for its own selection. Why the sound, phonetic, *run*? It springs from nowhere. Furthermore, Gans tells us that according to Girard's theory in order for discourse to emerge from this situation a mediator between those who desire the object and the object of desire must exist.[9] Yet once again Gans is unable to imagine who might function as a mediator or protector for the victim. It is quite possible that Gans, like Foucault, has fallen victim to his own sexist language, as he does not include women or children in his discussion. The invisibility of women in the theories of language origin and discourse development not only weakens the theories, but also perpetuates the silence of marginalized people, especially, in this case, women and children.

While Girard and Gans undoubtedly answer Mortensen's challenge for scholars to deal with the violent origins of language/\silence, they do so at the expense of women and children. They provide yet another theory (or theories) that silences women through invisibility.

In addition to the invisibility of women, another problem surfaces when these theories (i.e., Girard's theory of violence or Gans's theory of intentional nonviolence) are taken as universal explanations of the origin of language, silence, and institutions. The problem arises from the notion that both Girard (1972/1977) and Gans (1981) set their theories of violence and intentional nonviolence in a firm belief that prelinguistic people feared and hated those who were different. The theories are grounded on the premise of "debased otherness." Yet numerous cultures exist that did not and do not debase those who are different. For example, the Huron demonstrated a propensity to not only accept those who were different, but to place them in positions of authority. Trigger (1990) suggests that, "dwarfs, . . . often served as Shamans" (p. 13). "The Berdache in the plains Indian society was considered to be a powerful person who combined the attributes of male and female, . . . [and] acquired great super-natural power" (Cohen & Eames, 1982, p. 261). These individuals were respected rather than ostracized. Sexuality was not divided into categories of gender or orientation by many Native American cultures, instead several genders existed and those who may have seemed most unique often presided over sacred rituals. Furthermore, Cherokee men and women shared power, children were treated with respect, and women warriors were honored (see Mooney, 1900/1992). Difference had its place.

Although prejudice against "others" was absent among many Native American cultures, they did indeed have language, silence, and institutions. Thus, grounding the origins of language, silence, and institutions in violent attitudes towards those who are perceived as different does not explain the existence of language, silence, and formal organization among those people who are, at the very least, tolerant toward difference. I am not suggesting that Native Americans are the only people who tolerate and appreciate difference, nor am I suggesting that Native Americans did not act in violent ways in certain situations; rather, I am suggesting that no one universal theory of violence or intentional nonviolence can explain the origins of language, silence, and institutions. Furthermore, to ground a theory in the assumption that all people despise otherness, ironically marginalizes those who did not or do not fear or despise otherness.

Girard's (1972/1977) theory may well explain the origin of language, silence, and institutions for a prelinguistic European community, but it fails to make sense for many other cultures. Thus, origins may be considered specific, relative, multiple, and unique. In other words, many theories are possible and these different theories can co-exist. Although in one community violence may have been the impetus to the development of language/\silence; in another community, nurturing and care may have given birth to expressiveness. Each theory of origins can in turn provide possibilities for explaining the past and understanding current social relations—for the theories we create speak volumes about who we are.

IMPLICATIONS OF THE ORIGIN OF SILENCE/\LANGUAGE

The current rendering of the origin of language, suggests that in the first words we spoke, the first symbolic gestures we made, the first clicks of language, we articulated silence. This rendering does not totally negate the theories of the Port Royal, nor does it negate the theories of seventeenth- and eighteenth-century etymologists, environmentalists, or evolutionists. Rather, it draws upon certain criteria (i.e., proposition, articulation, designation, and derivation) in order to establish a rigorous grounding for a feminist perspective that explains how silence and language are self-contained. However, this position rejects early notions that summarize the role of language as purely a representation of reality and embraces a notion that any reality we have is bound up in discourse and silence, in expressiveness and lived experience.

This theory answers Bickerton's (1981) criticism that the early origin of language theories are weak due to their reliance on a Cartesian heritage. Nevertheless, the current rendering holds a place for early theories as well as comparative, evolutionary, and etymological linguistic solutions to the puzzle about the origin of language. Finally, it acknowledges the postmodern concern over the irony of human existence and the violent materialist character of social relations, but most importantly it provides a space for women in one of the most creative and monumental achievements of the human species, the development of language and silence as significant forms of expression.

This approach makes room for Burke's (1966) language origin theory as dependent upon the negative and Foucault's concept that a search for the origin reveals the end. Yet it moves beyond either of these approaches by providing what Burke refers to as an *essential irony* and one that includes women, children, and men. Burke's (1966) concept of irony is discussed in several of his essays. Here I am referring to his essays on the origin of language, which establish irony as essential to language. According to Burke, the rationality of language rests on the negative. In order to say what *is*, we must be able to say what is *not*. Although this irony may be essential, I believe Burke neglected an additional and even more obvious, yet elusive irony. That is, the *essential irony is that the first symbol, the first gesture, the first word was silence*.

Postmodern perceptions of the origin of language focus on the paradoxical and ironic aspects of origin itself. For Foucault (1966/1973) it is not origin that gives rise to history, rather it is "historicity that . . . makes possible the necessity of an origin" (p. 329). Origins are impossible for "the origin is that which is returning . . . the return of that which has already always begun . . . the origin is visible through time; but this time it is the recession into the future" (pp. 330–332). Foucault argues that,

> it is not a matter of rediscovering some primary word that has been buried in it, but of disturbing the words we speak, of denouncing the grammatical habits of our thinking, of dissipating the myths that ani-

mate our words, of rendering once more noisy and audible the element of silence that all discourse carries with it as it is spoken. (p. 298, also see Picard, 1948/1952)

Disturbing the discourse is exactly what numerous feminist theorists devote their research efforts toward. Interestingly, simply by including women in theories of language origin, the patriarchal discourse concerning language production is disturbed. Uncovering how language, in general, and its grammatical structure, in particular, acts to silence women, and all marginalized *others* lends itself to uncovering the disguised forms of domination. Furthermore, seeking the origin of language provides us with the origin of silence. An origin that is lived again and again through silenced groups. Although Foucault believes that the "origin of man [sic]" is not to be found in the primordial word, it can be said that in the origin of the primordial word, silence can be found, and there exist the *others*.

Silence can obviously marginalize and oppress members of society, but it can also express protection, resistance, and defiance. It may afford opportunities for emancipation or perpetuate the disappearance of the "other."

The present rendering of the origin of expressive activity (i.e., silence/\language) is not without limitations. As argued by postmodernists, any rendering of past events is vulnerable to challenges, as is this interpretation, which should be thought of less as a *theory* and more as a *possibility*—the possibility that silence and language emerged simultaneously and that women played a part, if not a central role in this process.

Silence and language create and re-create our social realities. From interpersonal relationships to the structuring of organizations, silent practices are pervasive and interwoven with linguistic practices. The alternative theory of the origin of language/\silence provided here is not only a possibility, but is also a creative expression. Just as Girard's (1972/1977) theory is an expression of one-world view (i.e., that language, silence, and institutions sprang from suspicion and loathing of others), the theory that I propose is yet another selective interpretation of the origin of language/\silence. And each of these theories contributes to the creation of our social realities. They are aesthetic expressions. They are narratives dressed as theory (Lyotard, 1984). As a narrative/theory of the origin of language/\silence, this *aesthetic expression* speaks of our abilities to *create possibilities* for new social realities. However, the acceptance, rejection, or modification of these social realities depends on the persuasive (or at time coercive) ability of the aesthetic expression, in this case, the narrative. "Narratives . . . are also subject to commodification, exchange, and consumption" (Clair, Chapman, & Kunkel, 1996, p. 255; de Certeau, 1984). They are produced and proffered. Furthermore, "The listeners are consumed by the aesthetic narrative. Thus consumption is linked not only to the economic notion of consumer, but also to the phenomenological notion of lived experience as artistic expression" (Clair et al., 1996, p. 255). But as deCerteau (1984) suggests, narratives are not necessarily passively consumed. Nor are they necessarily freely created. Thus, the narratives we live may speak of certain conditions while disguising others (Deetz, 1992; Giddens, 1979; Mumby, 1988). And some stories may be expressed while others are sequestered (Clair, 1993). The issues of power, politics, aesthetics, and economics are all part of the *organizing of silence.*

Although this rendering of the origin of silence/language may result in more questions than answers, it does provide a means of addressing expressive activity without bifurcating the concepts. As Picard (1948/1952) so eloquently put it: "Speech came out of silence, . . . and in every silence there is something of the spoken word" (p. 24). Because they are born of the same breath, these expressive activities give significance to each other. The following chapters of this book will attempt to make clear how expressive activities can be silencing and how silence can be expressive.

CHAPTER 2

Silencing Communication

... silence cannot be dismissed as trivial or peripheral.
—Philip C. McGuire, 1985

In chapter 1, I focused on how the expressive activities of language and silence were born of the same breath, giving significance to each other. Brown (1966) eloquently argues the vital importance of this position when he writes:

> Speech points beyond itself to the silence, to the word within the word, the language buried in language, the primordial language, from before the Flood or the Tower of Babel; lost yet ready at hand, perfect for all time; present in all our words, unspoken. To hear again the primordial language is to restore to words their full significance. (p. 258)

Understanding the significance that Brown speaks of rests in the ability to hear the unspoken, which van Manen (1990) suggests can be achieved by experiencing the phenomenon of our everyday lives as poetry. Van Manen entreats us to view life through a phenomenological lens:

> Phenomenology, like poetry, intends to be silent as it speaks. It wants to be implicit as it explicates. So, to read or write phenomenologically requires that we be sensitively attentive to the silence around the words by means of which we attempt to disclose the deep meaning of our world. (p. 131)

The silences around the words are as powerful and as numerous in meaning and valence as the words themselves. As suggested in chapter 1, silence may range from the poetic to the political with a variety of forms, functions, and outcomes. The words we speak, the actions we employ, express a rich and complex world beyond the surface reflection that we generally take for granted.

Our language of words and actions are usually taken as the means to reflecting our realities by conveying our thoughts and feelings or describing our lived experiences. Yet a more nuanced vision of communication has developed over recent decades that asserts that communication is more than a reflection of our social realities, it creates our social realities (e.g., see Baudrillard, 1988a; Berger & Luckmann, 1966;

de Beauvoir, 1949/1952; Foucault, 1966/1973, 1978; Heidegger, 1926/1962; MacKinnon, 1993). Silence, in all its diverse forms, contributes to the creation of our social realities, from the mundane micro-level practices of our everyday expressions to the structuring of our macro-level institutions and back again. Subsequently, silence, as a topic of scholarly interest, has been explored from diverse philosophical approaches.

TREATISES ON SILENCE

In 1916, Charles Courtenay undertook the charge of compiling what he argued was the first full treatment on the subject of silence. He points out the irony of having to break silence in order to know silence. In his book *The Empire of Silence*, Courtenay suggests that political silence covered a widespread area geographically and crossed generations throughout time. Nevertheless, he argues that women suffered most at the hands of disciplinary silence. Children were controlled through rules concerning speech, but Courtenay suggests that women, like no other group, were consistently submitted to the tortures of forced silence.

In Foucaualdian fashion, Courtenay describes the atrocities put to women in order to silence them. The ducking stool and metal bridle are rivaled only by his depiction of yet another torture:

> Akin to this, and even worse, is what Brandt tells us in his History of the Reformation in the Netherlands:—"They prepared two little irons, between which the tongue was screwed, which, being seared at the tip, would swell to such a degree as to become immovable and incapable of being drawn back." (p. 137)

This blistering torture may well have been forced upon both men and women, but disciplinary silence for men seems to come and go with political or religious upsurges. Women's silence is continuing and pervasive.

Courtenay (1916) provides not only a look at the disciplinary side of silence, but also develops the beauty of silence, the power of silence, the humor of silence, and a wealth of other perspectives concerning the subject. He includes praise for the Montessori technique of teaching children the essence of silence through gentle and artful practices. Punishment and torture produce only temporary silence. Children cannot learn to appreciate the aesthetics of silence, if forced into silence. As Courtenay suggests, "A silence which is noisily created is in constant need of being re-created, since it is made from without" (p. 343). Teachers who scream for silence, who threaten and punish children into silent submission, will never know a lasting silence or silence that is filled with thoughtfulness. Lurking within the forced silence is a scream of resistance.

Although Courtenay discusses the disciplinary silencing of women and children as shameful, he still labels women and children among the primary offenders of obnoxious loquaciousness. He accepts ancient "truisms" of women and children as incessantly chattering disruptions and is most concerned that while it is shameful to forcefully silence women, what really ought to be done is to give credit and praise to women who are graciously silent (see pp. 183–187).

Women's talk, Courtenay suggests, "provides a vent for superfluous energy . . . much talk cannot be wise talk, and in letting off steam somebody is apt to be scalded" (p. 183). What women speak of, Courtenay claims, represents "small subjects" (p. 184). And although they should not be dealt with harshly, they should not be encouraged to take any but the high road, that of silence. By the way, his book is dedicated to his wife—"A true comrade and the best of helpers"—a silent woman, I presume.

Courtenay's (1916) early work on silence has grown dusty on library shelves. For example, Dauenhauer (1980) credits Max Picard (1948) with writing the first full-length volume on silence. Subsequently, Dauenhauer reinvents some of the categories for silence that Courtenay had already justified in his work. Nevertheless, Dauenhauer (1980) provides an insightful look at silence through a phenomenological lens. Relying on the work of Picard, as well as Husserl, Heidegger, and Merleau-Ponty, he asserts that silence and discourse are bound together and that it is the "interpenetration of discourse, silence, action, and desire" that need to be explored (p. 138). Dauenhauer views silence as an active performance that is intertwined with discourse.

Although Dauenhauer (1980) neglects the work of Courtenay, I believe he is correct in asserting that Max Picard may have been the first *Western* philosopher to contribute a full treatment of silence that asserts that *speech and silence exist simultaneously.* Max Picard's book, *The World of Silence* is not only evocative, but also eloquent in its descriptions of speech and silence. Picard (1948) wrote: "the word not only brings the things out of silence; it also produces the silence in which they can disappear again" (p. 141). Dauenhauer (1980) senses similarities between Picard's (1948) work and the early writings of Heidegger on the relationship of discourse and silence. Furthermore, Dauenhauer incorporates the rich insights of Merleau-Ponty on the topic of silence and speech. Dauenhauer's phenomenological perspective is both enlightening and constraining, because in Jaworski's (1993) opinion, Dauenhauer's perspective fails to develop the political and pragmatic meanings of silence and discourse.

In 1993, Jaworski presented his volume on the *Power of Silence* in which he addresses Dauenhauer's attempt to provide the reader with the answer to the questions—What is the essence of silence? and, What is the ontological significance of silence? Jaworski concludes that Dauenhauer fails to answer these questions: "Dauenhauer's book seems to ramble on in search of the true meaning of silence only to conclude at the end that the book has failed to achieve its primary goal and that it probably can never be achieved" (Jaworski, 1993, p. 33). Jaworski dismisses essentialist approaches to the study of silence. He argues that

> silence and speech do not stand in total opposition to each other, but form a continuum of forms ranging from the most protypical instances of silence to the most protypical instances of speech. However, the decision as to which linguistic form should be treated as speech or silence will ultimately depend on a theoretically motivated decision of the researcher and not on some natural features of the form in question. (p. 34)

Jaworski (1993) finds the feminist perspective on silence useful for understanding the disciplinary side of silence. He credits feminist scholarship with advancing our understanding of how women are silenced. However, he suggests that women's silence can be explained via a more encompassing theory of sociopolitical silencing. He suggests that Leach's anthropological work on ambiguous status supplies the groundwork for a theory of political silence. In brief, he argues that those who are classified as abnormal, "dirty," or as the "other" are those who do not fit neatly into social categories. Women have been defined historically as "deformed males" (Hill, 1986, p. 42) and as such have subsequently been silenced.

Although I appreciate much of Jaworski's work, I must raise two concerns. First, it is not clear why Jaworski credits Leach with this theory of the ambiguous other. I am much more inclined to credit the existential philosophy of Jean-Paul Sartre and Simone de Beauvoir for advancing the notions of "otherness." Even if Jaworski wished to remain, theoretically, among anthropologists, Mary Douglas should be given at least partial credit for developing the notions of the ambiguous other from an anthropological perspective (Douglas, 1966; also see Wuthnow, Hunter, Bergesen, & Kurzweil, 1984). Her work brilliantly explains how some people and practices fail to fit neatly into particular category systems and are therefore defined as "dirty." Jaworski, to his credit, provides an excellent overview that explains how women have been defined as ambiguous others especially in terms of their being either clean or dirty (see pp. 125–129).

Second, while women, children, and minorities may fall into

ambiguous categories, it is of the utmost importance to remember who is creating the category system. No category exists in nature. Categories are discursive constructions (Foucault, 1970/1966) that play themselves out in material and practical ways; they are invented, as Bateson (1972) would say. It may be tautological to argue that women do not fit neatly into the category of "mankind" because they are deformed males and therefore they are ambiguous others. Nevertheless, the conclusion Jaworski draws from all this is an important one. He concludes that the ambiguous other is considered a taboo that must be silenced. Having established this case, he applies these theoretical positions to the study of silence and the Solidarity movement in Poland.

Feminist works on the topic of silence do not fit easily into the linear progression I have thus far provided. Their works are numerous and span decades, yet these works were often marginalized and difficult to find. Because women's scholarly work is not embedded within the mainstream texts, women seem to reinvent themselves every generation (Spender, 1983). Further complicating an overview of feminist work on silence is the practice of many feminists during the second wave of feminism to reject the notions of ownership and privilege with respect to their ideas. For example, bell hooks (1996) explained that she chose to use lowercase letters for her pseudonym as symbolic of the desire to reduce the emphasis on ownership of thought and increase the emphasis on what was being said. Therefore, although there are numerous feminist writings on the topic of silence, I am sure that my select presentation cannot do justice to the richness and quality of these works. Nevertheless, I will attempt to provide at least a partial rendering of the contributions that feminists have made to the topic of silence.

FEMINISTS SPEAK OF SILENCE

Two books written in the 1940s acted in concert to provide a grounding for feminist perspectives on the phenomenon of silence. Although neither of these authors were directly providing a treatise on silence, each offered rich insights for the development of future feminist work. First, I will briefly discuss Simone de Beauvoir's (1949/1952) existential understanding of the status of women as it relates to current studies of silence. Then, I will discuss Susanne Langer's (1942) book *Philosophy in a New Key* as an additional impetus to future work on silence.

Simone de Beauvoir (1949/1952) based her existential feminist philosophy on the premise that women are defined as "other" in relation to men. She exposes male-dominated theories of gender difference (e.g., biological theories, psychological theories, and psychoanalytic theories) as perpetuating the definition of women as objects that are subjected to men. She even-handedly discusses the trap that this oppression has set for both men and women. Men are trapped by the image of superiority that they create for themselves and that is always in danger of being uncovered for its bad faith. As women play out their object role as other, they far too often perpetuate their own oppression. Although men and women both would benefit from women's liberation, de Beauvoir is not so naive as to think men would willingly give up their superior and privileged position. The charming woman has much to offer the male, as de Beauvoir writes:

> When the charming woman shows herself in all her splendor, . . . under her tinted hair the forest murmur becomes a thought, and words issue from her breasts. Men stretch forth avid hands toward the marvel, but when they grasp it it is gone; the wife, the mistress, speak like everybody else through their mouths. (p. 687)

Simone de Beauvoir (1949/1952) argues that man is "caught between the silence of nature and the demanding presence of other free beings" (p. 687). Woman, therefore, is absent while present, her existence speaks of her silence.

Furthermore, de Beauvoir (1949/1952) recognizes that although the trap affects both men and women, it is women who must exist in a male-dominated culture, where their breasts speak louder than their mouths. Women, according to de Beauvoir, are socially constructed and until their economic, cultural, moral, and social constructions are modified they cannot emerge as new women.

Simone de Beauvoir (1949/1952) set the stage for much feminist scholarship. She points out: that it is by "definition" that women are made to be "other," that their status as "other" positions them as inferior in a male-dominated society, and that although woman's character may be a mythic creation, "the experiences for which she is the source or the pretext are none the less real" (p. 687). In other words, de Beauvior provides the initial impetus for future work on the linguistic construction of identity, the base for discussions of the subjected subject as object, the ironic interplay between presence and absence, and the reality of pretext. In many respects, even if it has not been credited, de Beauvoir's feminist existentialism has contributed to current social constructionist and postmodern positions. In addition, her influence on feminist work has allowed for the development of such theories as standpoint theory (Harstock, 1987), muted group theory (Ardener, 1975; Kramarae, 1981), and many others, all of which contribute to understanding patriarchal silence.

Susanne Langer (1942), also writing in the 1940s, described humans as beings whose activities are centered around the making, using, and abusing of symbols. Langer's work is "key" in moving a social constructionist perspective forward. She places emphasis on how language can both emancipate as well as trap us. Furthermore, this language need not be relegated to the spoken and written word alone. However, Langer does privilege "naming" through verbal form (oral, written, signed) as paramount to the expression of identity.

Fascinated by Helen Keller's early life of silence, Susanne Langer studied Keller's life history. There she finds the key to the origin of language. For Langer, language began with naming. In short, Langer claimed that the power to express our world through naming was central to our very being. Specifically, she provides Helen Keller's description of how her life changed as she realized that she could name w...a...t...e...r.

Naming became a central concern for feminist approaches to understanding silence and silencing. For example, we have Friedan (1963) to thank for exposing *the problem without a name*. In addition, Catharine MacKinnon (1979) was instrumental in "naming" sexual harassment. Her work has been followed by several feminist and pro-feminist writers who discuss the power of naming (Wood, 1992, 1994) and the ways in which sexual harassment acts to silence at both the interpersonal and institutional levels (see Bingham, 1994; Conrad & Taylor, 1994; Kreps, 1993; Taylor & Conrad, 1992).

Second, Langer's work contributed to unmasking the tyranny of words (also see Chase, 1938, as cited in Langer, 1942). Constrained by a Cartesian-style of language, she argued that we were virtually unable to break free of the world created through discussions of mind/body, subject/object, and logic/emotion. Specifically, she argued language impacts on the very philosophic questions that we ask. And far too often, the framing of the question asserts like-minded answers.

This challenge to current constructions of society and especially Cartesian and positivistic principles encouraged feminist scholars to look seriously at how language created and sustained their position in society. Langer's work encouraged women to ask questions in a new light.

One of the earliest scholars to explore language as a gendered practice is Robin Lakoff. Although Lakoff's (1975) early work was pivotal in exposing language differences, it was also "constrained by some of the sexist assumptions of the linguistic paradigm in which she worked" (Spender, 1980, p. 8). Ideas that centered around the opinion that women were not inferior in any way but rather trapped by a *man-made language* surfaced in the wake of Lakoff's work. This feminist cultural upsurge provided an exciting new way of understanding the linguistic construction of gender and the silencing of women.

Spender (1980) moved the discussions of language from a gender-difference model to a socially constructed model in her work *Man Made Language*. Spender's insights were nurtured by numerous feminist scholars including linguists like Julia Stanley, whose work explores how grammatical structure and syntax contributes to an oppressive language. Stanley's (1990) *Speaking Freely: Unlearning the Lies of the Father's Tongue*, which is authored under her liberated pseudonym of Julia Penelope, exposes the patriarchal aspects of language that reinforce an oppressive ideology. A second influence on Spender was Kramer, who also liberated her name by changing it to Kramarae (see Spender, 1980, for the stories surrounding these name changes). Kramarae (1981) exposed the injustices perpetuated by stereotypical constructions of women, especially those based on their linguistic competence. Feminists continue to contribute to this area of understanding language and silence. For example, Hill (1986) not only provides an overview of this literature that she aptly describes as "a decade of linguistic revolt," but also provides further insights into the silencing aspects of language.

Simone de Beauvoir and Susanne Langer were not the only philosophers to surface as primary figures in the feminist movement to understand silence. Two other important contributors made their voices heard on the topic of silence during the 1960s and 1970s. They are Mary Daly and Tillie Olsen.

Daly (1973) spoke of the "Great Silence" that makes women invisible throughout history and erases all clues that a matriarchal society could have existed prior to patriarchy. Her treatise, *Beyond God the Father*, addresses the institutional enforcement of silence. Specifically, she argues that religious institutions, especially the Catholic Church, are grounded in the principle of silencing women in order to promote patriarchy. Others have followed Daly in the unmasking of institutions that seem at the surface level to be gender-neutral, yet at the deep level are permeated with patriarchal oppression (see e.g., Ferguson, 1984; Hearn, Sheppard, Tancred-Sheriff, & Burrell, 1989; Hearn, 1994).

Tillie Olsen's (1978) work on silence, which began in the 1960s and culminated with her book *Silences*, launched a series of explorations into the topic of silence and silencing (Hedges & Fisher Fishkin, 1994). Olsen highlighted the ways that women writers are silenced through their everyday experiences as wife and mother, how their works are marginalized by the academy, and how they are virtually erased from anthologies of classic writers. Combining Olsen's work with that of Adrienne Rich's (1979) work set the stage for feminist writers to explore the cultural practices that reinforced the silence of women. Audre Lorde

(1984), who discussed the tyrannies of silence both paralleled and developed Olsen's treatise on the silencing of "others" (Hedges & Fisher Fishkin, 1994). Current literary feminists both expand Olsen's work as well as extend it into the realm of understanding silence as resistance (see Hedges & Fisher Fishkin, 1994).

Not all feminists developed their work on silence with the same radical passion as Daly and Olsen, or with the poetic passion of Lorde, Rich, or Morgan. In the 1980s, Tannen and Saville-Troike compiled a series of essays on the topic of silence that developed along a less radical path.

In their edited collection, Tannen and Saville-Troike (1985) intentionally privilege silence over speech in order to heighten awareness of the richness of the concept of silence. Working primarily from a linguistic perspective, the contributors approach silence through a variety of cultural situations. The essays contribute to an overall understanding of silence as a complex phenomenon that occurs at a variety of levels. For example, at the micro-level, the tiniest bit of silence juxtaposed to a consonant or a vowel contributes to the making of language. At a more intermediary level, silence is used as an indicator to stereotype certain groups of people (e.g., New York Jews as talkative or "Silent Finns"). At a microfunctional level, silence acts as a form of control and resistance within the classroom (Gilmore, 1985). Yet it would not be difficult to move this analysis to the macro-level in order to understand the silencing of subordinate groups on a grander scale. This macro-level example does not quite fit within what Saville-Troike calls "institutionally-determined silence" (p. 16).

Saville-Troike's "institutionally-determined silence" (p. 14), the broadest, most macro-level on her continuum, includes organizations' creating rules of silence (e.g., churches and libraries) as well as social taboos against speaking out of turn with higher-status individuals. This category of institutionally determined silence, comes close to providing a place for political, patriarchal, and ideological silence. However, it does not develop the cultural/political practices related to how numerous institutions legitimize their existence by silencing women, children, and minorities, as discussed by Daly. (For an example of bureaucratic silence, see Chapman, 1994.)

Daly (1973) and Olsen (1978) did not provide the final word on silence (pun intended); rather, they influenced a number of scholars who have continued to break silence in order to reflect on silence. For example, MacKinnon's work exposes additional forms of silence that range from the personal to the institutional level.

MacKinnon (1979, 1993) addresses patriarchal silence as enacted through the horrors of sexual violence perpetrated against women and children who are further silenced through the institution of patriarchal laws under the guise of freedom of speech. MacKinnon (1993) writes:

> Imagine that for hundreds of years your most formative traumas, your daily suffering and pain, the abuse you live through, the terror you live with, are unspeakable. (p. 3)

And even if women find outlets to speak, they are once again silenced by the patriarchal conclusion that freedom of speech allows men to pornographize, sexually harass, and even rape women (MacKinnon, 1993).

MacKinnon's (1979) early work on sexual harassment revealed that not only did the personal or private means exist to silence women, but also the legal means, which were set forth and legitimated through courts of law. Judges were insistent that sexual harassment could not be treated as a crime or it would surely overload the judges' dockets. This ironic and patriarchal form of logic perpetuated the silence of an obviously pervasive condition.

Together with Andrea Dworkin, Catharine MacKinnon "proposed a law against pornography" (MacKinnon, 1993, p. 22). They argue that pornography is an expression of encouragement to men to objectify and assault women, which both *is* and *leads to* their ultimate and complete silence. MacKinnon stresses the importance of what pornography *means* to women, children, and even men who are used and abused through pornography. Returning to what certain *expressions mean* for people's everyday lived experience positions the discursive practices in a place and time that has actual impact. MacKinnon (1993) argues that "discrimination does not divide into acts on one side and speech on the other. Speech acts. . . . [And] acts speak" (p. 31). It is state power that protects patriarchy, "silencing those who are hurt by it and making sure they can do nothing about it" (p. 40).

In short, MacKinnon (1993) argues that words and images embody experience: "Words [carry] a lived reality" (p. 59). This lived reality can be one of silence that is further silenced through legal institutions. MacKinnon tells us that when equality is achieved,

> silence will be neither an act of power, as it is now for those who hide behind it, nor an experience of imposed powerlessness, as it is now for those who are submerged in it, but a context of repose into which thought can expand, an invitation that gives speech its shape, an opening to a new conversation. (p. 110)

MacKinnon's approach to silence is sensitive to both gender and racial issues. Nevertheless, "other others" have contributed to feminist views of silence by providing powerful arguments concerning silence, dialogue, speaking, and being heard when one is marginalized twice over through gender and race. As Audre Lorde (1984) suggests:

> Certainly for Black women our struggle has not been to emerge from silence to speech but to change the nature and direction of our speech. To make a speech that compels listeners, one that is heard. (p. 124)

Audre Lorde (1984) both appreciates the unique situations of women of different backgrounds; race, religion, sexual orientation, class, and so on as well as the commonalities that bridge these differences. She believes that what is most important must be spoken; that silence must be transformed into action; and that what she most regretted in her life were her silences.

These insights came to her most clearly after she had been told that she needed breast surgery. The possibility of death, what she considers the "final silence," lead her to ask herself a question—what was I afraid of? Lorde continues:

> My silences had not protected me. Your silence will not protect you. [She continues to explain that] The women who sustained me through that period were Black and white, old and young, lesbian, bisexual, and heterosexual, and we all shared a war against the tyrannies of silence. (p. 41)

Silence and speaking out are a shared, yet unique experience among women. Feminist approaches to silence cover a wide variety of philosophical perspectives. These perspectives converge and diverge, dip and dive, through the waters of words and actions that compel silence.

Despite the impossibility of listing and discussing all of the contributors from the feminist school of silence, I hope that this overview provides the reader with some insights into the magnitude of the contribution that feminists have made to understanding silence.

CRITICAL AND POSTMODERN VIEWS ON SILENCING

Concerning silence, feminist contributions did not exist in a theoretical vacuum. To the contrary, both critical and postmodern thinkers were talking about silence, as well. Many feminist theories developed overlapping positions that incorporated critical theory, postmodernism and poststructuralism. Furthermore, we are now beginning to see scholars, who have advocated critical and postmodern positions, support the incorporation of a feminist perspective with these philosophical positions. Again, it is beyond the scope of this book to provide a detailed analysis of each of these schools of thought. However, I will briefly discuss the position of two influential scholars who have contributed to exposing the silencing aspects of communication. First, from the Frankfurt School, Jürgen Habermas provides a theory of discursive closure that addresses how communication can silence and how the "ideal speech act" can emancipate. Second, Michel Foucault, who is considered one of the most influential postmodern thinkers, sets forth an illuminating discussion of discourse, power, knowledge, and resistance.

Neither of these two theorists explicitly articulate that they have been influenced by feminist work on silence. Nor do they focus on the silencing of women, in particular. Feminists have argued that the critical and postmodern perspectives, in part, marginalize and ironically silence the oppression of women. I will take up this feminist critique following these brief overviews of Habermas and Foucault.

DISTORTED COMMUNICATION
AND THE IDEAL SPEECH ACT

Without a doubt, Habermas is considered the most influential critical scholar of today. His works encompass a wide variety of critiques aimed at understanding oppression in society. In this brief overview, I will focus on his theory of communicative action.

Habermas (1979) argues that social exchanges can be discussed in terms of three practices: work, interaction, and power. For Habermas, work is associated with material existence; interaction is associated with symbol systems; and power is associated with practices of domination and emancipation. Each of the practices act in concert. Work interests, for example, as embodied through private business, set forth certain interests that are often at odds with the other interests. Subsequently, the capitalist or technical interest might be disguised through communicative practices. These practices represent distorted communication.

In order to achieve emancipation, the distortion must be revealed. Habermas (1968, 1979) details a theory of communication competence that suggests that competent communication at a variety of levels will lead to emancipation as people move toward the "ideal speech act."

Habermas's concept of competence is not restricted to the level of skills in eloquence or articulation. To the contrary, he suggests that in addition to being a persuasive speaker, one must also provide validity and sincerity. In addition, ultimately, or ideally, power distinctions must be eliminated in order for speakers to speak freely so that no person is silenced. Habermas explains that speech has far too often been *systematically distorted* to privilege some persons or groups of people over others.

A POSTMODERN APPROACH TO DISCOURSE AND SILENCE

In contrast to this modernistic approach to communication and control, Foucault (1973a, 1973b, 1978, 1979, 1982) provides a postmodern position on power, discourse, silence, and resistance. Foucault centers his discussions of power and resistance around the concept of discourse. Foucault suggests that our worlds are created, sustained, and challenged through discourses. These discourses are not reflections of reality, but rather *are* reality. Discourses create knowledge regimes that in turn affect power relations. In a vicious circle, these power relations further legitimate the knowledge regimes. Power, for Foucault, does not exist as something someone or some group has; rather, power exists in the discursive practices:

> we must not imagine a world of discourse divided between accepted discourse and excluded discourse, or between the dominant discourse and the dominated one; but as a multiplicity of discursive elements that can come into play in various strategies. . . . Discourse transmits and produces power; it reinforces it; but also undermines and exposes it, renders it fragile and makes it possible to thwart it. (1984, p. 180)

Foucault (1972) intends the term *discourse* to encompass any representational practice. As Mumby (1988) proposes, even the practice of punching in on the time clock can be viewed as a discursive practice. Deetz (1992) also explains, "a manager may have a closer parking space, or a larger office, or dress differently. . . . Each of these is a discourse, a signifying, representational practice" (p. 260).

As discourses or discursive practices combine they develop what Foucault (1972) calls a *discursive formation*. These formations address a context in which the discourse can be interpreted. Deetz (1992) continues his example of the manager who has a larger parking space, or a larger office as combining to form a "managerial" discursive formation. Each discursive formation exists among many discursive formations with some of these formations being privileged over others. Discursive formations exist within discursive fields. These *discursive fields* are sites or sociohistorical contexts that illuminate political and economic practices.

According to Foucault (1972), as discursive formations are privileged they *enunciate* or *articulate* a particular social order. The privileging of certain discursive formations can marginalize alternatives, weakening our ability to recognize other discursive choices (Laclau & Mouffe, 1985; Weedon, 1987). Subsequently, people often begin to see the current social order as a given (Giddens, 1979). In short, Foucault's vocabulary provides us with a theoretical and heuristic means of discussing the silencing aspects of communication. However, Foucault's vocabulary on resistance is limited to counterdiscourses or reverse discourses, which fails to capture, fully, the essence of resistance (see Ramazanoglo, 1993).

Without a doubt, both the critical and the postmodern movements have contributed to the linguistic turn of theoretical events. Among the leaders of the postmodern movement, Michel Foucault may have contributed the most insightful and artistically rendered discussions of discourse and silence, resistance and oppression, the position of the subject, and how these realities simultaneously play themselves out at micro- and macro-levels. Furthermore, Foucault is the master of irony. He draws on the ancient works of Heraclitus to uncover the self-contained opposite. He breathes new life into Nicholas of Cusa's fifteenth-century treatises on the *coincidentia oppositorum*. His rhetoric is passionate, insightful, and persuasive. Nevertheless, I recognize that his work must be approached and applied tentatively for it has provoked deserving controversy.[1]

CHALLENGING FOUCAULT

First, and ironically, Foucault has been criticized for establishing a "performative contradiction" in his own work (Best & Kellner, 1991; also see Fraser, 1989). Best and Kellner (1991) describe "Foucault as a profoundly conflicted thinker whose thought is torn between oppositions such as totalizing/detotalizing impulses and tensions between discursive/extra-discursive theorization, macro/micro perspectives, and a dialectic of domination/resistance" (p. 36). Furthermore, he is charged with philosophical hypocrisy. "He is a conflicted thinker, . . . destroying the subject and resurrecting it, assailing forms of domination but eschewing normative language and metadiscourse," presenting the "new era," "new body," and "new forms of subjectivity" only to abandon postmodern pathos and "descend into the dusty archives of antiquity" (Best & Kellner, 1991, p. 73).

In addition, Fraser (1989) argues that Foucault disavows "the problematic of *normative* justification" (p. 21) by presenting his interpretation of the power/knowledge regime as neutral in terms of its legitimation. Yet he continually uses passionately disturbing rhetoric to describe oppression and "calls in no uncertain terms for resistance to domination" (p. 29). Fraser believes this is a clear example of his conflicted thinking. Furthermore, Foucault's work is challenged on the grounds that it presents "truth" as an effect of discourses, which leaves us with no means to justify Foucault's own work.

Phelan (1990) points out that many feminists fear that Foucault's belief in widely varying sources of domination through discourse will "deprive women of making any claims against a sexist society" (p. 430). Radical feminists assert that *woman* cannot be located and created in discourse alone or she will become a fiction and eventually invisible (Martin, 1982). Foucault, like other postmodern writers, is criticized for relegating gender or women to passing references, thus contributing to the marginalization of women. For example, MacKinnon (1991) responds to Foucault's *History of Sexuality* by asserting that "the silence of the silenced is forgotten in the noisy discourse about sexuality which then becomes its history" (p. 4). Furthermore, MacKinnon (1991) reprimands Foucault for his failure to take into account the pervasive sexual abuse of women and children. He minimizes the oppression of women to "hysterization" at the expense of women and the promotion of male pleasure. Subsequently, many feminists (see Ramazanoglo, 1993) reject Foucault's writings as lacking instrumentality to a feminist cause or at worst for being blatantly misogynistic.

With these caveats in mind, Weedon (1987) suggests that "if Foucault's theory of discourse and power can produce in feminist hands an analysis of patriarchal power relations which enables the development of active strategies for change, then it is of little importance whether his own historical analyses fall short of this" (p. 13). Foucault's greatest contributions lie in his ability to expose subtle forms of domination, to render the power/knowledge regime visible and to make clear the discursive construction of the subject. His work offers feminists a framework for contextualizing experience in "its constitution and ideological power" (Weedon, 1987, p. 125). Furthermore, his unconventional, passionate prose challenges us "to dereify our usual patterns of self-interpretation and renew our sense that, just possibly, they may not tell the whole story" (Fraser, 1989, pp. 65–66). Furthermore, his aesthetic portrayals combine imagination with rigorous rationality as they expose the ironies of the lived experience. As such, his work may be instrumental in developing a position on silence that is surrounded by the aesthetic.

With these critiques and caveats in mind, I turn to the commonalities that cross these diverse works concerning silence. Four themes that weave their way into almost all discussions of ideological silence include, (1) the dynamic relationship surrounding language and silence, (2) signifying subjectivity, (3) the micro/macro-level dialectic, and (4) the tensions between oppression and resistance.

THE DYNAMIC RELATIONSHIP
SURROUNDING LANGUAGE AND SILENCE

A dynamic relationship exists that allows communication to both express and at times silence individuals, issues, and interests. There also exists the possibility for silence to sequester as well as express experience. Silence and discourses are bound up in innumerable ways. Their many nuanced meanings and functions are woven together into a complex tapestry. In the following sections, however, I limit my discussion to two possibilities from this complex array: silencing forms of communication and expressing forms of silence.

Silencing Forms of Communication

Certain forms of discourse act to distort power relations, disguise inequity, sequester resistant discourses, and ultimately close emancipatory forms of communication. In short, communication can be silencing. These are not new thoughts. A variety of scholars have each provided pieces to the puzzle of how communication silences. Nevertheless, Hedges and Fisher Fishkin (1994) argue that our work is not done. There are more silences to be uncovered.

For instance, Deetz (1992) draws from a wide body of scholarship to develop a list of communicative practices that act to silence individuals. These practices include: naturalization, neutralization, topical avoidance, subjectification of experience, meaning denial and plausible deniability, legitimation, and pacification. In 1991, I presented a conference paper, which was published in 1993 and appears as chapter 4 of this book, that provides a similar list of practices that act to prematurely close communication or, as I put it, to sequester stories. I was unaware of Deetz's categories when I wrote the above mentioned article. Since then I have reviewed his work and wish I had been aware of it earlier because it provides an excellent framework for discussing communicative closure.

There are several overlapping categories between Deetz's list and my own, yet there are distinctions as well (see Chapman, 1994). An example of an overlapping similarity between categories is evident in Deetz's (1992) description of discourse called naturalization (also see Giddens, 1979; Mumby, 1987, 1988). This form of discourse closes off communication by framing oppressive events as natural to the point of reification. I have a similar category called reification, which highlights that what is discussed as natural seems beyond our ability to change. With respect to sexual harassment, invoking a biological excuse for sexually harassing behavior suggests that we simply cannot change this behavior. For example, to say "boys will be boys" implies that males are biologically determined to behave in certain ways toward women. This is a *discursive practice* that takes on a biologically deterministic *formation* that supports gender differences. Relying on this formation to frame oppressive practices supports a broader *discursive formation*—patriarchy. Patriarchy, in turn, *enunciates* or *articulates* the position of women as inferior and men as superior. By combining the discursive practice of invoking biology with the discursive formation of gender differences, patriarchy is supported as a natural way of organizing our social relations. Alternatives are marginalized and women are virtually silenced.

An example of a category that did not overlap is my notion of personalizing and privatizing discourses (see Chapman, 1994 for a discussion of overlapping and unique categories with respect to my categories and Deetz's categories). These discourses frame events in such a way that they will not be brought into public view. They are what Fraser (1989) would describe as uncontestable. One way to maintain silence is to sequester the events. In chapter 4, I supply an example of a woman who chooses to frame sexual harassment at the interpersonal level by suggesting that her boyfriend will handle the matter. Here the organization and public, in general, are relieved of any accountability and the issue is virtually silenced.

There are numerous ways in which communication silences. Researchers have barely begun to uncover the ways in which distorted communication acts as communication closure and articulates a system of privilege.

Expressing Forms of Silence

Recognizing that discourse does more than communicate, realizing that discourses also articulate grand social systems, and discovering that discourses can silence certain people, specific issues, and particular interests, demands our attention. Of course, we need to continue exploring how communication silences, but we also need to explore how *silence communicates*.

From Burke (1966) to Derrida (1973, 1967/1976), theorists have suggested that we need to search for what is absent yet present. A trace of the marginalized and silenced other can be found in what is said or written. The negation, or silence, we are told, is never complete. In chapter 5, I rely on the work of Derrida to uncover the traces of what *is not said* in what *is said*, but I do so in order to expose, once again, how communication can be silencing. I believe, in order to learn how silence communicates a different approach is called for. Specifically, I advance an aesthetic perspective for exploring how silence communicates.

The aesthetic perspective embraces paradox and searches out the ironies of life. It is a companion approach to the postmodern perspective. Aesthetics encourages that the lived experience be viewed *as expressive activity.* Like the postmodern approach, *discourses* are viewed as integral, but the materiality of the world is not considered secondary. Furthermore, the aesthetic perspective discourages the separation of communication and creativity from all other "things," as is advocated in more traditional approaches. For example, past models position variables in relation *to communication*, while the postmodern prescription is to explore these variables *as communication.* Numerous scholars are following this postmodern move. For example, we can understand sexual harassment *as* a discursive practice (Bingham, 1994; Clair, 1991, 1993a,b,c) or the glass ceiling *as* an articulation of a social order (Buzzanell, 1995) or pay inequity *as* both a discursive and a material practice (Clair & Thompson, 1996).

To add an aesthetic element to current theoretical moves is to allow for the unexpected. Aesthetics deepens the shadows and raises the highlights. It recognizes, explores, and recapitulates obscure relationships. Not only are subjects viewed as communication, but they are investigated for their creativity, their aesthetic aspects, their sensuous and seductive elements, and the ways in which they express, create, sustain, and challenge the lived experience. Ramirez (1996) suggests that the aesthetic perspective is like "the inscription on the facade of Le Museé de l'Homme, at Palai Chaillot, in Paris [which] reads. . . . ['Here are beautiful things, wisely assembled, which instruct the eye to see, as never before, the things which are in the world']." (p. 240). Aesthetics provides a means for silence to escape and become expression, and an aesthetic perspective allows us to see it. Yet few scholars are exploring the possibilities of the aesthetic approach (for an exception, see Calas & Smircich, 1996). There exist artful practices of resistance (Aptheker, 1984; de Certeau, 1984) that we have barely touched upon and expressions of silence that are invested with the aesthetic and embedded in our daily lives. An aesthetic perspective provides a way of exploring how silence is expressed.

SIGNIFYING SUBJECTIVITY

Silence as communication and communication as silence act in ways to position people within the social order. Stuart Hall (1985) demonstrates the power of naming as a means of "interpellating" who he is in relation to others. He tells the story of when he was brought home from the hospital as a baby and his older sister described him as a "coolie." To describe him as an infant of darker skin is to position him in an inferior status. A long history of intermittent slavery and uprisings, colonization and emancipation, resulted in an intricate system of racial categorizing. For example, the racial history of Haiti, not unlike Jamaica, demonstrates that whites, of course, were most privileged; mulattoes received special privileges, but not full status; and the darkest Africans were placed lowest on the social scale. Thus, no more than a few days old, Stewart Hall was initiated into the Jamaican racial system that signified his subject position.

Not only does history impact the position of subject, but so too does place. Moving from culture to culture, Hall describes how he is positioned differently in distinct countries. He explains these cultural, political, sociohistorical, and economic influences as contributing to *chains of signification.*

Silence as communication and communication as silence both create and perpetuate these subject positions. People are *named* into certain subject positions, but the notion that those positions carry with them privilege or disprivilege is silenced. This silence, in part, is achieved through the taken-for-granted labeling, naming, "hailing," or interpellating people as subject positions. To complicate matters, no individual carries a single subject position. Each person can be labeled and treated according to a plurality of subject positions (Laclau & Mouffe, 1985). For example, Stuart Hall is not only interpellated according to race, but he also holds subject positions in terms of gender, sexual orientation, age, class, intellectualism, able-bodiedness, and so on. This plurality of subject positions contributes to a complex system of signifying subjects in society.

Stewart Hall's story suggests that signifying practices take place at both the personal level and simultaneously at a cultural or macro-level. In the following section, I provide a brief overview of the dynamic relationships surrounding the micro- to macro-levels.

MICRO- AND MACRO-LEVELS OF COMMUNICATION

Everyday practices have been distinguished from more formal and global practices by way of the terms *micro-* and *macro-level exchanges.* These terms may at first glance indicate a bifurcation between local interpersonal communicative activities and the policy and practices of institutions such as government, education, or religions. However, scholars are arguing against viewing micro- and macro-level exchanges as dichotomous variables. For examples, Ritchie and Price (1991) suggest that "[h]uman communication behaviors are complex, and they implicate processes at several levels" (p. 133). Subsequently, micro- and macro-levels are only two of many levels. Or, as Eulau (1986) contends, the micro- and macro-level exchanges should be thought of as existing on a continuum. Taking this a step further, McDermott and Roth (1978) suggest that by exploring the everyday practices we come to see that there is no distinction per se between micro- and macro-level practices; instead, "there are no macro- and micro-constraints, no macro- or micro-behaviors, but people leaning on each other in specifiable contexts" (pp. 323–324).

Burawoy (1991) suggests that he used the terms *micro* and *macro* in order to distinguish his extended case method from other hermeneutic approaches. Specifically, he states:

> The considerable divergence between the methods requires categories that are so abstract and ahistorical that they are of little use in examining the appropriateness of a given method for a particular phenomena. We have to re-specify the meaning of micro and macro to appreciate the relevance of the extended case method. (p. 283)

Burawoy (1991) draws from the critical perspective as advanced by Habermas (1979) to explain his position. He argues that isolating interpretations of everyday practices to the everyday life world without extending it to include the larger system that organizes social practices fails to provide a full picture of resistance and oppression. Burawoy notes that those who limit their interpretations to the micro-level "ignore distortions brought about by the economic and political systems, particularly through the incursion of the universal media of exchange—money and power" (p. 285).

The critical perspective is an important one for defining the distinctions as well as the connections between the micro- and macro-level exchanges (Banks & Riley, 1993). Giddens's (1984) structuration theory provides a means of viewing micro- and macro-level exchanges less as dichotomous variables and more as interwoven activities of expression. The emphasis is on recognizing that "all social systems, no matter how grand or far flung, both express and are expressed in the routines of daily social life" (Giddens, 1984, p. 36). Ideological assumptions are embedded within the "taken-for-granted" everyday exchanges. In turn, the exchanges impact the macro-level organization of society and the macro-level reinforces the micro-level exchanges (Clair, 1996a). The result is what Weick (1979) calls the vicious cycle and is similar to what others have named "self-producing," "self-referential," and "autopeitic" (see Deetz, 1992, pp. 180–187), as well as "reproductive" (Giddens, 1979) or "co-productive" (Smith, 1990, 1993).

Foucault (1978) encourages us to extend our thinking of the micro- and macro-levels to a multitude of complex interrelated levels. Just as his discussion of formations occurs at one level and articulation at yet another level so too, power relations are occurring simultaneously at several levels of exchange.

Although each of these scholars has contributed to our understanding of how different levels of symbolic exchange produce one another, there simultaneous aspect was probably put most eloquently and parsimoniously by feminist activists during the 1960s when they raised placards that announced that "the personal is political." In short, the micro is the macro. Since that time feminists have asked us to view our realities as ongoing dialectical exchanges (Glennon, 1983), centered around "be-ing" (Daly, 1973) and communicating. Fraser (1989) suggests that privatizing and personalizing issues has contributed to the invisibility and silencing of women because as issues are privatized they are considered incontestable. Thus, we must see micro and macro, personal and public as discursive practices, as personalizing or publicizing, rather than as places or individual discreet events. As Dervin (1993) explains "communicating is where the micro becomes the macro, the macro the micro . . . where hegemony and resistance meet" (p. 52).

RESISTANCE/\OPPRESSION

Resistance and oppression are well-developed themes in feminist scholarship. This is not to say that one unified theory of resistance and oppression has been set forth by feminists. To the contrary, just as there are varied forms of feminism (see Tong, 1989, for an overview), there are varied approaches to conceptualizing resistance and oppression. Feminists have drawn from rhetoric ranging from liberal to Marxist in order to explain oppression and resistance within a patriarchal system. For some feminist scholars, Marx provides a sufficient theoretical framework for understanding patriarchal oppression. For others, Foucault provides the complex set of criteria necessary to illuminating the concepts of resistance and oppression. Others rely primarily on their own footing (e.g., de Beauvoir and Daly). Yet there are feminists who find both the traditional radical structuralist approach as well as the more slippery postmodern approach to be insufficient for explaining women's oppression and, especially, women's resistance.

Aptheker (1989) tells us that "[t]he word *resistance* is freighted with historical interpretation and nuance. We bring many assumptions to this word because of the way in which it has been defined in general (by men) in society" (p. 169). She suggests that three crucial assumptions invade our thinking and theorizing about oppression and resistance. First, the male view privileges oppression and resistance at the public level. This, she argues, marginalizes the private injustices that women face. Second, she proposes that resistance has been "counterpowered to ideas about accommodation and collaboration" (p. 170). For women, accommodation and collaboration may be forms of resistance. Finally, Aptheker suggests that traditional ways of speaking about oppression and resistance lead us to view emancipation in terms of grand political shifts in power.

Aptheker (1989) credits feminists with exposing the personal injustices as social injustices. She encourages researchers who study the everyday practices of oppression (e.g., sexual harassment, divorce laws, child support issues) to continue to contest the boundaries between personal and public. However, she believes that women's resistance is not isolated to moving these issues into the public domain. "There is a women's resistance that is not *feminist, socialist, radical,* or *liberal* because it does not come out of an understanding of one or another social theory, and it is not informed by experience in conventional politics" (173). The resistance, Aptheker (1989) speaks of, resides in everyday practices. Aptheker describes the networks that women form as well as personal responses to their situations, which help them to resist a patriarchal definition of reality. Their everyday art speaks of their everyday silences. And their everyday talk speaks of their resistance.

Like Aptheker (1987), Foss and Rogers (1994) repeat the call for more research in the area of resistance and coping when they suggest that we not only expose the personal as political, but also the political in the personal. Credit for this insight can be traced to Gloria Steinem (Conti, 1997). In response to "The Personal is Political" Steinem (1992, as cited in Conti) suggested: "It's time to turn the feminist adage around. *The Political is Personal*" (p. 17). However, Foss and Rogers, who focus on the everyday practices of resistance, are concerned about overlaying "expert" interpretations grounded in traditional critical or radical feminist theories.

While Aptheker (1987) and Foss and Rogers (1994) fear imposing grand theories as the explanation of women's oppression and resistance, Bingham (1994) argues that extremes in either direction can be dangerous. Relying on the work of Wood and Cox (1993), Bingham writes:

> The challenge for researchers, . . . is to devise theoretical orientations and methods of study that respect the integrity of individual experiences while also recognizing the influence of discursive practices and material life on individual subjectivity. . . . Without this layering of knowledge we fail to offer any illumination, much less

critique, of prevailing social structures and practices that have legitimized sexual harassment and other forms of oppression. (pp. 174–175)

With these thoughts in mind, I draw from several theoretical orientations to guide my investigations of the organizing of silence. I hope that layering different perspectives will further illuminate the complex issues surrounding patriarchal and political silence as well as the discursive practices that encourage resistance and emancipation.

CHAPTER 3

Organizing Silence

... then our silences must lead us to a wider, deeper listening.
—Kate Adams, 1994

To date, Antonio Gramsci has provided one of the most compelling foundations for theories that explore the silencing of individuals and groups of individuals. His work has been refined by critical scholars, and poetically exploded into useful fragments by postmodern scholars. In this chapter, I briefly review Gramsci's development of coercion and hegemony as explanation for the control of mass populations, especially European masses under a fascist regime. Second, I describe the feminist challenges to Gramsci's definition of coercion and the feminist post-modern challenge to his definition of hegemony.

COERCION, HEGEMONY, AND SILENCE

Antonio Gramsci, relying on Marxist thought, explains the domination of mass populations across Europe during the reign of fascism. Gramsci (1971) notes that the "democratic-bureaucratic system has given rise to a great mass of functions which are not all justified by the social necessities of production, though they are justified by the political necessities of the dominant group" (p. 13). According to Gramsci, in order for the dominant group to control the masses both coercion and hegemony are required. No dominant group can rely entirely on coercion. For if the dominant group uses physical force and threats of death or other punitive measures as its sole means of control, it will expend huge amounts of time and energy in the control process. Furthermore, complete control through coercion is more likely to lead to resistance through revolution or rebellion because coerced people have little to lose. Eventually, systems of control become "normalized" into everyday practices, which are regulated through institutions such as the family, education, religion, systems of law and law enforcement, medicine, and general administration. These systems guarantee "relations of domination and effects of hegemony" (Foucault, 1978, p. 141).

Gramsci defines hegemony and coercion, respectively, as:

1. The "spontaneous" consent given by the great masses of the population to the general direction imposed on social life by the dominant fundamental group; this consent is "historically" caused by the prestige (and consequent confidence) which the dominant group enjoys because of its position and function in the world of production.
2. The apparatus of state coercive power which "legally" enforces discipline on those groups who do not "consent" either actively or passively. This apparatus is, however, constituted for the whole of society in anticipation of moments of crisis of command and direction when spontaneous consent has failed. (Gramsci, 1971, p. 12)

Gramsci's development of a theory of coercive and hegemonic control is both notable and problematic. It is notable for its addition of hegemony as a subtle means of controlling the masses—force by consent—and for its conceptualization of hegemony and coercion acting in concert to enforce control. Yet each definition (i.e., hegemony and coercion) is problematic for several reasons. First, I address the limitations of Gramsci's version of coercion and follow with a discussion of hegemony.

Limitations of Gramsci's Definition of Coercion

Gramsci's definition of coercion is fundamentally insightful. He suggests that the masses cannot be controlled through either hegemony or coercion exclusively. The possibility for physical force must be apparent yet used with restraint. Specifically, Gramsci's definition suggests that "legal" forms of discipline can be used against individuals who do not "consent"; or, government discipline can be enforced upon the masses during moments of crisis when "spontaneous consent has failed" (p. 12). Gramsci explains:

> The "normal" exercise of hegemony on the now classical terrain of the parliamentary regime is characterized by the combination of force and consent, which balance each other reciprocally, without force predominating excessively over consent. Indeed, the attempt is always made to ensure that force will appear to be based on the consent of the majority. (p. 80)

Taken together, Gramsci's conceptualization of coercion and hegemony suggests that physical discipline resides primarily in the state and that it is the state that exercises forms of coercion in times of hegemonic crisis. Specifically, he writes:

> [B]ecause huge masses (especially of peasants and petit-bourgeois intellectuals) have passed suddenly from a state of political passivity to a certain activity, and put forward demands which taken together, albeit

not organically formulated, add up to a revolution. A "crisis" of authority is spoken of: this is precisely the crisis of hegemony, or general crisis of the State. (p. 210)

This characterization of coercion may be appropriate for understanding the workings of a fascist regime, but it fails to address the oppression of marginalized members of society who face coercive practices in their everyday lives. I am not suggesting that marginalized groups have not encountered physical coercion from the government, indeed they have. For example, stories of state-sanctioned or state-enacted violence against protesters or people suspected as threats to "authority" are not uncommon in American history. Certainly, stories abound concerning coercive action taken to silence groups that have failed to "consent," such as civil rights activists, including Native Americans (e.g., Wounded Knee—both over a century ago and in the 1970s), suffragettes (see O'Neil, 1986, for the story of the beating of suffragettes who were led by Alice Paul), Japanese who were confined in internment camps during World War II, and Vietnam War protesters (e.g., the students at Kent State University who were shot by National Guard troops). Although each of these examples demonstrate how marginalized groups are treated during a "crisis of authority" or a "crisis of hegemony," they do not depict the whole story of coercion. As Gramsci suggests, these acts of coercion are necessary to maintain control over people. However, other forms of coercion exist for marginalized groups that may be equally influential in the control process.

Neglecting to include the everyday violence and coercion faced by women and minorities into theories of oppression has been a source of frustration to many feminist activists. MacKinnon's (1991) dynamic response to Foucault's *The History of Sexuality*, clearly and forcefully reminds us that women have been oppressed through sexual coercion both at the level of everyday practices as well through institutions; in other words, both *civil* and *state* influences are at work to use Gramsci's terms. Relying on Diana Russell's (1984) work, MacKinnon notes:

that 44% of all women had been victims of rape or attempted rape at least once in their lives, . . . abuse of women of color was more frequent . . . 38% of young girls had been sexually molested by some person in authority or a family member, . . . before they reached the age of majority . . . about a tenth, it would appear, of rapes are reported. . . . If you add up all the forms of sexual harassment, . . . she [Diana Russell] found that only 7.5% of women reported none of them, ever. (p. 5)

The Women's Action Coalition (WAC) compiled statistics of violence faced by women in their everyday lives. These statistics are too numerous to report in detail here, but a few examples follow:

- Every 15 seconds a woman is battered in the United States.
- 60% of battered women are beaten while they are pregnant.
- 1 in 4 suicide attempts by women [in general] is preceded by abuse, as are half of all suicide attempts by African American women.
- In 1991, 2.7 million reports of child abuse were recorded nationally; 15% (or 404,100) were child sex abuse cases. (WAC, 1993, pp. 55–57)

In addition, Connell (1987) provides an overview of everyday physical violence perpetrated on those people who fail to demonstrate qualities consistent with "hegemonic masculinity." These statistics of domestic violence, rape, beatings, and murder of men, women, and children, especially of marginalized status, are attributed to a collective structure that privileges a violent and powerful image of white, heterosexual masculinity. Connell's statistics reinforce the claims that violence against these marginalized groups crosses countries and cultures of varying economic and sociopolitical systems. He singles out gender, race, and sexual orientation as the primary subject positions that challenge *hegemonic masculinity*. Clearly, scholarship points to the everyday violence that these others face (Cockburn, 1991; Daly, 1973; hooks, 1992; MacKinnon, 1979, 1989, 1993; West, 1993).

Thus, the recent moves to privilege hegemony over coercion as the primary explanation of oppression, control, and silence is unsatisfactory for explaining the domination of marginalized groups of people, especially women. Coercion is not only enforced by the state, nor is it only called upon during times of crisis. To the contrary, violent coercion surfaces at every level of society and is in part reinforced through institutional and state apparatuses. In short, although Gramsci's definition of coercion is insightful and his conceptualization of hegemony and coercion acting in concert with one another is illuminating, the definitions do not fully explain the oppression of marginalized people, especially that of women. Gramsci himself noted that sexual politics and the oppression of women is an especially complex matter. His views on the subject are far from clear as he calls for the independence of women from males; yet he is also concerned about "unhealthy *feministic* deviations" occurring in society (p. 298, also see footnotes in Gramsci, 1971, that attempt to decipher his meaning).

Limitations of Gramsci's Definition of Hegemony

Gramsci's conceptualization of hegemony suggests that individuals *spontaneously* consent to the general direction of the social order as prescribed by the *dominant fundamental* group. Furthermore, this consent is bestowed due to the privileged position the dominant group holds. Their historically grounded elitism rests on their privileged position in relation to production. This definition of hegemony excited scholars who spawned new studies that extended Gramsci's discussion beyond fascist European social relations. However, as the theory was applied more widely, gaps and fissures became apparent. Gramsci's hegemony needed to be reshaped to fit the postmodern concepts of the world.

The first challenges were directed at his notion of one dominant fundamental group. The idea that one dominant group controlled society worked well for theories of fascism, but failed to satisfy numerous modern-day scholars. Chantal Mouffe provided one of the earliest critiques against the *one dominant group* theory.

Mouffe (1979) argues that the political struggle cannot be reduced to class struggle; "it did not consist in a simple confrontation between antagonistic classes but always involved complex relations of force" (p. 180). These insights were further developed into a theory described as radical democracy that accounted for multiple social relations based on a plurality of subject positions (Laclau & Mouffe, 1985).

To further complicate, and at the same time illuminate, the relations between subject identity and hegemony, Laclau and Mouffe (1985) argue that these subject positions are continuously constructed through discursive practices. These discursive constructions evolve into systems of differences that are continually unfolding. We are faced with an "irreducible plurality" (p. 139); and "the problem of power cannot, therefore, be posed in terms of the search which constitutes the center of a hegemonic formation, given that, by definition, such a center will always elude us" (p. 142). For example, an individual holds subject positions in terms of economic class, gender, sexual orientation, religion, physical or mental acumen, race, ethnicity, and age—to name a few. Thus, a plurality of subject positions exist (Cockburn, 1991; Daly, 1973; Deetz, 1992; Hall, 1989; Laclau & Mouffe, 1985; Mouffe, 1979).

Laclau and Mouffe (1985) also question the degree of coercion that is subtly built into a system that interpellates people according to subject positions that are already constituted as *inferior* or *other* in some way. Thus, the coercion is more intricately embedded in social relations than surface appearance would indicate.

Hall (1989) reiterates that all too often researchers take a simplistic approach to the concept of hegemony failing to recognize "that the notion of hegemony is not the old notion of determinism in a new guise" (p. 51) (also see Mouffe, 1979; Mumby, 1987, 1988; Smart, 1986). Hegemony is not the "struggle between already constituted blocs—them over there and us over here—battling like mastodons on a field" (Hall, 1989, p. 51). Rather, hegemony is a constant struggle in the creation of positions; a struggle over identities, issues, and interests that are never fixed, but are always open to the malleable practices of communication (Clair, 1993b).

As Foucault (1979) explains, domination is dependent on "dispositions, maneuvers, tactics, techniques, functionings; that one should decipher in it a network of relations, constantly in tension. . . . Furthermore, this power is not exercised simply as an obligation or a prohibition on those 'who do not have it'; it invests them, is transmitted through them; it exerts pressure upon them just as they themselves in their struggle against it resist the grip it has on them" (pp. 26–27). Thus, the concept of hegemony, as defined by Gramsci, is still useful in describing social relations and the silencing of individuals, but with a reduced emphasis on a single dominant group as hegemonic.

New conceptualizations of hegemony emphasize the plurality of subject positions and the role that discourses play in creating, sustaining, and challenging current social order. Incorporating this complex view is a challenge to scholars.

An example of how daunting the task is to explicate the complexities of hegemony are evident in Condit's (1994) work. Condit develops a perspective of hegemony that calls for researchers to look at *polyvocality of concordance* as demonstrated through rhetorical strategies invoked by varied interest groups. This theory of hegemonic concordance focuses on the alliances achieved between groups. Although this theory is quite insightful, useful, and draws directly from Gramsci's insights, it still fails to capture the full complexity of hegemony. Condit focuses on groups as they relate to the issue of *in vitro* fertilization. These groups include doctors, infertile couples, the Catholic Church, to name a few. Condit recognizes multiple discourses coming from the varied groups who each hold varying levels of power. But Condit does not develop Laclau and Mouffe's (1985) notion of a plurality of shifting subject positions. In other words, doctors are discussed as doctors, while the idea that they may also be infertile or Catholic or male is never mentioned. Both themes and interest groups are selected by the researcher who attempts to critique them individually for their multitude of implications for all parties concerned. Yet the researcher *names* those interests and individuals and *judges* the impact based on textual materials. Certain groups are bound to be left out or misjudged. In other words, while Condit provides a healthy dose of viewing the world as a complicated social process, even she is unable to serve up all the complex intricacies in one article. I do not mean to criticize Condit; to the contrary her work is provocative. However, I do mean to highlight the incredibly complex nature of the problem. (For another example of applying a critique of concordance, see Consalvo, 1996.) Despite limitations, each attempt to understand oppression and silence brings us closer to understanding the complex nature of social relations.

Radical feminist philosopher Mary Daly (1973) also struggled with how to deal with the plurality of oppression. She wrote:

> It is also true that men are castrated by such a social system in which destructive competitiveness treats men who are low on the totem pole (e.g., black males, poor males, noncompetitive males, Third World males, etc.) *like women* (p. 10). [As long as Daly is using the totem pole reference, let us not forget Native American males among her oppressed male population.]

Although Daly encourages the focus on practices, specifically patriarchal practices, it is difficult not to find those practices privileging an elite white male heterosexual population. We seem to return to a nameable dominant group.

In an attempt to develop the notions of patriarchal practices as silencing a plurality of people, Connell (1987) explores the influences that perpetuate this patriarchal system through practices that reinforce male violence and heterosexual privilege. As mentioned earlier, he names these practices *hegemonic masculinity*. Connell's work begins by including race as a position, which is subject to the ravages of hegemonic masculinity, but his discussion of race, along with age, religion, mental acumen, and so on, gives way to a focus on gender and sexual orientation. Lesbians, gays, and heterosexual women seem to be the primary targets of male aggression, and males themselves are caught up in a vicious cycle of violence.

Catharine MacKinnon (1993) recognizes the plurality of subject positions, as well. She unapologetically focuses on gender and race as examples to provide a thought provoking comment on the unique and shared aspects of oppression:

> Racial and sexual harassment, separately and together, promote inequality, violate oppressed groups, work to destroy their social standing and repute, and target them for discrimination. . . . Yet each also has a particular history, occupies its own ground, and works in its own way both as an expression and as an inequality. (p. 56)

It seems clear that Gramsci's original conceptualization of hegemony fails to provide for the complex practices and plurality of subject positions that more recent scholars have pointed out. Nevertheless, Gramsci's notion of hegemony has also been quite illuminating. The theory suggests that marginalized members participate in their own oppression. Feminists may have been the most vocal group to acknowledge this possibility and explore it for the ability to raise our consciousness concerning domination.

Specifically, Daly (1973) wrote of a dynamic process of "co-optable reformism that nourishes the oppressive system" (p. 6). Other feminists suggest that both men and women have "participated in the construction of the dominant discourse" and that "women have not been simply passive victims" (Ferguson, 1984, p. 166). "At the interpersonal level it is not a conspiracy among men that they impose on women. It is a complementary social process between women and men. Women are complicit in the social practices of their silence" (Smith, 1987, p. 170). Although women may be complicit in the social practices of their own silence, it may be naive to suggest that *no* conspiracy exists. In other words, it is important for all marginalized groups to be wary of their own participation in oppressive practices, but equally important to note that groups have been systematically, intentionally, and maliciously conspired against.

All scholars who take on the challenge of exploring how silence is politically enforced should be praised for their accomplishments. Each bit of new knowledge opens the dialogue. Attempting to understand oppression using these new insights (e.g., plurality of subject positions or hegemonic polyvocality of concordance) can leave scholars feeling as if they are wrestling a bear. At times, I am tempted to and do wrestle with only one part of the bear. In the following sections, I wrestle with the idea that marginalized members of society not only participate in their own oppression according to one subject position, but they can and, at times, do participate in the domination of other groups through a hegemonic process.

The idea that people hold a plurality of subject positions and that a complex set a social relations drive hegemony suggest that we need to explore *how* marginalized groups act in ways that support dominating aspects of the system—not simply by viewing how one marginalized group seems to be situated in relation to a dominant group; but, rather, how marginalized groups situate themselves and each other with respect to the ordering of society. In order to understand oppression, we must question how certain marginalized groups establish their supposed superiority over other marginalized groups. Thus, how these groups enact *privilege* and how they *abandon* "others" will be further discussed. Furthermore, if we are to understand how coercion interacts with hegemony, it would be fruitful to explore practices that clearly evidence both discursive and physical aspects. I have chosen sexual harassment to frame the following discussion. It is both physical and discursive. It lends itself to the possibilities of both coercion and hegemony.

SEXUAL HARASSMENT

Sexual harassment has been described as "violence out of history" (Taylor & Conrad; 1992, p. 414). It is, without a doubt, a coercive practice; yet it can be described as a discursive practice as well. I will briefly address each of these perspectives separately and then discuss the relationship between the two.

The coercive aspects of sexual harassment were described in the early and notable works written by Farley (1978) and MacKinnon (1979). These works not only illustrated sexual harassment, but also named it. MacKinnon's work was instrumental in exposing how the legal system framed sexual harassment in such a way as to make it invisible. By making it invisible, judges and lawmakers were in essence attempting to silence the voices of those who had been sexually harassed. Early definitions of sexual harassment were argued and debated at length. Eventually, a definition was set forth by the Equal Employment Opportunity Commission (EEOC) that was supported by the Supreme Court. This institutional definition of sexual harassment is not without flaws and we should be careful not to reify it as though it were set in stone (Crocker, 1983). Nevertheless, I will provide this definition as a heuristic tool:

> In 1980 the EEOC established parameters for the definition of sexual harassment, which includes unwelcome sexual advances, verbal or physical in nature, and which are deemed sexual harassment when (1) submission to the advances is a term or a condition of employment, (2) submission to or rejection of the advances is used as a basis for making employment decisions, or (3) such conduct interferes with a person's work performance or creates an intimidating, hostile or offensive work environment. (also see Konrad & Gutek, 1986, p. 422)

Furthermore, the pervasiveness of sexual harassment in the workplace cannot be underestimated. Approximately 42% of female and 15% of male government workers reported sexual harassment experiences over a two-year period (U.S. Merit Systems Protection Board, 1981). These figures remained virtually unchanged during the decade (U.S. Merit Systems Protection Board, 1988; Clode, 1988). Estimates of sexual harassment perpetrated against private sector workers are even higher than percentages reported by public sector workers (LaFontaine & Tredeau, 1986; Loy & Stewart, 1984). Educational institutions evidence no immunity to the possibilities of sexual harassment. College campuses host alarming rates of sexual harassment (Dziech & Weiner, 1990; Paludi, 1990; Grauerholz & Koraleski, 1991).

The epidemic proportions with which sexual harassment occurs is only part of the problem. Its insidious nature impacts on victims in negative physical, emotional, and behavioral ways (Crull, 1980/1979; McKinney & Maroules, 1991). Women report suffering from nervousness, irritability, uncontrolled anger and crying, stomach problems, weight loss, and sleeplessness (Loy & Stewart, 1984). In some cases the severity of the harassment leads to posttraumatic stress syndrome, where women suffer from nightmares and wake with cold sweats and muscle tremors for months after the harassment has occurred (Castaneda, 1992). Many women report being unable to work effectively (Taylor & Conrad, 1992). Victims also endure economic hardship as a result of sexual harassment. It is not uncommon for women to be transferred, fire, or forced to quit due to an unbearable working environment (Loy & Stewart, 1984; MacKinnon, 1979). Targets of sexual harassment are not limited to adult women, males of all ages and girls are also subject to these practices. Early scholarship may have downplayed the sexual harassment of males for fear that it would jeopardize the feminist political movement to create laws against such behaviors.

It is widely accepted that sexual harassment is a coercive or material practice, whether that is achieved physically or verbally through quid pro quo or creating a hostile environment. What is less widely accepted and or developed is how sexual harassment is an articulation. Certainly, we recognize that discursive practices (i.e., verbal and nonverbal) are used to perpetrate sexual harassment as well as to resist sexual harassment. We generally think of these practices as occurring at the micro-level (i.e., communicative exchanges between individuals at a personal level). Yet the communicative aspects of sexual harassment do not end with the micro-level exchange.

Relying on the definitions provided in chapter 2, I argue that sexual harassment is a *discursive practice* at the micro-level and an *articulation* at the macro-level in the sense that it articulates a gendered construction of society that silences the marginalized members of society, and reinforces patriarchal practices. Sexual harassment is symbolic of women's oppression; and, at the same time, it contributes to the construction of that very oppression.

Returning to the notion that hegemony and coercion are complex matters, which are both evidenced through sexual harassment, I explore the complex relations within and between marginalized groups. If hegemony is consent by the subordinated to a system of oppression, then we need to explore how these subordinated groups provide support for the oppressive system. I especially focus on how these marginalized groups address privilege and abandonment with respect to each other. The discursive practices of privilege and abandonment that marginalized groups engage in at the micro-level sustain a macro-level articulation.

HEGEMONY, COERCION, AND THE DISCURSIVE PRACTICES OF PRIVILEGE

Privilege denotes special rights and advantages. It is an articulation of dominance. "[P]rivilege turns difference, diversity, and plurality into debased Otherness. Granting esteemed status upon certain individuals, structures, and practices, privilege relegates 'others' to the margins of society" (Clair, 1996b).

Focusing on how marginalized groups treat each other, I suggest that privilege can occur in at least three ways that are relevant to understanding hegemonic/coercive domination: *within group privileging, between groups privileging,* and the *privileging of practices* or structures. Within group privileging refers to acts that are primarily confined to one group as described according to one subject position. For instance, we may talk of how women, as a group, treat each other or how black males as a group treat each other (see Albrecht & Hall, 1991, for a discussion of women privileging and marginalizing each other from networks). Of course, these discussions are limiting because, as pointed out earlier, no one has but one subject position or identity. Moreover, these subject positions can be shifting through their discursive construction. Thus, to speak of women as a group is simplistic to say the least. Women also represent a variety of races, religions, ages, ethnicities, classes (and the list goes on), as do black males.[1]

SEXUAL HARASSMENT AND THE
DISCURSIVE PRACTICES OF PRIVILEGE

Discursive practices that construct a system of privilege are varied. The three reviewed here may not be exhaustive, yet they provide an initial means of addressing the discursive practices of privilege. The three forms discussed are between group privileging, within group privileging, and the privileging of practices. Each are discussed in more detail with respect to sexual harassment.

Within Group Privileging

Within group privileging suggests that victims of sexual harassment may privilege some victims over others. Both men and women have developed a caste system within the class of gender. For women, several theories have been suggested to account for this female antifemale behavior including psychoanalytic theories (Dinnerstein, 1976), socialization and poststructural theories (see Epstein, 1988; Ferguson, 1984), and radical feminist theories (Daly, 1973). For the current purposes, postmodern and radical or critical feminist theories are more consistent with the general direction being taken.

"Feminine antifeminism," as Daly (1973) refers to it, is an extreme form of disprivileging, exhibited by women who discourage other women from pursuing career goals that offer the privilege that they themselves have achieved. Daly (1973) argues that women who promote antifeminism by discouraging other women from achieving their potential are acting as "patriarchy's puppet" (p. 52). Yet this is just one means of promoting privilege within the general group of women.

To define some women as more or less "deserving" of harassment than others is to acknowledge privilege. To accept the harassment of some victims more readily than others or to argue against the harassment of some victims more loudly than others is a means of playing into a patriarchal game of privilege. For example, although some studies indicate that a small percentage of women (ranging from 0% to 17%) are flattered by some sexual behaviors in the workplace (Gutek, 1981, 1985; Littler-Bishop, Siedler-Feller, & Opaluch, 1982), half of all female respondents felt other women would be flattered by sexual behaviors (Littler-Bishop et al., 1982). One hundred percent of these same women reported negative feelings about sexual behavior in the workplace.

Several explanations might be proposed, one of which is that women see other women respond to sexual harassment in "feminized" ways. As Ferguson (1984) suggests women are expected and often do accept their plight with smiles and diplomatic gestures. Many women and men may misinterpret this behavior as condoning sexual harassment when it is more likely that women are only tolerating oppressive conditions in the best way they know or the only way in which they feel safe. For example, many women simply slip away or ignore the harasser while others "smile at them . . . and not let them know it gets to me" (Clair, 1993a, p. 127). These forms of resistance may be misleading. Or women may be projecting what they consider to be "socially appropriate" responses to male sexual behaviors, considering themselves to be social anomalies. In other words, years of socializing leave women under the impression that they are the only ones who dislike the sexual behavior enacted in the workplace and that most other women like this behavior. Women are thus isolated from each other's views. In either case, for women to expect other women to enjoy what they hate is to accept a patriarchal definition of what women like and don't like. They may privilege themselves as being more sensitive to sexual harassment when they perpetuate the myth that most women like being treated this way.

Even more dramatic in terms of privileging some women over others is indicated by the finding that a "woman was perceived as less likable and less desirable when the harasser touched or invited her to a private party than when the harasser had made a sexual comment" (Littler-Bishop et al., 1982, p. 144). The finding that the more "serious" the harassment the less women like the victim, was explained by Littler-Bishop et al. as an example of stereotyping that accompanies the "good girl"–"bad girl" image, with "bad girls" asking for or deserving what they get. This may explain why harassment associated with a consensual relationship has taken so long to achieve legitimacy from policymakers. When outrage over sexual abuse is apparently linked to the privileged status of the victim (e.g., when nuns are granted more privilege than prostitutes), the hegemonic relation is vitalized.

Between Group Privileging

Between group privileging suggests that some members of the subjugated group will enact different discursive practices with members of the dominant group who have been ranked differentially in terms of status. This status might rely on occupational status, socioeconomic status, religious affiliation, sexual orientation, political power, or authority, to name a few. When the status of the harasser is taken into consideration by the victim, as a valid criteria for legitimating the harasser's actions, a hegemonic relation may exist. Reifying the system of privilege, especially between group privileging with respect to sexual harassment, is exemplified in the following studies.

The finding that women affectively respond to sexual harassment scenarios differently when the status of the harasser is manipulated (Livingston, 1982, as cited in Littler-Bishop et al., 1982) indicates a system of privilege. First, Littler-Bishop et al. (1982) found that higher-status harassers engaged in more frequent and more serious forms of harassment than lower-status harassers. Furthermore, the authors found that female flight attendants reported more negative *feelings* when touch was initiated by a lower-status male employee than an equal or higher-status male employee. This study demonstrates the plurality of subject positions in the sense that in general men are privileged over women, yet some women are attributed higher status than males with respect to specific job duties/titles (i.e., female flight attendant vs. male airplane cleaner). It further illustrates the notion that privilege is a defining characteristic of oppressive practices, especially sexual harassment.

In addition, women report different *behavioral responses* to different status harassers. A restaurant server explained in an interview that when she handled sexual harassment, the techniques varied depending upon the status of the harasser. For example, she suggested that if it was a manager who was harassing her she usually would just "blow 'em off," but if the harasser was one of the cooks in the restaurant, she would "blow 'em off and tell them to keep away" (Clair, McGoun, & Spirek, 1993, p. 212).

Status of the harasser has been shown to impact upon affective responses as well as behavioral responses to sexual harassment. Both males and females promote the system of privileging. Men do this by harassing women and subordinate men and by harassing more often and more "seriously" as they gain power and prestige. Women accept privileging by attributing more negative feelings or different responses to the same harassment from lower-status harassers.

Privilege is not limited to the placement of persons in society. Practices and principles can also be privileged, as the next section demonstrates.

Privileging Practices of Oppression

Privileging practices or acts that link the two groups and sustain the domination of one group over another function as a part of the hegemonic process. Victims have reported varying levels of indictment toward sexually harassing behaviors. For example, one woman said that the manager would come up and put his arm around the female workers. "But he never really, I mean he never really, you know, never really tried anything," she said (see chapter 4). Another woman, who contacted an agency to deal with the sexual harassment she had encountered, later dropped the charge due to lack of support from her coworkers and described the sexual harassment as "just touchy-feely" (see chapter 4).

Suggesting that certain forms of harassment are privileged is *not* to deny the fact that sexual assault, rape, and quid pro quo harassment are traumatic events often resulting in physical and emotional pain. Privileging more "serious" forms of harassment, however, makes it all the easier to trivialize sexual innuendoes, degrading remarks, and sexually oriented disrespectful behaviors. Although these examples focus on the micro-level exchanges, it should be noted that sexual harassment itself has long been framed as a trivial concern (see MacKinnon, 1979), as has women's oppression in general.

HEGEMONY, COERCION, AND THE DISCURSIVE PRACTICES OF ABANDONMENT

Abandonment occurs when one marginalized group accepts privilege to the disadvantage or neglect of another marginalized group. The practices of abandonment are particularly sensitive to the concept of plurality of subject positions. Furthermore, the following examples suggest a relationship between privilege and abandonment.

In 1840 Lucretia Mott and Elizabeth Cady Stanton were refused the right to speak at the World's Anti-Slavery Convention because they were women. Recognizing their own marginal status as women, they devoted their efforts not only toward the abolition cause but also toward women's liberation. Fredrick Douglas and Sojourner Truth were invaluable allies to Stanton, Anthony, and Mott (Gruening, 1971). This harmonious alliance between African American females and males with white females was limited, at best. Racist attitudes still prevailed among white feminists (Campbell, 1986, p. 434) and sexist attitudes still prevailed among African American men. The uneasy alliance between these groups took a disconcerting twist with the onset of the Civil War. Women from the northern states, both black and white, gave up their legislative activities directed at the protection and enfranchisement of women. Presuming they would be rewarded for their efforts at a future time, they devoted their energies to ending slavery through the war effort. To their surprise not only were they not rewarded, but almost all the legislative enactments that had been lobbied for and won were overturned; but the hardest blow was yet to come (Banner, 1986).

At the close of the Civil War, Wendell Phillips, president of the American Anti-Slavery Society, announced "This hour belongs to the Negro" and committed himself and his group to the enfranchisement of black males. Stanton answered with "Do you believe the African race is composed entirely of males?" (O'Neill, 1986, p. 100). The clamor of the feminist voice was ignored. Passage of the Fourteenth Amendment, ensuring all male adults the right to vote, confirmed the inferior legal and political status of women.

By accepting the vote, black males accepted the notion of privilege and abandoned other marginalized groups (i.e., women of all races). Some white women were quick to retaliate by escalating bigotry, eventually abandoning other minorities, including racial and ethnic minority women.

Modern feminists attempted to renew their allegiances with men in the 1960s, only to be turned away again. Political activist Abbie Hoffman splintered any hope of an alliance when he stated "the only alliance I would make with the women's liberation movement is in bed" (as cited in Kipnis & Hingston, 1993, p. 72). Similar sentiments were voiced by Stokley Carmichael—"the only position for women in the SNCC [Student Nonviolent Coordinating Committee] is prone" (see Coburn, 1993, p. 6).

Abandonment is not limited to male minorities abandoning females. White feminists can also be charged with abandoning minority females, especially poor women, African American women, and poor African American women. Modern white feminists have continually been reprimanded for failing to see the plight of these multiplied disadvantaged women. For example, in the same year that Friedan (1963) released *The Feminine Mystique*, the state of South Carolina practiced sterilization of women who requested government welfare or medical assistance. The Supreme Court had ruled sterilization only unconstitutional when performed on males (Thomas, 1982). Yet *The Feminine Mystique* focused on the plight of well-educated, wealthy white women. The divide between wealthy white women and poor women of all races was more excruciating than Friedan realized. Abandonment of poor and minority women, whether through outright prejudice or ignorant neglect, has tainted the feminist vision. Yet Robin Morgan (1993) argues that this is a media construction, a *man*-made myth. Her argument rests on the fact the she wrote in 1970: "It seems obvious that a legitimate revolution must be led by, made by those who have been most oppressed: black, brown, yellow, red and white women—with men relating to that as best they can." It is difficult to say how the red, yellow, brown, and black women might respond, yet it should be noted that Lakota Indian women were being sterilized without their permission and both female and male Native American peoples were struggling to protect their lands from further encroachment (Crowdog, 1991), Japanese women and men were still recovering from their internment, Hispanics were struggling for economic survival, and African Americans were still facing segregation and the daily humiliations and physical coercion of prejudice.

Further criticism suggests that the white woman's liberation is based on the "desire" to work at challenging jobs while the black woman's liberation rests in being freed from the drudgery of manual labor. This particular criticism may be more media-engineered than substantive, according to Epstein (1988). Wealthy white women do indeed exist and Betty Friedan describes their existence as nothing more than a "comfortable concentration camp" (Friedan, 1963). However, statistics indicate that stereotypes of white women are as mythical as stereotypes of any other minority. While it is true that many influential feminists were and still are upper-class, well-educated females; they are few in number. The media painted a portrait of white women sitting at home watching soap operas and complaining about boredom, when in fact, in 1977, less than 16% of households in America fit the traditional description of a male head of household going off to work while his wife stayed home (Epstein, 1988). The myth encourages the notion that racial minorities (and at the time especially blacks as a group) encounter more prejudice than women as a group. This debatable point only increases tension between the two groups and leaves the minority woman (e.g., black women) tautly stretched between two rival groups. Furthermore, when women, as a group, are pitted against men and women of a particular group (e.g., African Americans) not only are subject positions complicated and confused, but other groups (e.g., racial and ethnic minorities, disabled, lesbians, bisexuals, and gays, and so on) are rendered nearly invisible.

Images of feminists as bra-burning, male-bashing, radicals is another media myth (Morgan, 1993). Negative images of one group, can result in other individuals or groups denying any affiliation with the ridiculed group.

This brief historical overview of abandonment suggests that abandonment may be occurring in three different ways. Like privilege, marginalized members may abandon members of their own marginalized group; they may abandon members of another marginalized group; or they may abandon principles, ideals, or goals. Each of these forms of abandonment are enacted as discursive practices. The following section will review sexual harassment situations for evidence of discursive abandonment.

SEXUAL HARASSMENT AND THE DISCURSIVE PRACTICES OF ABANDONMENT

Abandonment occurs in several different ways. First, examples of within group abandonment will be provided and followed by examples of between group abandonment. Finally, I will present an example of the abandonment of principles.

Within Group Abandonment

If a woman, for example, enters into a romantic relationship with a male of a superior status and subsequently receives favors that neglect or disadvantage other female or male subordinates, then the woman has abandoned her unempowered coworkers. It is not uncommon for this scenario to continue with further abandonment by the marginalized members of the workplace. Acts of sabotage against the woman are common, and generally unrelenting. Women in these situations are often forced by the pressures of coworkers to quit or are fired when their work fails to meet organizational standards even if this is due to a covert conspiracy by offended coworkers (Backhouse & Cohen, 1980). Here we see the subordinates, representing a class of people, abandoning each other.

Another scenario of abandonment comes from a graduate student who confided to a senior doctoral student that three male professors had made unwelcome advances. She did not divulge their names. Concerned over the issue, the senior graduate student called a meeting of his fellow graduate students. He believed this incident was not isolated and demanded attention. Several other graduate students feared that filing a complaint against their major advisor would result in ramifications affecting everyone. They not only discouraged the victim from coming forward, but turned her into the scapegoat. "Ironically, their advisor was not one of the three professors who had made the unwelcome sexual advances" ("Our Stories," 1992, p. 367). The group of students abandoned a fellow student for fear of retaliation. This is an expression of within group abandonment.

Abandonment also occurs when victims lodge formal complaints against a harasser, often with the knowledge that they are not the only ones who have been victimized, yet no one will come forward to support their complaint. Orphaned by this response, these people may feel more marginalized and more isolated than before they filed the complaint. For example, a woman who reported encountering sexual harassment from a superior called an agency that deals with sexual harassment in order to file a complaint; however, her coworkers who had also been sexually harassed by the same man, refused to support her story. Without support from coworkers, the woman rescinded her complaint ("Our Stories," 1992).

Another scenario depicting abandonment details the plight of the victim who does the abandoning. The professor was continually taunted by the chair of her department with sexually degrading comments, sexist jokes, and innuendoes. When she voiced complaints about his behavior, her anonymity was not protected. Specifically, the chair of the department was informally told that the professor was voicing complaints. Her review from the chair that year was replete with unfounded criticism. She was given a probationary contract and informed that tenure may be dubious at best. The professor continues her story:

> Tensions remained high but rather than risk backlash and further harassment, I maintained my silence. Shortly before my tenure review, a newly appointed female colleague, . . . filed a grievance against the chair after he uttered a series of harassing remarks. . . . The female acting-provost counseled me about my precarious situation in offering supporting testimony. Out of fear, I chose silence. Out of frustration, my colleague abandoned her petition and resigned. ("Our Stories," 1992, p. 366)

Tragically, this story conveys not only the pain of sexual harassment but also the consequences of abandonment. This story reflects within group abandonment in the sense that one victim of sexual harassment abandons another. Both women are silenced. As Taylor and Conrad (1992) put it: "This last story suggests how bureaucratic conservatism and male power divide the members of powerless groups—here, women—against each other, rewarding them for their silence and complicity, for placing self-interest over gender solidarity" (p. 412).

Between Group Abandonment

An ironic example of between group abandonment, with respect to sexual harassment follows. On Thursday, November 12, 1992, the National Association of Student Personnel Administrators (NASPA) presented a live interactive teleconference entitled "Confronting Sexual Harassment on Campus." Five nationally renowned experts participated in a panel discussion that was moderated by a Washington, D.C. attorney and former talk-show host. The host, an African American female, told the panel of experts that sometimes men call women names when they ask them to stop the harassment. Specifically, they may be called "feminists." The moderator proceeded to inquire of the experts how a woman could stop sexual harassment and protect herself from being linked with "feminists."

Although this was only one woman, the sentiment against feminists is hardly unknown. This demonstration of renouncing feminism exemplifies how even the more marginalized of the marginalized can abandon other groups (i.e., the teleconference host was both female and African American). Furthermore, it is bitterly ironic for this woman to wish to be separated from the women (i.e., feminists) who have done the most to define sexual harassment and make it illegal, when confronting a male who is perpetrating this crime.

Abandonment of Principles

A target is not always visible in the case of abandonment. For example, a single mother of two was attempting to survive on a meager salary in an academic setting. She was subtly propositioned by a superior who had the power to increase or decrease her work load and with it her pay. The woman wrote that she still experiences a "heavy sense of dread and uneasiness . . . whenever I recall the events" ("Our Stories," 1992, p. 373). Her uneasiness stems from the fact that she "did not challenge his actions. . . . Instead, I chose my job and position over the higher ethic of claiming my moral ground" (p. 373). Sometimes, principles are abandoned.

INSTITUTIONALIZING SILENCE

At the surface level, the previous examples seem to focus on the micro-level exchanges between people; however, as Taylor and Conrad (1992) point out, organizational structures such as bureaucracy contribute to the practices of privilege and abandonment. Institutional silencing is not limited to particular practices. Institutions themselves contribute to the silencing of marginalized members of society.

Legal, religious, and educational institutions are based upon patriarchy and each promote the current organization of society. Foucault (1978/1976) traces this system back to early Roman laws. We are indebted to feminists like Catharine MacKinnon (1979, 1989, 1993) for challenging the taken-for-granted structures of the legal system with respect to patriarchy in general and sexual harassment in particular. Legal supremacy of the male continues today and is collaborated by other patriarchal societal structures, including formalized religion and educational institutions.

With respect to religious institutions, we are indebted to feminist Mary Daly for her brilliant and dynamic philosophical resistance to religion, especially the Catholic Church and its relation to other institutions of patriarchy. Daly (1973) writes: "*God* then functions to legitimate the existing social, economic, and political status quo, in which women and other victimized groups are subordinate" (Daly, 1973, p. 19).

In addition, our educational systems are used to reinforce dominant worldviews (Deetz, 1992; Foucault, 1978/1976). For example, at the surface level our school systems are intended to educate the young; yet, as Willis's (1977) work points out, the educational system sustains the status quo and is particularly influential in perpetuating how working-class lads get working-class jobs. McRobbie (1981) and others move this work beyond the concept of class to include a feminist agenda. Current concerns over our educational systems are only beginning to uncover a host of sexist, racist, and homophobic practices, to name but a few problems.

The workplace is saturated with sexuality. Although management often argues for a Weberian-like rational, emotionless, and gender-neutral image (see Ferguson, 1984; Mumby & Putnam, 1992; Pringle, 1989), numerous organizations demonstrate gender discrimination. Gender discrimination in general and sexual harassment in particular are institutionalized in religious organizations (Daly, 1973), government and private service organizations, political agencies, and trade unions (Cockburn, 1991). DiTomaso (1989) found gender discrimination and sexual harassment in industrial manufacturing, nonmanufacturing, and public agencies. Findings by Collinson and Collinson (1989) corroborate the existence of sexual politics at work in industrial shops, trade unions and insurance companies. Even residential care organizations are sexually politicized (Parkin, 1989). No organization is free from gender or sexual politics. Thus, organizations play a role in hegemonic formations.

Gendering of organizations contributes to the oppression of women. Generally, women are relegated to lower-status positions with lower pay (Buzzanell, 1995; Clair & Thompson, 1996; Epstein, 1988;

Kanter, 1977). This phenomenon is not restricted to American working women. "The concentration of women at the bottom of all occupational strata holds for socialist and communist societies as well as Western capitalist societies" (Epstein, 1988, p. 152). Women in western society are steered toward stereotypically female occupations (Kanter, 1977; Pringle, 1989) where their sexuality is often "harnessed" to provide benefits to the organization (Tancred-Sheriff, 1989). Russian women may dominate what is considered to be "male" occupations in America, such as physicians, but they fail to hold prestigious positions in medical academies (Coser, 1981). American women who enter male-dominated professions or attempt to reach male-dominated echelons also face the much publicized "glass ceiling" (Buzzanell, 1995; Solomon, 1990). The European community, in general, does not demonstrate any significant exemption from gender discrimination (Kerr, 1986). Nor do Eastern countries demonstrate a freedom from female oppression. Both Japan and China have recently noted high levels of sexual harassment in their countries (see Goozner, 1993; *Sexual Harassment*, 1992, respectively).

Gender discrimination, especially through sexual harassment, is not isolated to any one society or country. It is a primary means of controlling and silencing women (Cockburn, 1991; Hearn & Parkin, 1987; MacKinnon, 1979; Tancred-Sheriff, 1989) and marginalized men, which results in a worldwide phenomenon with sociopolitical and economic ramifications (Tancred-Sheriff, 1989).

The pervasiveness of sexual harassment attests to its "normalized" place in society, which was not legally challenged until the 1970s. As a reified practice, it carries a general message to the members of society which clearly articulates that some people are privileged over others.

ORGANIZING SILENCE

To suggest that organizing silence is a simple, systematic practice that can be explained via the old notions of hegemony and coercion would be inadequate, at the very least. The present chapter suggests that organizing silence is anything but simple to explain. Numerous scholars have advanced Gramsci's notions of hegemony and coercion, allowing us to see that multiple voices are positioned in a variety of places within an ever shifting and changing set of social relations. Nevertheless, certain groups of people have either never or rarely experienced a shift into a leading position. Many voices are marginalized if not *totally silenced*.

Silencing groups of people may take on a multitude of forms that we have only begun to explore. Silence may be achieved through coercion or through hegemony. It may be created through discursive practices that privilege some and abandon others. Silence may be systematically structured through institutions or informally imposed through informal conversation. Furthermore, silencing people may be achieved through incessant and noisy discourses (Foucault, 1978). For example, Warren (1996) employed a Foucauldian approach to the study of how the media covered the story of Dr. Margaret Bean-Byog, a psychotherapist accused of sexually abusing one of her male clients. The media coverage was extensive (e.g., it was covered by *Newsweek*, *Time*, the *New York Times*, and several national television shows). Warren argues that this noisy discourse of one woman's story of therapeutic abuse effectively silences the vast majority of women's experiences of being abused by male therapists. Specifically, she writes: "and indeed, the male physician who abuses is in a limited space, a betwixt and between—utterly central to our understanding, yet remarkably absent in much of the writing about it" (p. 19).

Warren (1996) suggests that breaking silence about therapists' sexual abuse of patients by highlighting the exception only perpetuates the silence that has been taken for granted. As Clegg (1994a) points out, openness does not necessitate a democratic utilization of voice. I made a similar observation in chapter 1 of this book, that is, at times even the most articulate are silenced and the least articulate, based on their association with a privileged group, are granted positions from which to speak. Drawing directly from Clegg (1994a), who writes "Control is never total" (p. 163), Warren (1996) suggests that "Silence is never complete" (p. 22). Both writers were influenced by postmodern precepts. Scholarly pursuits to shatter the oppressive aspects of silence and give radiant voice to the resistive aspects of silence may provide possibilities for a new social order.

CONCLUSION

In this chapter, I have painted a bleak picture concerning social relations. It is not my intent to overwhelm the reader with injustices too numerous and vile to be overcome. For if there were not possibilities for change, this book would be an exercise of feminist futility and the reader might do well to characterize me as a masochist, but such is not the case. To the contrary, there are examples of resistance to hegemony and coercion; there are examples of marginalized members of society denouncing privilege and supporting one another; and there are discursive practices that turn silence into expressions of freedom, responsibility, and care. Appropriating silence and expressing resistance and change are developed in part III of this book.

Believe me, I am as anxious as you to step into the world of possibilities where silence is turned into a cacophony of resistance. Nevertheless, before proceeding to a detailed discussion of the self-contained opposite and its possibilities to demonstrate a dynamic means to challenging patriarchal constructions of the world, it is imperative that I provide empirical evidence of the claims that I have made in chapters 2 and 3.

I argued that discursive practices culminate in articulations of a grander scale than one might initially expect. In addition, I argued that social relations exist in a variety of dialectical tensions that are self-contained and that require exploration of where hegemony and resistance meet, of how communication and silence function simultaneously, of how subject positions create and re-create a complex system of social relations, and how the everyday practices played out at the micro-level are concomitantly creating macro-level articulations and practices. Evidence of this complex structure can be seen through everyday practices such as that of sexual harassment. Therefore, in Part II I provide three empirical studies that explore these complex issues. These chapters move from the dominant paradigm approach to a more pluralistic perspective.

PART II

CHAPTER 4

The Use of Framing Devices to Sequester Organizational Narratives: Hegemony and Harassment

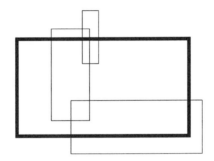

Stories of pubic hair, pornography, and pressure for dates were included among allegations of sexual harassment voiced by Anita Hill against Supreme Court nominee Clarence Thomas.[1] Initially reluctant to go public, Hill explained that she had confided in a few close friends at the time of the harassment, none of whom advised her to lodge formal complaints. Sequestering of sexual harassment stories is not limited to the actions of the harassed employee. Public sentiment keeps stories of a sexual nature out of the mainstream as well. President George Bush's reply to the question of whether victims of sexual harassment should come forward reflects the tendency to sequester stories of sexual harassment: "I say they should come forward. But let's do it in a climate so people are not destroyed in the process. And that's why I'm saying let's do it behind closed doors" (McFetters, 1991, sec. 4, p. 3).

While some researchers devote their efforts to exposing and explaining sexual harassment, others contribute to its low profile. For example, Martin, Feldman, Hatch, and Sitkin (1983) suggest that mainstream organizational stories demonstrate both positive and negative images of the organization, yet their analysis fails to provide any stories from a sexual genre. Even more striking is the study conducted by Murray and

Gandz (1980) who interviewed 590 MBA and BBA graduates in order to collect stories of organizational politics. Although the authors report "33 percent of our managers thought that politics frequently played a role in how much people were paid . . . as a result of a superior's unreasonable ethnic, gender, or other prejudices" (Murray & Gandz, 1980, p. 15), they relegate gender discrimination to one of the "minor varieties of politics" and never mention any other stories of sexual harassment. In defense of these authors, it should be noted that the deep-structure games that distort reality are so embedded within our culture that it is difficult even for researchers to explicate, discover, and understand them (Frost, 1987).

The power of narratives in the cultural and ideological development and reproduction of organizations is well documented (Deetz, 1982; Feldman, 1990; Frost, Moore, Louis, Lundberg, & Martin, 1985; Mumby, 1987, 1988; Pondy, Morgan, Frost, & Dandridge, 1983; Putnam & Pacanowsky, 1983; Smircich, 1983). In the past, researchers frequently selected and interpreted organizational stories that were easily obtainable due to their public status. Mumby's (1987) interpretive analysis of a common and freely exchanged organizational narrative at IBM addresses the deeper meaning (i.e., the political meaning) embedded within the story and how those meaning systems create and perpetuate dominant interests.

Now it is essential to investigate those stories that do not receive the same public exposure, legitimation, or respect within the organization that more commonly reviewed stories reach and receive; that is, sequestered stories. The term *sequestered* refers to stories that are set apart from the mainstream. As Boje (1991) suggests, "there are implicit rules in storytelling (who can tell it, to whom, and where)" (p. 124). Stories of sexual harassment are passed on to coworkers and close friends or relatives outside of the organization, but are rarely considered proper material for public anecdotes. In addition to *who tells it, to whom,* and *where*, it is important to address *how* organizational members tell their stories. *How* organizational members frame their experiences and accounts may severely impact the kind and amount of exposure the story will receive.

The purpose of this study is to provide an empirical-interpretive analysis of sexual harassment stories with respect to how such stories perpetuate or challenge the dominant interests. The term *dominant interests* refers to those concerns shared and promoted by members of the privileged group. Generally speaking, with respect to the discursive concept of gender, males, regardless of their race, religion, or socioeconomic status, have enjoyed the privileged position relative to females. Thus, the dominant ideology can be captured by the terms *patriarchy* and *fraterarchy* (Buzzanell, 1990; Cockburn, 1991; Daly, 1975, 1984; Ferguson, 1984, Fine, 1993; MacKinnon, 1979, 1989).

The privilege of patriarchy is maintained through coercion and or hegemony (i.e., when the leadership of one group dominates another group through the subjugated group's unwitting acquiescence or active participation). The present study devotes special attention to the framing of sexual harassment stories as a hegemonic device in maintaining the dominant interests of the privileged group.

The account offered here is not inconsistent with the reports of men being sexually harassed. To the contrary, patriarchy is seen as an ideology that promotes hierarchy, class division, and oppression usually at the expense of women, but other marginalized members of society are also subject to oppressive practices. Since people hold a plurality of subject positions, only the most privileged of privileged would be exempt from the indignities of sexual harassment.

How hegemony functions to suppress marginalized members of society can be viewed from several different perspectives including: differentiation and fragmentation perspectives (Frost, Moore, Louis, Lundberg, & Martin, 1991; Martin & Meyerson, 1988; Meyerson & Martin, 1987; Meyerson, 1991a), critical-interpretivism (Clegg, 1989; Deetz, 1982; Habermas, 1984; Mumby, 1987, 1988; Rosen, 1985, 1988), postmodernism (Foucault, 1978; Laclau & Mouffe, 1985; Anonymous Authors, 1991), and Marxist, socialist, radical, or postmodern feminism (see Buzzanell, 1990, for a review of the feminist perspectives). The commonality among each of these perspectives is that they reject a functionalist orientation, promote the study of ambiguity, and seek to uncover the "deep structures" of oppression. More specifically, the fragmentation perspective and postmodern feminist perspective support the existence of "diversity in cross-cultural, racial and class arenas" (Buzzanell, 1990 p. 9; Meyerson, 1991b), which is relevant to understanding sexual harassment as a political tool of oppression. The use of hegemony as an explanatory principle concerning sexual harassment relies on the well-developed work of critical theorists who can be credited with explicating the concept of hegemony (Gramsci, 1971); yet it is also dependent upon the advances of feminist theory that expand beyond class distinctions to sex distinctions (MacKinnon, 1989). Hegemony will be discussed in relation to sexism rather than classism in the present chapter. Although this chapter does not fully develop a postmodern critique and deconstruction of sexual harassment, it does draw from certain postmodern principles by asking the reader to *"think culturally* rather than to *think of culture"* (Anonymous Authors, 1991, p. 316). With respect to sexual harassment, this view discourages the perspective that sexual harassment is some "thing" that exists "within" the organization (see Smith, 1992, for a critique of reified containment views of organization). Rather, to *think culturally* about sexual harassment is to encourage the view that sexual harassment is discursive action that hegemonically reproduces an oppressive organizational society.

While hegemony is considered an interactive process, the present chapter devotes its attention to how the subjugated members reinforce or challenge their own domination. Specifically, this chapter analyzes how sexually harassed workers participate or refuse to participate in their own domination through the framing of their sexual harassment experience.

SEXUAL HARASSMENT

Exposure of numerous certain organizational issues could be damaging to the dominant interests of an organization and thus subject to sequestering. For example, stories of conflict resolution (Aram & Salipante, 1981), wrongful discharge (Ewing, 1983), employment at will (Gorden & Infante, 1987; Sanders, 1987; Werhane, 1987), discrimination (Osigweh, 1987), and dismissal or harassment due to whistleblowing (Stewart, 1981) may be subject to sequestering through reframing. Although each of these issues deserves to be addressed in relation to how narrative framing acts to promote and reproduce the dominant ideology, this investigation will focus on sexual harassment for two main reasons: (1) sexual harassment is widespread, and (2) it is unlikely to reach public view.

Sexual harassment is pervasive in the workforce. Fairhurst (1986) reports statistics from the U.S. Merit Protection Board of 1981 that state that 42% of female and 15% of male government workers reported having encountered sexual harassment in the previous two years. Approximately 50% of working women drawn from a random telephone survey of men and women in Connecticut "experienced at least one form of sexual harassment" (Loy & Stewart, 1984, p. 36). Similar levels were reported for 1991 (Ukens, 1991). However, these statistics may vary according to sex ratios. For instance, Lafontaine and Tredeau (1986) suggest that over 75% of women in traditional male occupations encounter sexual harassment. Although no difference has been found between blue-collar and white-collar occupations for sexual harassment frequency (MacKinnon, 1979; Tangri, Burt, & Johnson, 1982), some occupational arenas demonstrate a lower frequency of sexual harassment (e.g., higher education, sciences, and public administration), but these findings were reported with some trepidation (Lafontaine & Tredeau, 1986).

In 1981, 3,456 formal sexual harassment complaints were filed with the Equal Employment Opportunity Commission (EEOC). By 1990, the number of complaints reached 5,694 (Lee, 1992). Although there may be some debate over these figures, as Terpstra and Baker (1988) set the figures for 1981 complaints at 4,272 rising to 7,273 by 1985, they demonstrate just how pervasive sexual harassment is when these figures are linked with statistics for how many victims of sexual harassment actually file complaints. Estimates place the frequency of female complaints somewhere between 0% (Ukens, 1991) and 5% (Tangri et al., 1982).

Organizations rarely encourage open discussion of issues of sexual harassment and often call for confidentiality when dealing with the complaints. Furthermore, women rarely go through formal channels to report sexual harassment because they expect their complaints will be ignored or trivialized, they receive no guarantee that they will be protected from future retaliation, they expect that the male-dominated hierarchy will "team up" against them, or their time will be wasted because the organization has an ineffective sexual harassment policy (Collins & Blodgett, 1981). Gruber (1989) reports that women's most common reaction to sexual harassment is avoidance. Specifically, only 22% of female sexual harassment targets tell anyone about the incident (Ukens, 1991).

Sexual harassment cannot be viewed strictly from the perspective that these interactions are solely the personal experiences of the victim if we are to understand the complex role sexual harassment plays in society. Gender discrimination through sexual harassment oppresses the victims and encourages a power imbalance among organizational members (Cockburn, 1991; Kanter, 1977; Loy & Stewart, 1984; Mills, 1989; Tancred-Sheriff, 1985). Furthermore, sexual discrimination acts as a means of controlling and defining the structure of economies and cultures (Tancred-Sheriff, 1989).

The sequestering of sexual harassment stories acts to maintain the established dominant structure, contributing to the hegemonic process. The sequestering of these stories is achieved through a variety of framing devices. Specifically, the present investigation assesses the use of framing devices by the subjugated group and examines the ways in which these framing devices promote or challenge the dominant ideology.

FRAMING

Anthropologist Gregory Bateson has been credited with originating the concept of "framing" (Goffman, 1974). Bateson draws from the work of several famous philosophers including Whitehead, Russell, and Whorf (Bateson, 1972). According to Bateson, frames delimit "a class or set of messages (or meaningful actions)" (1972, p. 186). Like a frame around a picture, people perceive and evaluate social interactions by separating figure from ground. Specifically, "the frame is involved in the evaluation of the message . . . as such the frame is metacommunicative" (p. 188); it comments upon the discursive event.

Bateson argues for a theory of schizophrenia rooted in the concept of framing. Individuals who are continually faced with double-binding situations (i.e., paradox), which they are incapable of reframing or transcending, will eventually escape through the fantasies of schizophrenia, the only sane answer to an insane communicative environment.

Goffman (1956, 1959, 1963, 1974) applies Bateson's premises to situations with less radical outcomes. Specifically, he views everyday events as vulnerable to the organization of individuals' perceptions, their transformations and even retransformations of events. Goffman (1974) assumes "that definitions of a situation are built up in accordance with principles of organization which govern [social] events—and our subjective involvement in them" (pp. 9–10). Framing situations in a way as to embarrass a coworker or client confuses the roles by altering what is generally acceptable in the social situation and incapacitates the recipient of the message in a similar, yet less dramatic, fashion as the schizophrenic described by Bateson. Goffman detailed a number of examples, one of which describes a physician who prescribed himself to his female patients as a sex therapist who could relieve their medical problems through sexual intercourse. Wood and Conrad (1983) apply the concept of framing to the double-binds faced by professional women. The authors propose how women may communicatively perpetuate, reframe, or transcend the paradoxes of organizational life.

Similarly, Ferguson (1984) presents "femininity" as one overarching frame of subordination. Femininity is created through institutions of dominance and subordination. In other words, "feminized people" are powerless people who are confined "to the depoliticized status of reactive spectators" (p. 173). Furthermore, "strategies of femininity" are implemented "to ensure survival" (p. 145). Participation in patriarchy through feminine survival strategies may be a reflection of hegemony.

HEGEMONY

Rooted in Marxist ideology, the concept of hegemony was first popularized through the prison notebooks of Antonio Gramsci (1971). Gramsci contemplated the persuasive process involved in the fascist domination of large European populations (Gitlin, 1980). While it was not Gramsci's charge to provide a fully developed theory of hegemony (Gitlin, 1980), the concept offers a valuable means of understanding organizational control (Clegg & Dunkerley, 1980).

Hall (1985) defines hegemony as a process in which the dominant class both dominates and leads the people to accept subordination as the norm. Although coercion and passive acceptance are means to domination, active participation by the subjugated group is more pervasive (Gramsci, 1971). This supports Mouffe's (1981) proposition that hegemony is achieved through "the ability of one class to articulate the interests of other social groups to its own" (p. 183).

The concept of hegemony has been used to understand the social movement of feminism as well as specific issues such as sexual harassment (Cockburn, 1991). "At the interpersonal level it is not a conspiracy among men that they impose on women. It is a complementary social process between women and men. Women are complicit in the social practices of their silence" (Smith, 1987, p. 170). Furthermore, Ferguson (1984) states that both men and women have "participated in the construction of the dominant discourse" and that "women have not been simply passive victims" (p. 166). However, because their social reality is rooted in "feminization" it is difficult to decipher between their "integrity" and their "victimization" (pp. 166–167). Yet little research has been devoted explicitly to *how* women participate in this hegemonic process. Scholars have developed theoretically and conceptually the relationship between framing and hegemony from a feminist perspective, yet few have empirically tested it (Fine, 1993).

FRAMING DEVICES

Framing devices are rhetorical/discursive practices that define or assign interpretation to the social event by the actor or actors. Stahl (1989) suggests that such discourse acts as a "kind of metanarrative that influences interpretation but is not part of the content" (p. 49). Six framing devices are especially pertinent to the sequestering of organizational narratives. The first three are drawn from the work of Giddens (1979): "accepting the dominant interests as universal," "simple misunderstanding," and "reification." The fourth framing technique, "trivialization," is rooted in Goffman's work and has been developed by political mass media researchers (Gitlin, 1980). The fifth framing device, "denotative hesitancy," relies on Schiappa's (1991) interpretation of Perelman and Olbrechts-Tyteca's (1969) rhetorical treatise on definition as a matter of choice. Finally, the sixth framing technique, "private/public expression and private/public domain," is rooted in the notion that communication is generally expressed in either a public or private format within either a public or private setting (Sennett, 1977). Its academic heritage and link with women's oppression can be traced to Engels (see MacKinnon, 1989).

Giddens (1979) suggests that sectional interests are strategically concealed by the dominant group through three ideological forms:

1. Representation of sectional interests as universal, as when the dominant group attempts to represent its own particular sectional interests as the interests of all (Mumby, 1987) or the dominant group attempts to represent dominant interests as universally shared

2. The dominant group attempts to deny or disguise system contradictions through ideology, which is often accomplished through confusing or paradoxical statements of purpose, but also may be achieved by suggesting that the other individual simply misunderstood

3. Dominant interests are reified.

Dominant group members may frame harassment in the following three ways: (1) "To bring a sexual harassment suit against one employee is not in the best interests of the company," (2) "No, we would never let one employee harass another, but we really feel that you may have misunderstood the man's motives," and (3) "This behavior is tolerated because it is natural; boys will be boys." These examples show how the dominant group might frame sexual harassment. The examples are derived from the work of Giddens. However, the focus of the present study is to investigate how the subjugated group frames harassment and whether they use similar techniques that might be more readily expected of the dominant group members. Subsequently, the three framing devices will be discussed briefly from the perspective of the targets of sexual harassment.

Accepting Dominant Interests

Once again, accepting dominant interests is to agree that "organizational" interests take precedence over secondary or personal interests. Targets of sexual harassment accept dominant interests when they define sexual harassment as a less important problem to the organization's survival than other concerns presented as crucial by management. Ironically, judges have argued to protect overloaded courts from sexual harassment cases on the grounds that there would simply be too many cases (MacKinnon, 1979, p. 96). Thus, the dominant interest is protecting overworked judges and overloaded court dockets so that more "important issues" can be handled. Targets of sexual harassment who agree with this interpretation promote the hegemonic relation. An example of how a target of sexual harassment might discursively play this out in an organization is as follows: "I'll just quit my job instead of filing sexual harassment charges because that will be easier for everyone."

Simple Misunderstanding

Simple misunderstanding is based on the notion that organizations must disguise contradictions inherent to the system. Targets of sexual harassment incorporate the framing device of simple misunderstanding when they accept and justify contradictions. For example, if targets of sexual harassment agree with judges who argue that an inordinate number of complaints could be expected by the courts due to women misconstruing flirting as sexual harassment (MacKinnon, 1979), they have accepted the contradiction that everyone has the legal right to be protected from sexual harassment except women who do not know the difference between harassment and flirting. Thus, the simple misunderstanding frame may be employed when a worker explains harassment in the following way: "I'm not sure if it was sexual harassment or if the man was just flirting with me."

Reification

Reification gives permanence and a sense of tangibility to abstract ideology. In other words, what may well be a political construction is viewed as a permanent aspect of the structure or process of an organization. Mumby (1987) uses the concept of hierarchy to exemplify reification. Hierarchy is a political construction that has been granted a sense of permanence within most organizations. The dominant ideology could reify itself by suggesting, "That's just the way it is," which further implies that "the way it is" is immutable (Mumby, 1987). Targets of sexual harassment who agree with or support court rulings that excuse cases of sexual harassment on the grounds that sexual harassment is "natural" or "biological" with a tone of "you can't change *that*" (MacKinnon, 1979, p. 90) are supporting the hegemonic condition. Within the organizational setting, targets of sexual harassment who employ reification might offer the following frame: "There's nothing you can do about it. Men are just that way."

Trivialization

A fourth way that the dominant group may sequester stories is to deny their existence or trivialize the harassment, thus, effectively invalidating the situation. Trivialization denies the validity of the individual's experience; it reduces the significance of the act and invalidates the target's feelings (Giffin, 1970; Watzlawick, Beavin, & Jackson, 1967). Trivialization as a form of negation can be accomplished through "humor, ridicule, or metaphor" (Metts, Haefner, & Konsky, 1987). "Trivialization of sexual harassment has been a major means through which its invisibility has been enforced" (MacKinnon, 1979, p. 52).

Trivialization may be achieved by making light of the narrative event (e.g., turning it into a joke). As Daly (1984) suggests, harassers often frame their actions in terms of "harmless entertainment," which provides further criticism of the woman if she challenges their behavior: "Can't she take a jock/joke?" (p. 209). The most prevalent form of sexual harassment is in the form of "unwanted sexual teasing" (Bureau of National Affairs, 1988). Framing harassment as a harmless joke not to be taken seriously disguises its deeper implications that women are not respected in the organization (Duncan, Smeltzer, & Leap, 1990). While trivialization may well be a form of framing incorporated by the dominant group, the question remains whether the subjugated group trivializes sexual harassment.

Denotative Hesitancy

An institution's vocabulary is a powerful tool for defining an institution's reality and plays a significant role in the ability to frame organizational experiences by both the dominant and subjugated groups. Ardener (1975) refers to the subjugated group as the "muted" group; the group that has no language to express itself and thus accepts its own limited definition of self as dependent on the dominant group. Domination through vocabulary and definition constitute a form of hegemony that Spender (1984) calls "internalization of oppression" or "conditioning" (p. 204) and its pervasiveness and power to control cannot be underestimated (Daly, 1975). Spender (1984) suggests that if the dominant group can control the language of the culture, then it is possible that the subordinate group may be without the means of expression necessary to convey their own narrative or define their own experience. As MacKinnon (1979) points out (crediting both Sheila Rowbotham and Adrienne Rich), "the unnamed should not be mistaken for the nonexistent" (p. 28).

Following Perelman and Olbrechts-Tyteca's (1969) notion that definitions are a matter of choice, Schiappa (1993) argues that "definitions are rhetorical in the sense that they function as strategies of social influence and control" (p. 2). When new terms are introduced into a language system (e.g., sexual harassment) their definitions must be contested before the language-users reach consensus about their denotative meaning. Shared understanding and adherence to the definition by the linguistic community results in "denotative conformity." Furthermore, Schiappa argues that "a successful new definition changes not only recognizable patterns of behavior, but also our understanding of the world" (p. 3).

It is important to note that denotative conformity is preceded by tentative use of the term and its definition by unempowered groups (Schiappa, 1991). For example, the legal term "sexual harassment" is more likely to be used by groups who have been empowered to do so (e.g., attorneys, legislators, experts in women's studies, and officials of women's organizations). Women without legal expertise are less likely to use the term "sexual harassment" when describing encounters of a sexually harassing nature.

Public/Private Expression-Public/Private Domain

Sennett (1977) argues that there are two types of expression: public and private, which are typically practiced within corresponding domains. Expressions refer to characteristics of communication or text. For example, private expression is spontaneous, emotional, symbolic, sincere, and reactive; public expression is codified, repeatable, and signlike. Private expression and public expression are not equivalent to the private and public domains. Domains are more contextual in nature; they represent a definition of a situation. The public domain is that contextual situation that is environmentally and communicatively open to people as a whole. The private domain is environmentally closed to outsiders and usually kept within the confines of close family and friends. Labeling sexual harassment as "personal" or "private" can be construed in several different ways; however, "one function of all the uses of the term is to individuate, devalue, pathologize, and isolate women's reactions to an experience which is common and shared" (MacKinnon, 1979, p. 87). Furthermore, it contributes to the "mystification" of harassment and relegates it to an interpersonal level.

The dominant ideology can frame sexual harassment as part of the private lives of the employees, thus dismissing it as an organizational problem and relegating it to the private domain. It is also possible for the subjugated group to frame their own stories by bringing in elements from the private domain. For example, if a woman responds to sexual harassment by framing her experience or the account of it in a way that brings in the personal life of the characters, then she is moving the story from the public arena to the private domain (e.g., "When my husband hears what you did, he's not going to be happy"). Furthermore, if the victim retells the story with spontaneity and emotions, especially those that promote passivity (e.g., embarrassment or fear), then s/he is using private expression, which is more likely to maintain the dominant ideology.

Based upon the foregoing review, six primary framing techniques are proposed. They are accepting dominant interests as universal, simple misunderstanding, reification, trivialization, denotative hesitancy, and displaying private expression or incorporating the private domain.

METHOD

Each of five undergraduate female students volunteered to conduct semistructured interviews with ten working women. Women were selected due to their higher rate of exposure to sexual harassment. A total quota sample of fifty women were selected for participation based on demographic characteristics intended to match the U.S. Census statistics. These characteristics included type of occupation, marital status, race, and full-time or part-time employment.

The sampling strategy included reviewing the U.S. Census figures for women employed outside of the home in nonvolunteer positions and calculating the ratio necessary for a sample size of fifty women. Then a grid was devised on paper to accommodate the categories. The five interviewers used a network system to fill the quotas. Specifically, they sought out relatives, friends, and coworkers who might fit the description. Then they moved on to friends of friends, acquaintances, and strangers until they exhausted the required number of women for the categories. All fifty women were selected from a midwestern urban area. The students met on a regular basis to determine which categories were not yet filled. An exact match in quota ratios was not achieved in the area of job type, mainly because the students' perception of how a particular occupation would be listed under the U.S. Census category was not in agreement with the perception of the woman who held the position. Thus, slight deviations were accepted across categories (see table 1).

The undergraduate students who conducted the interviews were given interview training during three meetings. The college students also participated in wording the questions and arranging their order for the interview (see Clair, 1993a for a complete interview schedule).

The women were asked general questions focusing on what they liked or disliked about their jobs, what they considered the most frustrating aspects of their job, and how they expressed that frustration. Finally, the interviewer asked the respondents if they had ever experienced sexual harassment or job discrimination.

All interviews were audiotaped by the undergraduate students with

TABLE 1
Percentage of Sample Sought, Sample Achieved,
and Reported Sexual Harassment

	Sample Census Percentage (Sought)	*Sample Percentage (Achieved) (n = 50)*	*Percentage Reporting Sexual Harassment (n = 24 [48%])*
Marital Status			
Married	59%	54%	41%
Single	25%	32%	50%
Divorced/Widowed	15%	14%	71%
Race			
White	82%	82%	51%
Black (African American)	11%	11%	50%
Hispanic/Other	7%	7%	0%
Part/Full Time			
Part-Time	23%	34%	41%
Full-Time	63%	66%	52%
Career/Job Title			
Managerial/professional	24%	24%	42%
Technical sales/administrative	45%	42%	33%
Service	16%	18%	89%
Production	2%	6%	100%
Operators/fabricators/laborers	8%	2%	100%
Farming/forestry/fishing	1%	2%	0%

Source: Statistics are based on the following sources: U.S. Bureau of Labor Statistics, *Employment and Earnings*, 1987; U.S. Bureau of the Census, *Current Reports*, series P-20, No. 427; and U.S. Bureau of Labor Statistics, *Population Bulletin* 2307 (1988).

the verbal consent of the interviewee. A graduate student transcribed all fifty interviews. The author read all transcriptions and listened to the tapes. Then the transcriptions were reviewed by the author who used the six framing techniques to guide the interpretations of the stories. After examining the stories for specific examples of framing devices, the author and a graduate student listened to the selected tapes to verify the correctness of the transcription.

Of the fifty women interviewed, one reported sexual harassment without being prompted. Once asked if they had encountered sexual harassment, 48% of the women reported having encountered sexual harassment on the job.

The stories these women tell can be considered "personal narratives; that is, "a prose narrative, relating a personal experience," which are often characterized as "single-episode" experiences (Stahl, 1989, pp. 12–13). Personal narratives can be interpreted at a variety of levels including discourse, type, and style (Stahl, 1989). The present interpretation is directed at the discursive level that "is used to designate examples of rhetoric or aspects of a situation that either move the story along or frame it" (Stahl, 1989, p. 49). Consistent with the literature presented earlier in this chapter, Stahl (1989) argues that frames of reference define the personal and social reality of the participants. Thus, the framing techniques, like a template, are laid over the personal narratives of sexual harassment to assess how the proposed ideological frames act to sequester sexual harassment.

Finally, it is important to note that a frequency of framing techniques is not specifically provided in the interpretation section. Stories were selected for their ability to offer rich descriptions of the framing techniques. Some of the women's stories include more than one framing device and are repeated in a second section. Occasionally, a story readily displays the use of one framing technique. For example, Elizabeth's story will be discussed under the heading of reification, but the reader should note that Elizabeth also avoids direct use of the term "sexual harassment" to explain her situation. Thus, her story might also fit well under "denotative hesitancy." For the sake of brevity not all stories incorporating more than one framing technique are repeated. However, every story reflecting the first three framing devices are included because such devices were so rarely employed. Most stories include some form of denotative hesitancy and trivialization; exceptions to this are provided. All stories incorporating public/private expression and public/private domain are placed under their respective heading. Again the stories affecting public/private may also incorporate denotative hesitancy or trivialization, but they were not necessarily repeated in those sections due to the abundance of stories to represent the framing techniques of trivilization and denotative hesitancy. Furthermore, framing techniques that emerged from the data, but had not been previously expected, are discussed in the concluding section.

INTERPRETATION OF NARRATIVES

Narratives Accepting Dominant Interest as Universal

Giddens's (1979) first function of ideology suggests that if the narrative is not representative of universal interests, then it is not supportive of the dominant ideology. The perception that one's own interests should be second to the interests of the organization were implied by the following woman's story.

Abbey,[2] who currently works as an office manager handling purchasing, invoicing, and general financial issues, considers herself a "committed" and "loyal" employee who handles conflict by taking the boss's side. For example, she said, "When I'm frustrated I take my boss's side . . . explain to him what needs attention and have him take it from there. I'm not the kind that needs to be loud. . . . I don't want anyone to think that I'm a rat. I'm just looking out for the best interest of that individual." She told us that she encountered the most sexual harassment when she worked at a bar. The interviewer asked her if she had ever encountered sexual harassment from an employer or manager. She said "Yes" and that eventually she thought "What's more important, this job or finding another job?" The harassment had "started out as joking" but it became "more persistent and more serious." Abbey did not detail the actual harassment but did tell us that:

> I felt that I was jeopardizing my job, and that individual's [the harasser's] job. And I saw that there was no reason for that, so I had to leave.

Abbey suggests that she is jeopardizing her job. Usually, to say that one's job is in jeopardy is to be fearful of losing one's job. Although fearful of losing her own job, Abbey sacrifices that very same job in order that her harasser should not lose his job. It is a "feminized" frame that defines the oppressed as responsible for the situation, for example, "*I* was jeopardizing my job and that individual's job." Even more to the point, it is the victim who must suffer the consequences of the actions: "so *I* had to leave."

In Abbey's case, the harasser is her superior. She therefore makes the "logical" decision that she must leave. According to patriarchy, a superior is more valuable than a subordinate, a man more valuable than a woman. Abbey's narrative reflects how some women participate in hegemony by devaluing themselves or their interests.

Narratives Suggesting a Simple Misunderstanding

Stories of sexual harassment lend themselves to being framed as simple misunderstandings between the participants because harassment often begins with ambiguous nonverbal overtures which may be confusing (Hickson, Grierson, & Linder, 1991; also see Goffman, 1974, for a detailed description of ambiguity with respect to framing). For example, Barbara said she had encountered sexual harassment at work and when asked to elaborate by the interviewer, she said:

I know there's a couple of people where I work, really there's quite a few, if I think about it. I guess as I got older I realized more that it's sexual harassment since it's come out more. Like when I first started as an LPN, a lot of times, you know, I took it more as flirting. If a doctor flirted with me, I thought, well you know he's the doctor and you looked up to him. And you know. And, but, yeah, I encounter it a lot and now that it's out in the open I've actually said to people on the job, "You better not do that. I'm only going to tell you once. That is sexual harassment."

Barbara's story suggests that sexual harassment can at times be framed as flirting as seen in the statement "I took it as flirting." However, now that "it's come out more" she is more likely to define it as "sexual harassment." For Barbara there is now no mistaking flirting for sexual harassment.

Cassie, a sales representative, said sometimes the men at work critique her clothing or rub her knee. She explained that the men want "it to come across as a joke," but she interpreted their actions as intentionally trying to make her "feel uncomfortable." Darla, a fax operator at a law firm, said she encountered sexual harassment at her previous job where she worked as a telemarketer. As she put it: "It wasn't blatant, but I could tell."

Personal stories in this study were framed in such a way that the women clearly did not attribute the behavior to a simple misunderstanding. Rather, women were inclined to embrace the notion that harassers want you to think it is a joke or a misunderstanding, but they see through this deceptive framing technique. Thus, the framing device of simple misunderstanding might be used by harassers in order to sequester stories, but is not common to the harassed.

It may be that targets of sexual harassment do not employ a "simple misunderstanding" frame for two reasons: (1) it shifts the blame to them, and (2) it denies them the right to reality (see Goffman, 1974). For the woman to claim misunderstanding is to do more than save face for the harasser; it also shifts the blame to the woman by suggesting that she is in error, unable to correctly interpret and identify communicative behavior. Therefore, the problem is her fault. Furthermore, to claim that you misunderstand is to forfeit your right to acknowledge the difference between illusion and reality and with it the right to sanity. A sane person can distinguish between deception or illusion, and reality. The women interviewed in this study were unwilling to accept the blame or forfeit reality. Thus, by not accepting the "simple misunderstanding" frame, which they claim men supply to them, they are challenging the status quo or at the very least are sidestepping what Goffman calls a "frame trap."

Narratives Supporting Reification

Elizabeth is currently employed as a cashier at a gift shop. She reported being happy with her current boss. Although they have disagreements that at times can be "frustrating," Elizabeth feels as though she is on an equal level with her boss and said she was able "to share my feelings with her." This easy-going superior-subordinate relationship has not always characterized Elizabeth's organizational experiences.

Elizabeth explained that when she was sixteen years old she worked at a restaurant where her boss sexually harassed her. "It was a terrible job" where she "wasn't treated like a person." She said, "He used to touch me in the back room and he used to rub my back and hug me." He asked her, "When are you going to be old enough to go to a hotel room with me?" The company was family owned and Elizabeth liked half of the family members, which may have some bearing on her final assessment of the situation:

> I felt bad, I was close to the family. And I thought it was normal, but it was very, very abnormal. And it used to make me so mad inside. It's a terrible position to be in when it's your job and you like working there but your boss is a real jerk.

The contradictory assessment of the normality and abnormality of sexual harassment at first supports the framing technique of reification by suggesting that this behavior is a normal part of society. Yet the immediate retraction that what was thought of as "normal" is really "very, very abnormal" contradicts the framing technique of reification. Reification as a framing technique, is neither strongly embraced nor totally abandoned.

Similarly, Franny's story both reifies sexual harassment and yet denotes an awareness that life does not have to be this way. Franny explained that organizational life is *pre-dominated* by male chauvinism (i.e., male attitudes are both preponderate and dominate). Although their are several frustrating aspects of a male-dominated system, she is particularly incensed by the way women are treated as inferior and the way some women are coopted by the system as they are promoted. She encountered sexual harassment when she worked for a company in an upper-middle-class suburb. It was during the 1970s. "I worked again as an assistant for several men and they would make jokes. They would make suggestions. It got beyond joking." Franny was bitter about her experiences. She had also encountered sexual discrimination in other forms and had taken the issue to court where she lost on a "technicality." She said that we live in a "very egocentric, very male-dominated" country and "that's just the way it is." Furthermore, we will have "to look to other countries" for better and more feminine systems of organizing. "There are other countries that do not have that mentality." Thus, Franny reifies the status quo and with it sexual harassment when she says "that's just the way it is," yet it is not conceived of as completely immutable. While it seems to be immutable in America, it does not exist in all countries. Thus, reification is again an incomplete matter; a framing technique not totally embraced by these women.

Narratives Evidencing Trivialization

Women trivialize sexual harassment by joking about it, even though it makes them angry or uncomfortable. Cassie explained:

> Well, if it's subtle, and it's jokingly, and it's not hurting me or my position, I'm okay with it, because it's not harming me. And it's nothing really direct. But then it annoys you and you say something about it. You almost want to dish it back, really bad.

Cassie offers contradictory descriptions of her response to sexual harassment. She is both "okay with it" and annoyed enough to "want to dish it back." "Feminization" as described by Ferguson (1984) does not allow for a woman to assert herself or "to organize around common interests" in order "to oppose the powerful" (pp. 148–149). Instead she must show "patience . . . and a high tolerance for ambiguity and for insult" (p. 147). Trivialization represents the overarching frame of feminization.

Gabriella told us that at both a previous place of employment and the restaurant where she currently works both the managers and the cooks sexually harass the waitresses. She told us that the manager "used to come up to all the girls and put his arm around them and schmooze them. But he never really, I mean he never really, you know, never really tried anything." The qualifiers that the manager "never really tried anything" implies that sexual harassment is perceived of in varying degrees and that unwanted arms around the waitress is a lesser offense and therefore more easily trivialized. Gabriella, like many other women in this study, "just blow it off" if they are dealing with "higher-ups," but tell coworkers to leave them alone and "blow it off." Helen, a medical technician, had a boss who "kept wanting to, I don't know, touch you. . . . I would joke with him about it and make light of it and just kind of blow him off." Irene said, "My former boss would come up behind me and rub against me." She explained further "that it got to be kind of a joke" in that she would watch for him and slip away when he got close. Several other women reported similar responses. Judy said, "I sort of got up and walked away and made a joke of it." Similarly, Karen responded, "Blow it off. Smile at them . . . and not let them know it gets to me."

Lisa trivialized what happened to her although she felt she had been harassed. She contacted an organization that dealt with sexual harassment and discrimination cases, but found she had no support from her coworkers although several of them had been harassed by the same person. Later, Lisa described his actions as "*just* touchy-feely" and after some time she "made a joke of it."

Trivialization may act as a coping mechanism or, as Ferguson (1984) might explain it, as a feminized strategy for survival. To frame the situation as though it is a trivial matter may reduce the anxiety associated with assertively challenging the status quo and justify the lack of action or follow through.

While some women may trivialize their experience, others did not. To the contrary, they pointed out the debasing ramifications of sexual harassment. Melissa, an M.D. specializing in surgery, relayed the following feelings to us:

> When you're a surgeon and you do surgery on women, and there are male surgeons, there are lots of inappropriate comments made—often sexually based, often degrading comments that they would never make if the woman patient was awake, and that as a woman surgeon bothers you a lot. . . . [Some men have] preconceived notions of women as people and how they are as patients that I don't consider to be valid.

The surgeon did not trivialize the situation. Her organizational status may allow her to break away from the more feminized strategy of trivialization. The same can be proposed of Natalie. Although she has only been with her present company for nine months, she is thirty years old, a sales representative, and earns between $30,000 and $39,999 per year. Natalie told us that when she says something that stumps her boss, he often uses sexual harassment to belittle her in some way. For example, she told us that he might say, "Go take your nice ass and get out of here." Instead of trivializing this kind of objectification, she says that she would respond with a statement like "You know, you don't have to say that." Furthermore, she recognizes and acknowledges that sexual harassment is "demeaning," saying "they look at you like you are a lower class" or "not a serious business person" and as if you "were there just for their amusement or their sexual jollies." While Natalie does not hold the same social status as a surgeon, she is a well-paid professional woman, a status that may contribute to her challenging her boss's behavior.

Narratives Demonstrating Denotative Hesitancy

The women in this study were intentionally given no prior definition of sexual harassment. By supplying the women with a definition of sexual harassment, perhaps the one offered by the Equal Employment Opportunity Commission (EEOC), the researcher would be establishing artificial parameters. Supplying a definition may limit the quantity or content of stories that women consider sexually harassing, but are not included in the definition. Conversely, the argument can be made that without supplying a definition of sexual harassment some of the women who did not report sexual harassment in this study actually did encounter it, but were unsure if their experiences should be considered sexual harassment. Since not forcing a definition on the participants left the door open for women to test the validity of their experiences, it was judged to be the better choice for this exploratory endeavor.

Lack of terms and denotative conformity can successfully sequester a story. For example, Franny, who recounted a past experience of sexual harassment, said:

> And at that time, in the middle 70s, there was not this big thing about sexual harassment. Had there been, I would have found a lawyer immediately. I would have gotten a lawyer immediately. But, it just wasn't the topic of the day. In other words, I would have been shown to be leading them on.

Odelia, a fifty-year-old sales administrator, also reflected on the past. She explained that when she first started working "sexual harassment" was not part of the vocabulary, so she couldn't be sure whether she had been sexually harassed. More recently, Barbara, in reference to sexual harassment occurring in the 1990s, commented that "I realize more that it's sexual harassment since it's come out more."

The *more it's come out* may reflect the early stages of denotative conformity. As the term and topic gains greater visibility and acceptance, it is easier for marginalized members of society to use the term.

While the "topic" limited these women's ability to develop their stories, other women were limited by inadequate definitions of sexual harassment. When Pat, a telephone repair person, was asked if she had ever encountered sexual harassment, she answered: "Yeah, I guess you might say that. It depends how you define it." She continued: "Guys telling real sexist jokes and talking *that* way about their wives." The interviewer asked her what she does in these situations. "I would just leave," Pat answered. Then she continued: "But as for me one guy propositioned me and I just talked to him. Another guy was blowing kisses and smacking his lips at me every time he saw me. He did it for about a year. . . . The thing is I don't have to be around them all the time. It's just in and out of the garage." Similarly, the response "Kind of" was offered by women who continued to tell stories that leave little doubt that sexual harassment was occurring. For example, Rachel said:

Uh, kind of. I mean, when I worked in the restaurant, I was quiet. . . . People think you are stupid. I let them think like this because I didn't really care about these people. I just wanted to do my job. I don't want to get close to anyone because they are not people I want to be around. And my manager . . . he always caught me, hugged me, you know. He wanted to touch my shoulders. He always says you are the very girl that I always dreamed of. . . . I worked with a lot of the black men. You know, they just want a white girl. And they just say "Oh look at her." You walk by. They just like to touch you.

One day, she was standing in the kitchen of the restaurant holding a heavy tray over her head with both hands. A male coworker came in and started saying,

"Oh, honey are you nice," and he touched my rib cage and almost touched my chest. I was almost in tears. I was so scared.

Then another male coworker came into the kitchen. He took the tray from her and threw the harasser into the wall.

I thought he was going to kill him. I was so scared and just wanted to get out of there.

The story leaves little doubt as to whether sexual harassment has occurred, yet Rachel begins this story by saying, "Uh, kind of." While it is possible she is merely showing verbal hesitancy (see Kramarae, 1981; Lakoff, 1975, 1990; Linell, 1991; O'Barr, 1982, for discussions of powerless speech forms) rather than denotative hesitancy, other examples clearly instantiate denotative hesitancy.

When asked the same question, Susan answered, "Possibly, a long time ago." Finally, Tina reported having to deal with "kind of sleazy" comments on the job from her boss like "Oh, what a bunch of beautiful girls," or "Oh, I like the skirts," but she was either unsure of what constituted sexual harassment or lacked empowerment to use the term. She said, "You could say it was harassment."

The term *sexual harassment* may have double-binding implications. On the one hand, it confirms the existence and illegal nature of the behavior. On the other hand, judgment and disciplinary action are relegated to male-dominated arenas (i.e., courtrooms and Congress). Victims of sexual harassment may assertively argue for their rights only to find themselves victimized by the "system." Thus, women may be torn between the term's empowering qualities and its disempowering qualities.

When Gabriella was asked if she had encountered sexual harassment in the workplace, she answered "yes and no." With reference to the yes, she said she had one job "where the manager used to come up to all the girls and put his arm around them." In regard to the "no," she said that many employees flirt with one another. Other women who were not included within the group of sexually harassed individuals gave equally tentative responses, such as: "Not really," "No, I don't think so." However, each of these women went on to describe interactions such as "flirting" or making "jokes" of a sexual nature that they did not consider to be "bothersome." It is difficult to categorize these comments. The women truly could have considered it flirting and joking and therefore did not consider it to be harassment, or they could have framed the incident through trivialization. In either case, they did not go on to offer a story. The other women simply reported "No" or "No, I cannot recall ever encountering sexual harassment."

In stark contrast, Melissa, the surgeon, embraced the term "sexual harassment." When asked if she had ever encountered it, she replied without hesitation, "Absolutely!" This exemplifies a consistency between her condemnation of sexual harassment, her refusal to trivialize it, and her lack of denotative hesitancy.

It is important to note that even if women are supplied with a definition of sexual harassment, they may not share the story with an interviewer for numerous reasons, one of which may fall under the rationalization that the story is too personal to tell.

Narratives Acknowledging Private Expression or Private Domain

Narratives acknowledging either private expression or that were framed in a way that places them in the personal domain rather than in the public domain are more easily sequestered within the organization. First, stories can be viewed as too embarrassing to be passed along as in the following example offered by Uta:

> When I was in nursing school I was in surgery and I was extremely nervous, the surgeon was one of the big guys on the staff. They were doing surgery on a woman; and they were cutting her abdomen open; and, they got down to her pubic hair and were joking about it. They looked at me and made some comment about my red hair and then made a comment about whether my pubic hair matched the hair on my head. I thought I would die.

Women who define the situation as too embarrassing are also supporting the hegemonic relationship. By expressing guilt, humiliation, or embarrassment, or considering the stories too disconcerting to tell, women protect themselves from feelings of debasement, but fail to express their feelings of rage (Daly, 1984). If women expressed rage, rather than humiliation, then they would be expected to take action. Incidents that are too embarrassing to tell are certainly too embarrassing to act upon. This framing device successfully sequesters stories of sexual harassment and keeps the dominant ideology intact.

Sequestering a story because it is too embarrassing to tell is probably the most difficult framing technique to assess. As reported earlier, two women reported encountering sexual harassment but preferred not to talk about it. This may be due to its personal nature since sexual topics have been generally taboo in public discussion. Furthermore, one cannot be sure that other women who said they had not encountered sexual harassment were not doing so in order to keep from talking about what they consider to be a sensitive topic.

Another way of sequestering a story is to frame it or the harassment in terms of belonging in the private domain. For example, Vanessa, a nurse, reported that a doctor who was "pretty handsy" and harassed several nurses,

> came up to me a couple of days ago and said he gets turned on by pregnant women [the respondent was pregnant at the time]. I told him I felt sorry for him. . . . It was really an injustice to his wife.

Rather than claiming that it was inappropriate behavior, especially within the organization, or that it was an injustice to her, the nurse brings in the personal life of the doctor. Similarly, yet more sarcastically, Winona suggested that the man bring his wife along when he made advances of a sexual nature. Finally, Yvonne frames the story by bringing her own personal life into the organization to solve the situation:

> I had an operator . . . who would constantly ask me for sex. Every morning he be waiting to ask me for sex; and, he would always tell me he'd pay me, that he'd give me his check. Whatever it took for me to have sex with him. I brought my boyfriend on the job and he stopped [respondent laughed].

Women seek justice not from an oppressive male-dominated organization or legal system that has tolerated these actions for years but rather, they seek justice based on their private-interpersonal relationships. However, those relationships frequently are rooted in heterosexual male-dominanted foundations. By framing the incident in a personal and private way, targets of sexual harassment are suggesting that this is not an universal organizational interest. By calling on the boyfriend or husband to protect the interests of the woman, they make those interests separate from organizational interests. Consequently, the organization is relieved of its accountability/responsibility in the matter and the dominant ideology remains undamaged.

EMERGENT AND PROPOSED FRAMES

The power of narratives to provide organizational members with a sense of "reality" has been well documented (Mumby, 1987, 1988). Past studies relied on highly visible narratives. The present study provided a look at organizational stories that are usually sequestered, rarely afforded the same exposure as stories intended to reify or support the dominant ideology.

How these personal narrations of organizational life are framed contributes to or challenges the dominant ideology of organizational life. Certain framing techniques either reinforce or challenge the dominant ideology. Specifically, the subjugated group, in this case female targets of sexual harassment, framed their stories in such a way that sexual harassment incidents were generally sequestered or kept out of the mainstream of organizational communication. The women experiencing these events are subject "to gendered institutional assumptions about what they are and are not supposed to say, feel, and think about in a given cultural context" (Meyerson, 1991b, p. 2). At times, their own discourse is embedded with biases that partially disguise or contradict alternative discourses that they provide. For example, Elizabeth told us that the harassment was "normal" and "abnormal" and Cassie claimed the harassment was "okay," but she wanted to "dish it back, really bad." These contradictions suggest that another framing technique might exist; one where the subjugated individual both accepts and rejects the dominant ideology (i.e., "mutual negation"). Thus, the individual negates not only the dominant discourse, but also their own discourse. Perhaps, it is safer for the subjugated individual to negate both. On the other hand, both Elizabeth and Cassie give their negative assessments of sexual harassment after either reifying or trivializing them, which may simply indicate that "feminized" individuals react first in subservient ways, but are capable of overcoming these characteristics during the course of an interview. Only future research can provide answers to questions of (1) whether this is a viable framing technique; (2) if this is a viable framing technique, whether it is predominantly employed by either the dominant or the subjugated individuals; (3) whether the interview itself gives targets of sexual harassment the encouragement to speak out against the dominant ideology, and (4) if open discussions of sexual harassment encourage women to come forward, how will this affect framing techniques in the future?

Another framing device emerged from the data that was not suggested in the discussion of proposed framing techniques. Sexual harassment is often defined in terms of its intensity (i.e., from looks and verbal comments to threats and physical assaults); however, at least one woman in this study framed the harassment in both spatial and temporal terms. For example, Pat said with respect to harassment that "It's just in and out of the garage," which suggests another framing technique, "minimalization." She did not trivialize the harassment itself, but suggested that it occurred intermittently from either a time or space orientation (e.g., "It's just in and out" suggests brief periods of time, not often, and "in and out of the garage" suggests that the harassment is only occurring in one place, not everywhere), allowing for the incident to be minimized. This framing technique may have greater implications in terms of hegemony than a cursory look would reveal. For example, researchers have focused on the frequency of sexual harassment often to the neglect of its more complex meanings in society (Gutek, 1989).

Two other techniques that may be used to frame sexual harassment include "self-defacing" and "self-effacing/erasing." Self-defacing is represented in stories where the women demean themselves in some way whether it be a past inability on their part to deal with sexual harassment or a current lack of skill often attributed to naiveté or youth. This framing technique surfaced occasionally in the stories and is deserving of further investigation. Self-effacing/erasing is different from self-defacement. Self-effacing/erasing is utilized when individuals frame the experience so that they seem to disappear from the story. Some women described their response as slipping away or walking away, which would exemplify self-effacing/erasing. Self-effacing/erasing may be a common technique that parallels the general sequestering of sexual harassment (i.e., the invisibility of the subject). Self-erasing should be considered in future research endeavors.

Future research should also address a limitation of this study. Due to the methodological procedures focusing on recall of sexual harassment, several issues may be raised. First, recall data are always subject to the possibility of distortion over time (i.e., we may forget things or remember them differently). Second, the question can be raised as to whether these data address the temporal character of how respondents came to understand their experience. Future work might address this concern by conducting a longitudinal study. Perhaps personalized case histories would provide richer data to address this limitation.

CONCLUSION

Of the several framing techniques proposed, those based upon the work of Giddens were least fully developed by the subjugated group. Specifically, women did not frame their experiences as simple misunderstanding, nor did they wholly embrace reification. Future research might investigate whether these framing techniques are more natural to the dominant group than the subjugated group. Techniques that were implemented by the subjugated group include: accepting universal interests, trivialization, denotative hesitancy, and private domain/private expression. Accepting universal interests might be combined with trivialization; to trivialize the issue is to relegate it to a matter of less importance. While each of these framing techniques and their relationship to the hegemonic relation deserve more attention at the individual level, it would also be of benefit to study these framing techniques at different levels of society (e.g., how do formal organizational policies, the mass media, Congressional acts and bills, and juridical laws frame sexual harassment). Currently, organizations are aflutter with activity to meet federal guidelines on sexual harassment. The discourse they select to use in their policies, procedure statements, and brochures could be laced with framing techniques that should be investigated.

Furthermore, future studies should investigate the interactive aspect of hegemony. What responses do women anticipate or actually encounter from family, friends, coworkers, or superiors? How are those responses framed and so on. This study suggested that trivialization sometimes occurs as a group response to harassment where other females joke with the harassed individual. The group trivialization process may support the morale of the subjugated workers as well as support the patriarchal system. However, it is also interesting that Lisa, who voiced her complaint through an official organization, turns to the technique of trivialization when no one is willing to support her. It is unclear as yet why trivialization is the preferred fall-back technique. In other words, could Lisa just as easily have turned to the private domain at this point by asking her boyfriend or husband to intervene, or could she have selected another framing device such as accepting the dominant interests? Future research might consider this question.

The theoretical framework advanced here can be applied to understanding a variety of topics that organizational management may prefer to sequester. But more importantly, it can and should be applied to the study of how framing techniques are used to further subjugate already marginalized members of society. With respect to women, Cockburn suggests (1991), "oppression takes the form of an open secret that is continually exposed to view yet remains for ever unseeable and unsayable" (p. 170). The present interpretive analysis is a means of saying what has been silenced; a means of knowing how rhetorical framing techniques sequester as well as expose stories; a means of recognizing the oppressive and the emancipatory nature of communication.

CHAPTER 5

The Bureaucratization, Commodification, and Privatization of Sexual Harassment through Institutional Discourse: A Study of the "Big Ten" Universities

Your language is alien.
—Lillian Morrison,
1990

Sexual harassment[1] is a pervasive and serious problem in the workplace (Clair, McGoun, & Spirek, 1993; Collins & Blodgett, 1981; Fain & Anderson, 1987; Fairhurst, 1986; Lafontaine & Tredeau, 1986; Loy & Stewart, 1984; Tangri, Burt, & Johnson, 1982) and on college campuses (Dziech & Weiner, 1990; Grauerholz & Koralewski, 1991; Paludi, 1990). Gender discrimination in the form of sexual harassment impacts on the emotional, physical, and economic well-being of the victims (Clair, 1993; Loy & Stewart, 1984; MacKinnon, 1979; McKinney & Maroules, 1991). Physical and emotional symptoms ranging from headaches and an inability to eat or sleep to posttraumatic stress disorder have been reported by victims of sexual harassment (Castaneda, 1992; McKinney & Maroules, 1991). Many victims suffer economic hardships by being forced to quit, transfer, or relinquish their job due to unbearable working conditions ("Our Stories," 1992). Student victims of sexual harassment find their ability to study grossly impaired and they may even change majors in an attempt to separate themselves from the harasser (Dziech & Weiner, 1990).

These seemingly "individual"-level problems, which are exacerbated by their frequency,[2] impact at the macro-level of society. Sexual harassment is a macro-level discursive practice in that any single act of sexual harassment announces the "inferior" role of the victims, who are usually women (Clair, 1994a). (For a review of perspectives and theories that deal with gender discrimination and sexual harassment, see

Clair, 1994b; Epstein, 1988; Gutek, 1985.) "Sexual harassment is not 'personal': it is violence out of history" (Taylor & Conrad, 1992, p. 414), grounded in discursive practices that are enacted at the micro-level and that affect social relations at the macro-level (Clair, 1993, 1994; Conrad & Taylor, 1994; Strine, 1992; Tancred-Sheriff, 1989; Wood, 1992). Macro-level practices, in turn, reflect back on micro-level discursive practices. Thus, the micro-level and macro-level practices can be viewed as an activity of mutual constitution (see Giddens, 1979, for a discussion of mutual constitution, or Smith, 1993, for a discussion of coproduction). A discussion of micro-level and macro-level distinctions may imply an artificial dichotomy. Thus, it is important to note that a myriad of levels exist in the discursive practices of sexual harassment, all of which are intricately interwoven in the complex constitution of sexual harassment. For example, it can be argued that social relations that constrain the well-being of victims of sexual harassment are perpetuated through discursive practices that range from interpersonal exchanges (Bingham, 1991; Bingham & Burleson, 1989) to juridical and legislative enactments (MacKinnon, 1979) to managerial policies. It is beyond the scope of this investigation to analyze sexual harassment at all of these levels. Consequently, the present chapter focuses on one discursive area surrounding sexual harassment, that is, managerial discourse.

One reason that sexual harassment remains a pervasive and serious social problem is that organizational management has failed to address the problem effectively. Neugarten and Shafritz (1980) summarized the bleak state of organizational ability to deal with sexual harassment by asserting that "(1) management has failed to take the problem seriously . . . (2) organizations have lacked adequate policies and procedures . . . [and] (3) there is confusion regarding who it is in the organization who has responsibility" (pp. 7–8).

Focusing on the university setting, Dziech and Weiner (1990) believe that "most colleges and universities probably now have established policies prohibiting sexual harassment and have developed procedures for formal complaints" (p. xiii). The authors recommend researchers put their efforts into developing strategies to encourage victims to come forward. The presumption that universities have taken steps to establish sexual harassment policies and procedures may be based on two motivations. First, universities are motivated by their humanitarian mission to educate in an environment that is free of hostility. Second, universities are mandated by law (Title VII) to comply with government regulations opposing gender discrimination or to face the possible loss of federal funds. Thus, universities are a natural site for conducting a study of institutional discourse on sexual harassment. However, the presumption that policies and procedures are well developed and that researchers should focus their attention on how to get students to come forward may be premature if those assumed systems for dealing with sexual harassment are deficient or nonexistent.

The present study examines the institutional discourse of large federally funded universities to assess their oppressive or emancipatory qualities. First, the power of discourse is discussed. Second, an argument is set forth that institutionalized communicative techniques provide a sophisticated and complex form of gender construction by bureaucratizing, commodifying, and privatizing the issue of sexual harassment. Third, three forms of discourse are singled out as pertinent to the study of sexual harassment: taken-for-granted discourse, strategic ambiguity, and exclusionary discourse. University policies, procedures, and brochures about sexual harassment are examined and deconstructed to illustrate these forms of institutional discourse and their relation to bureaucratization, commodification, and privatization.

THE ROLE OF DISCOURSE

Communication is "the creation and maintenance of symbolic meaning systems" (Mumby, 1988, p. 5). These meaning systems are not neutral (Deetz, 1992; Habermas, 1984; Mumby, 1987, 1988). In other words, communication is denoted as discursive action that creates, enacts, and reproduces power structures that privilege certain groups over others (Giddens, 1979). Discourse has the ability to oppress as well as emancipate people.

Feminist theorists, who agree with these tenets of communication, believe that a critical analysis of language can aid in understanding (uncovering) political meanings (see Ardener, 1975; Buzzanell, 1990; Daly, 1973, 1975, 1984; Ferguson, 1984; Fine, 1993; Kramarae, 1981; Penelope, 1990; Spender, 1984). Feminist and pro-feminist theories integrate the concept of gender construction and sexuality with the concept of political production and reproduction (Hearn, Sheppard, Tancred-Sheriff, & Burrell, 1989). Thus sexuality, which subsumes gender, is a political construction of patriarchy (see Hearn et al., 1989; MacKinnon, 1982).[3] Understanding that sexuality is a political construction directly impacts on managerial theory and practice. Specifically, managerial discourse can support the current construction of gendering organizations or offer alternative forms of discourse that may alter the status quo.

Patriarchy has advanced three ideological practices directly related to sexuality: bureaucracy (Ferguson, 1984), the public-private dichotomy (Fraser, 1989; MacKinnon, 1989), and commodification (e.g., Daly,

1975; Tancred-Sheriff, 1989). Each is critical to the understanding of sexuality, discourse, and domination, as the following pages will explain.

The present argument suggests that women have been oppressed through a bureaucratic structure of organizing, through the objectification of their bodies as exchangeable commodities, and through the privatizing of their work and concerns. These same oppressive conditions are being incorporated as a means of "framing"[4] sexual harassment. First of all, bureaucracy,[5] for example, is the accepted structure and process at universities that promotes hierarchical decision-making and subordination of minorities and females (Ferguson, 1984). When applied to sexual harassment, bureaucracy can mean placing the power for eradication of sexual harassment in the hands of those who have perpetuated it. Second, sexuality has been equated with a commodity of exchange. This commodification of sex reduces women to objects and is dehumanizing. When applied to sexual harassment, commodification can turn the issue of harassment into one of an exchange, suggesting that victims of sexual harassment have a choice to be harassed or not as in a capitalist enterprise system. Finally, women, women's work, and sexuality have all been privatized. Privatizing women, their work, and sexuality sequesters abusive and oppressive behavior. When applied to sexual harassment, privatization creates an atmosphere of secrecy and promotes a personal definition that discounts the legitimacy, validity, and the cultural embeddedness of victims' complaints.

Essentially, I am suggesting that not only do the actions of sexual harassment perpetuate patriarchy, but more often than not, so do the "corrective" institutional discourses that surround it (e.g., label, define, advise). Institutional discourse intended to rectify the problem of sexual harassment is ironic because it is saturated with patriarchal ideology. The development of this assertion relies on three philosophies.

First, for Foucault (1978), the political construction of sexuality is highly dependent on the proliferation of sexual discourses. Control of individuals is achieved through multiple discourses from varying sources that range between the micropractices and the macropractices of politics. For example, Foucault asserts that confessional discourse is crucial to achieving a control of sexuality in modern society. We are deluged with experts (e.g., sex therapists, educators, doctors, psychologists) who establish a power/knowledge regime and who will guide our behavior and encourage us to discuss (confess) the topic of sex. This expert knowledge controls us by engaging us in discourse about what is appropriate sexual behavior.

Second, Baudrillard (1982/1988) suggests that discourse achieves a reality of its own:

In a profound sense, the referent is the reflection of the sign . . . the sign recovers and commands reality; better still it *is* that reality. . . . The crucial thing is to see that the separation of the sign and the world is a fiction, and leads to a science fiction. (pp. 83–84)

With regard to the present discussion, this means the discourse that surrounds sexual harassment takes on a reality all of its own. It cannot be viewed as a symbol reflecting a reality that exists outside of the sign/symbol; the sign itself is embedded with political-economic meaning. Therefore, it can be argued that not only do the discursive actions of sexual harassment have material aspects, but so do the discourses that surround these events.

The third and most profound influence on the proposed arguments stems from feminist theory. It is difficult to single out contributors of feminist thought as so many have aptly drawn from each other to develop an intertextual web of feminist philosophy and community. Daly (1973), whose work clearly precedes Foucault (1978) and Baudrillard (1982/1988), established the link between the early influence of the Catholic Church and the controlling discursive actions of modern psychology. Daly discusses the power of language to limit women and perpetuate patriarchy. Her focus on the Catholic Church lays the groundwork for Kanter (1977), Ferguson (1984), Mumby and Putnam (1992), and others who challenge bureaucracy as a patriarchal practice that defines gender and sexuality. Furthermore, Daly's (1984) constant etymologies contribute to theories that suggest that both the connotation as well as the denotation of the sign/symbol contribute to the oppression of women. This is important. It allows us to extend beyond Baudrillard's *political economy* of the sign to viewing the sign as *patriarchally imprisoned*. Thus, the reality espoused by the sign is one that perpetuates patriarchal practices. As discussed earlier, three of those practices are bureaucratization, commodification, and privatization.

Bureaucratization of Sexual Harassment

Bureaucracy is rooted in the ethics of rationality and efficiency; it promotes a logical and passionless perspective of organizing that has significant implications for the constructing/ordering of gender (Kanter, 1977). Specifically, Weber's (1947) bureaucracy encourages the normalizing of lengthy documentation, justifications, rationalization, hierarchy, and impersonalization of workforce relations. Bureaucracy, and especially rationalization, constrains emotionality, "privileges instrumental processes, [and] excludes alternative modes of organizational experience" (Mumby & Putnam, 1992, p. 480).

Ferguson (1984) proposes that bureaucracies are patriarchal institutions that create subordination and individuals given to passive, timorous, and subservient behavior. "Feminization" can be applied to *both males and females*. As Ferguson explains,

> Bureaucratic power creates an arena in which "feminization" of subordinates is encouraged. The victims of bureaucracy—both those who are the targets of control, especially the poor, and those who administer the control—have many of the attributes of femininity. (p. 98)

These include isolation, dependence, helplessness, and extreme image management. Patrimonial bureaucracy creates an environment that encourages "parochialism, timidity and self-effacement, praise-addiction, and emotionality," especially among female workers who are trapped by the structure (Kanter, 1977, p. 91). Bureaucracy encourages a "confessional" interaction between clients and their caseworker, explicitly expecting clients to reveal information about their "sexual behavior" including "child-bearing and child-rearing practices, and living arrangements" (Ferguson, 1984, p. 138). Bureaucracy disguises power imbalances in the organization behind a mask of rationality; behind discourse tangled with detail and stripped of emotion (see Putnam & Mumby, 1992).

Administrative bureaucratic control is achieved primarily through institutional discourse that arranges the social organization of jobs. Similarly, institutional discourse is applied to sexual harassment to control and rationalize it under the stolid eye of bureaucracy. Thus, the *irony* here is that the original acts of sexual harassment that perpetuate patriarchy (generally through displays of male dominance) are proposed to be rectified through bureaucratic control, which is simply another form of male dominance that contributes to an "organizational conspiracy of silence" (Taylor & Conrad, 1992; also see Conrad & Taylor, 1994).

Sexual harassment, however, also occurs in small family-owned businesses that do not rely on bureaucracy (recall some of the stories from chapter 4). Thus, other practices that contribute to harassment need to be explored, including commodification and privatization.

Commodification of Sexual Harassment

Women have been continually forced into positions of exchanging their sexuality for material survival. (See Spender, 1983, for a series of essays that deal with the objectification of women; see also MacKinnon, 1989.) Furthermore, women are the reproducers of the labor force, birthing and nurturing children (MacKinnon, 1989). Moreover, organizations are more than willing to take advantage of "wives" for their unpaid reproductive capacities (i.e., having offspring who will fill future labor needs). Wives also act as the support for husbands in need of someone to act as hostess and organizer for many organizational functions (Kanter, 1977; Papanek, 1973). Each of these situations highlights the objectification and materialist exploitation of women. More subtle forms of commodifying women's sexuality through adjunct labor (Tancred-Sheriff, 1989) or subjugated roles (Kanter, 1977; Pringle, 1989) are the focus of recent research.

This chapter extends the concept of commodification to include not just women's sexuality, but also sexual harassment and sexual harassment discourse. As Baudrillard (1987/1988) suggests, sexuality has been commodified to the point that its packaged identity has taken on a reality all of its own. The "hyperreal" is an exploitation of sexuality that has been pushed to the extreme, resulting in the creation of artificial desires for an artificial product (i.e., the simulation of sex).

Likewise, sexual harassment discourse has reached the level of hyperreal in the sense that it takes on a reality of its own. It is now exchanged as if it too were a commodity, from consultants' packaged videos (*Sexual Harassment*, 1991) to "how to" prevention books (Wagner, 1992). Articles on the legal and liable aspects for organizations are abundant. In addition to proliferating sexual harassment paraphernalia, the issue of sexual harassment itself may surface as a commodity of exchange. This concern raises the following query: Is sexual harassment described as something that can be offered and accepted or rejected in terms of an exchange system? The *irony* is apparent. The solution to the problem of sexual harassment is framed in objectification through commodification.

Privatization of Sexual Harassment

Commodification of women's sexuality is directly linked to the idea of women being privatized.[6] Based on Marxist theory, which viewed the family as the microcosm of the state that exhibits both "slavery" and "serfdom," Engels (1884/1983) addressed the issue of exploitation of women in the private realm for reproductive purposes. He argues that increased division of the private and public occurred during the transition from feudal economies to capitalism when the means of production and reproduction were separated due to the industrial revolution. Women became increasingly dependent on men for themselves and their children. "Household management lost its public service. It no longer concerned society. It became a *private service*; the wife became the head servant, excluded from all participation in social production" (Engels, 1884/1983, p. 110).[7]

The privatization of women's sexuality and work has channeled abusive situations to the hidden and often forgotten realm of society.

Specifically, although sexual harassment occurs in the public realm, it has been consistently treated as a private matter. Only recently, over the past decade, have the efforts of feminists publicized the issue of sexual harassment, suggesting it can be politically contested (Fraser, 1989). Yet sexual harassment is still labeled as "personal" or "private" and functions to "individuate, devalue, pathologize, and isolate women's reactions to an experience which is common and shared" (MacKinnon, 1979, p. 87). Women perpetuate this problem when they respond by bringing the harasser's personal life to the foreground, or their own (e.g., by chastising the man's behavior because he is married or by summoning their own boyfriend to rectify the situation—again recall the stories from chapter 4). It is not just the victims who privatize sexual harassment, recall that George Bush said that harassment should be exposed, but "let's do it behind closed doors" (McFeatters, 1991, sec. 4, p. 3). Once again an irony arises: Does *public* (i.e., managerial/institutional) discourse *privatize* sexual harassment?

Three questions that are proposed here concern sexual harassment discourse. Additionally, three strategic devices that may be used to promote patriarchal practices are proposed and described below. They are taken-for-granted meaning systems, strategic ambiguity, and exclusionary discourse.

COMMUNICATIVE STRATEGIES

Three types of discourse are discussed in further detail with the speculation that each may contribute substantially to the bureaucratization, commodification, and privatization of sexual harassment. They are (1) taken-for-granted meaning systems, (2) strategic ambiguity, and (3) exclusionary discourse. These three types of discourse are neither mutually exclusive nor exhaustive. Furthermore, they may be used within a variety a discursive genres, including organizational narrative (Mumby, 1987), personal narratives (Clair, 1993), metaphor (Deetz & Mumby, 1985; Smith & Eisenberg, 1987), social drama (Rosen, 1985, 1988), euphemisms (Schiappa, 1989), or simple memos (Putnam & Sorenson, 1982). Each of these three types of discourse will be explained in light of their relationship to bureaucratization, commodification, and privatization of sexual harassment.

Taken-for-Granted Discourse

Taken-for-granted meaning systems range from verbal pronouncements of stereotypes to unspoken assumptions of authority. They are discursive forms that casually reinforce the status quo as if it is the natural order of things. Their ideological function is to reproduce the current structure and process of socio-organizational life, as inevitable or natural systems (Frost, 1987; Giddens, 1979; Mumby, 1987, 1988). "Forms of signification which 'naturalise' the existing state of affairs . . . act to sustain such [dominant] interests" (Giddens, 1979, p. 195). As suggested earlier, taken-for-granted meaning systems permeate daily lives and are so embedded in our social interactions through discursive frames that even the most diligent researchers have trouble uncovering their deeper signification (Conrad, 1983; Frost, 1987; Lukacs, 1971).

Mumby (1987) explains taken-for-granted meaning systems through organizational decision-making. Decision-making is presumed to be guided by hierarchy. The more important the decision, the higher up the hierarchical chain of command one must go to reach an authoritative or valid decision. Such an assumption presupposes that hierarchy is the natural and inevitable structure for organizing rather than a political construction (Ferguson, 1984). Similarly, the construction of sexual harassment policy operates through organizational hierarchy. It is a taken-for-granted assumption that management is responsible for writing, disseminating, and enforcing policy. Furthermore, patriarchy encourages the assumption that management efforts uphold the employee's best interest.

Strategic Ambiguity

Strategic ambiguity is the use of discourse to foster multiple interpretations and promote unified diversity from organizational groups (Eisenberg, 1984). According to Eisenberg, consensus is achieved by allowing diverse groups to interpret a message (e.g., policy or formalized procedures) based on their own viewpoint. Multiple interpretations can be fostered through vague language, equivocal information, puns (Weick, 1979), and false deictics (Penelope, 1990). Constituent groups will interpret certain messages positively or at least in keeping with organizational values. Strategic ambiguity serves several functions within an organization including the promotion of "unified diversity" and the facilitation of "organization change" (Eisenberg, 1984, pp. 230–234). However, one function described by Eisenberg seems especially appropriate for the study of sexual harassment. Strategic ambiguity strengthens the present arrangement and "preserves privileged positions" (Eisenberg, 1984, p. 234). As Mumby (1987) suggests:

> If we tie together the notions of power and ambiguity, then, we can say that power is exercised when ambiguous or equivocal information is interpreted in a way that favors the interests of a particular organizational group; or, alternatively, when organization ambiguity is utilized and amplified to disguise the exercise of power. (p. 116)

Strategic ambiguity has been applied to sexual harassment at several levels including within the actions themselves, through rationalizations and justifications by harassers, and through the courts. According to one male argument, women often confuse flirting with sexual harassment (MacKinnon, 1979). Yet women clearly report that men want them to think it is flirting or joking, but they [the women] know better (as described in chapter 4). Thus, a question is raised that invites exploration: Does management use strategic ambiguity in sexual harassment policies, procedures, and brochures to preserve the existing power structure?

Similar to strategic ambiguity is exclusionary discourse. Whereas ambiguity offers the possibility of multiple interpretations, exclusionary discourse limits one's options. Yet both strategies may be used in perpetuating patriarchy.

Exclusionary Discourse

Maintaining ideological domination rests heavily "upon concealment versus disclosure" (Giddens, 1979, p. 193). Although the dominant interests could be concealed in a variety of ways, the most effective may be through minimization or trivialization, and through exclusionary practices. Sexual harassment has certainly been minimized and trivialized at the individual (Clair, 1993), the institutional, and the juridical levels (MacKinnon, 1979). These two forms of discursive framing (i.e., minimization and trivialization) may be less appropriate for the current study, which looks at the text of policy, procedures, and brochures. The existence of these documents suggests that sexual harassment is regarded as a serious organizational problem, not trivialized or avoided.

Exclusionary discourse may energetically address the concern yet frame the issue in a limiting way by excluding pertinent information. Penelope (1990) provides an example of exclusionary discourse. Dictionary definitions of manly include "strong, brave, determined, honest, and dignified," in short, all good qualities. Negative qualities about men are excluded from the definition. Furthermore, denotative definitions of womanly are terse and tautological—"like or befitting woman" (p. 53). Discourse defining women in general and men in a negative light have been excluded.

Penelope (1990) adds that the wording of actions to remove the agent (i.e., grammatically and syntactically) is oppressive (e.g., in the sentence "the woman was raped," no rapist is identified. Instead, the woman appears as both the subject and object of the action). Sexual harassment literature often focuses on the victim, to the exclusion of the harasser.

In summary, the bureaucratization, commodification, and privatization of sexual harassment may be promoted through strategies of taken-for-granted discourse, strategic ambiguity, and exclusionary discourse. How these discursive practices sustain and perpetuate oppression will be explored through an analysis of institutional discourse.

METHOD

The present chapter examines the institutional discourse of sexual harassment for elements of taken-for-granted meanings, strategic ambiguity, and exclusionary discourse. These types of discourse are examined through a critical interpretive analysis as well as through a deconstruction of sexual harassment policies, guidelines, and advice given through brochures. A link between these three types of discourse and the three patriarchal practices (i.e., bureaucratization, commodification, and privatization) is proposed.

The critical interpretation assesses both oppressive and emancipatory forms of discourse used in the policy, procedures, and brochures supplied by the Big Ten universities. A deconstruction of the advice that is most commonly given to targets of sexual harassment draws from the theoretical and methodological postulates provided by Derrida (1967/1973, 1967/1976) for deconstructing texts. The following critique and deconstruction of institutional discourse at the Big Ten universities is intended to shed light on how discourse might contribute to the oppression or emancipation of sexual harassment victims specifically through bureaucratization, commodification, and privatization.

Sample and Procedure

Eleven U.S. universities tout the title of Big Ten. All eleven universities were contacted via a letter sent to the office of the president. The letter requested a copy of their policies and procedures on sexual harassment, racial discrimination, and plagiarism, and any brochures or other communiqués that they might have surrounding the subject of sexual harassment. To ensure good faith, the host university's policy, procedures, and brochure (the brochure is not a product of the university; rather it was developed by the School of Liberal Arts) were mailed with the request. A few universities responded immediately. Those schools that did not respond immediately were contacted via phone. The phone call was placed to the Affirmative Action Office (AAO) of the university instead of the president's office because the responses from most schools came from the AAO (although in one case the response came from the office of the provost). The first follow-up phone call resulted in the respondent's offering unsolicited information. Thus, I engaged in further conversation with this person and added interviews to all other follow-up phone calls. Subsequently, further information was collected during the phone interview. No systematic schedule of questions had been previously developed. Nine out of the eleven schools participated.

DECONSTRUCTION

Broadly speaking, deconstructionism[8] "cannot be seen as an attempt to make present what the metaphysics of presence has obscured—to reveal, in the sense of making fully available and illuminated, a truth suppressed" (Dolan, 1991, p. 198). For the postmodernist, taken-for-granted, ambiguous, and exclusionary discourse "must not be taken as signs of a more primordial presence or absence, but as traces of the difference, of the 'presencing' that precedes both" (Dolan, 1991, p. 202). Within the text, one will find differences in the form of opposites, one of which has been "deferred," giving privilege to the first. For example, the term *patriarchy* refers to father rule. Fathers cannot exist without some form of "mother." Thus there are subtle traces of femaleness within the term *patriarchy* yet they are deferred or subverted; maleness becomes privileged over femaleness. This binary imposition can easily be reversed by offering the differed for "presence." For example, a reversal of binary opposition might be overthrowing patriarchy for matriarchy. Such a reversal merely gives us another binary opposition. Postmodernists, instead, wish to "escape" the dialectic of opposites not through synthesis of the thesis (e.g., patriarchy) and antithesis (e.g., matriarchy) but "through the discovery of an unassimilable third term that both founds and escapes the binary opposition" (Dolan, 1991, p. 191).

"Deconstruction always in a certain way falls prey to its own work" (Derrida, 1967/1976, p 24). This is because signifiers or terms lead to other terms, and meaning may be virtually undecidable. Likewise, one text can lead to another text creating "intertextuality" or a connection between texts. Like critical interpretation, the process can be never ending.

The present deconstruction is based on a reading of the most commonly given advice to victims of sexual harassment: "Say no," "Keep a record," and "Report it." First, the text is deconstructed in a search for binary opposites and the privileging of one term over another. Any discourse can leave "traces" of the marginalized voice, or the second term. Second, the binary opposites must be read for their "metaphorization" or the inevitability of the terms to "inhabit each other" (Cooper, 1989, p. 483) within a violent "hierarchy" (Dolan, 1991, p. 191). Then a third term is sought that both "founds and escapes the binary opposition" (p. 191). Any number of binary oppositions could be uncovered and reversed; however, I will focus on gender impositions created at the expense of the female voice.

"Say No"

Eight universities encourage victims to confront the harasser. Five universities (UA, UB, UC, UD, UE) take the assertive "say no" approach. University A (UA) tells victims in a rather authoritarian tone to "say no" as their *first* and *last* suggestion for "What to do?" The other four universities provide "say no" as the first step. It is a myth to believe that saying no will always improve the situation (Sandler, 1992). Women report mixed results with assertive strategies that focus on confronting the harasser, with 43% of the women saying that assertiveness had no impact on the harasser (Livingston, 1982). Furthermore, victims who confront the harasser are often subjected to further harassment. If victims are not prepared to face being blamed or insulted by a harasser, then it is not wise to encourage this action without training or consultation. University F (UF) asks victims to "consider" confronting the harasser and University G (UG) suggests that "sometimes you can stop sexual harassment by telling the person directly that you are uncomfortable." Finally, University H (UH) recommends that the target of sexual harassment "tell the harasser . . . to stop" but adds a section that explains the vulnerability of the victim and encourages any third party who is aware of sexual harassment to expose the harasser.

"Say no" is filled with traces of binary oppositions and lends itself readily to a postmodern deconstruction. Its imperative tone commanding the victim to be assertive reminds the reader of the stereotypically male/female binary opposition (i.e., females are passive and males are assertive) and consequently by telling the target to act more "masculine" is concomitantly devaluing the "feminine." "Say no" privileges an imperative over a request, verbal action over nonverbal action, and assertiveness over passiveness. The privileging of these oppositions is addressed in light of their reliance on strategic ambiguity, taken-for-granted meaning systems, and exclusionary discourse.

No one would consider "say no" ambiguous advice. It does not even slightly resemble strategic ambiguity. However, it does reflect a taken-for-granted meaning system that the individual has not said no. This is not a totally unfair assumption because the majority of sexual harassment victims ignore harassment in hopes that the harasser will stop (Clair et al., 1993; Gutek, 1985; Konsky, Kang, & Woods, 1992; Loy & Stewart, 1984). However, it also assumes that harassment will stop if the victim is more assertive. As previously mentioned, findings are generally mixed with regard to the assertiveness of the response and its effectiveness to stop harassment (Livingston, 1982). Finally, this discourse is exclusionary in nature because it fails to represent the variety of approaches available for addressing harassment. Numerous rhetorical strategies have been invoked by women to deal with harassment, few of which rely on the simplicity of "say no" (see Bingham, 1991; Bingham & Burleson, 1989, for proposed strategies; see Clair, 1993; Clair et al., 1993, for enacted strategies).

Furthermore, "say no" is easily linked to the popular antidrug slogan "just say no." The intertextuality is achieved through similar word choice and leads us, like one signifier to another, into the meaning of the "just say no" text as it plays on the "say no" discourse. "Just say no" discourse can be read as if the authors of the brochure's text are suggesting that sexual harassment has been offered as politely as someone might offer a drag from a joint. It carries a trace that presumes the harasser was misdirected and not participating in a patriarchal demonstration of chauvinism. Following this advice, the victim should say, "No, thanks. I prefer not to be harassed today." The idea is, of course, ludicrous. It is nearly as simplistic with regard to drug use in some situations. Such a presumption encourages the idea that the target is responsible for stopping this behavior rather than the perpetrator. Sexual harassment is often an insidious behavior that the victims should rarely, if ever, be obliged to rectify. Would we ask any other victims of abuse to confront their tormentor in this way? University H at least reduces the impact of this blow by urging others to expose, if not confront, the harasser for the victim.

It is important to point out that the "say no" discourse encourages the commodification, bureaucratization, and privatization of sexual harassment. In terms of commodification, "say no" assumes that sexual harassment can be turned down or turned away as easily as a door-to-door salesperson, when this may not be the case (Gest, Saltzman, Carpenter, & Friedman, 1991; Sandler, 1992).

The "say no" strategy assumes the harasser will act in a "rational" manner, encouraging the bureaucratization of sexual harassment as a neutral, innocuous, and easily manipulated behavior. Yet harassers have been known to respond with further harassment, sarcasm, and generally humiliating verbal or nonverbal statements when confronted by the victim (Gest et al., 1991). Furthermore, advising victims to talk with the harasser first sets up a hierarchy of solutions, suggesting that it should not be taken to "higher" levels until "lower"-level recourses have been exhausted. It should be pointed out that this advice may be a sincere attempt to rectify the problem of women losing court cases "by not adequately protesting his [sic] actions" (Gest et al., 1991, p. 39). Yet this supports traditional management styles that promote the idea that there is one best way (i.e., logical, efficient) of organizing. It excludes a variety of ways in which victims of harassment can make their disgust known.

Most obviously, "say no" perpetuates the privatization of sexual harassment by encouraging victims to handle the situation at the interpersonal level. Repeat offenders are free to move on to their next target. Privatization relieves the institution from having to be responsible and accountable for the harassment. However, in 1990, a California court ruling "established that even women who were not themselves damaged by harassment could sue on behalf of others" (Gest et al., 1991, p. 39). "Say no" attempts to individualize rather than encourage third party intervention, class action suits, or even simple support from coworkers.

"Keep a Record"

Seven universities instruct victims of sexual harassment to "keep a record" (UB, UC, UD, UF) or "document all events" (UH, UE). University B has no official university-wide brochure for sexual harassment. However, two brochures have been developed, one by the School of Liberal Arts, which does not tell targets of sexual harassment to document, and one provided by the Women's Resource Office, which does tell targets to "keep records."

Keeping a record or documenting all incidents concerning the sexual harassment encounter(s) is certainly consistent with bureaucracy. It is without a doubt sound advice in a bureaucratic system. However, the reasons undergirding this written formalization are indicative of the past treatment of women and sexual abuse. "Keep a record" suggests that the behavior is serious enough to be documented, but primarily is intended to offer a credible report of what happened. This line of thinking was promoted by Weberian bureaucracy. It privileges the written word over oral tradition and suggests a certain lack of credibility with references to the oral report. With respect to sexual harassment, it implies that the victim's word is not good enough when it is "his" word against "her" word unless her word has been written down on numerous occasions.

Consequently, women are forced to document their sexual harassment experiences in a bureaucratic fashion, devoid of emotion and saturated with patriarchal logic. For example, "keep a record" privileges several quantitative assumptions. First, one incident will not be enough, except in extreme cases, to support a strong case against the harasser (Gest et al., 1991). Second, little if anything will be done to rectify the situation immediately. Although the Equal Employment Opportunity

Commission (EEOC) expedites a few "urgent cases," generally the process is "painfully slow" (Gest et al., 1991, p. 39). Third, the victim can expect to go through several formal channels. The quantitative focus on sexual harassment is common even among researchers who spend an inordinate amount of time reporting the frequency at which sexual harassment occurs, much to the neglect of researching its more complex meanings (Gutek, 1989).

"Keep a record" is neither strategically ambiguous nor exclusionary; however, it does fall under the rubric of taken-for-granted discourse. "Keep a record" is laced with assumptions that victims are not likely to be believed and that bureaucratic "red tape" will result in a lengthy process of detailed documentation.

The documentation in and of itself bureaucratizes sexual harassment by enveloping it in an endless trail of written accounts and records. Although a cursory interpretation suggests that documenting sexual harassment makes it formal and public, this may not be the case. Documenting the incident says nothing of publicizing it. Many sexual harassment cases are documented and some are settled out of court, with the stipulation that the harasser, the university, and the results of the settlement should not be publicly discussed. Conrad and Taylor (1994) discuss this "organizational conspiracy of silence" (p. 45).

Documentation does not commodify sexual harassment in quite the same way as "say no," but traces of the exchange process are still evident. Documentation becomes the commodity of value that can be exchanged for formal attention to the subject. Sexual harassment lacks credibility and exchange value without documentation. For example, law professor Ronna Schneider explained, "A man probably can get away with one free sexual joke or one free pinch" (Gest et al., 1991, p. 39) and as one EEOC director explained—the first feel is a freebie.[9] The more documentation there is, the more sexual harassment is perceived as a "real" commodity. In Baudrillard's (1977/1987, 1987/1988) terms, a "simulacrum" is created in which sexual harassment documentation becomes an artificial reality or the pretense of action against harassment. It is only an interim action, one that is supposed to lend credibility to the victim's story. Documentation exists as its own reality, an artificial panacea to the problem. This is exemplified in the following statistic: "Roughly 2 out of every 3 cases go nowhere" (Gest et al., 1991, p. 39).

"Report It"

Four universities recommend that the victim of sexual harassment "report it" (UA, UB, UC, UH) (albeit this recourse is never suggested prior to "say no"). University D replaces "report it" with "ask for help." University F says to "talk to a staff member" of the AAO. University G suggests that sexual harassment can be handled "informally" or "formally." Before handling the complaint in an informal way, University G recommends the victim get advice from a trained university advocate. If the formal route is selected, then victims are told, "If you decide to file a formal complaint" procedures are supplied. Finally, University E never explicitly tells victims to "report it," rather it tells victims to (*a*) confront the harasser, (*b*) keep records, (*c*) look for witnesses, (*d*) get emotional support, and (*e*) research your options, then University G provides options of recourse in terms of whom to report it to.

"Report it" seems clear and direct at first glance, yet it is ripe with strategic ambiguity. First, to "report it" one must know what "it" is. Penelope (1990) has argued that "it" acts as a false deictic that creates ambiguity. Although "it" refers to sexual harassment, clear policy statements concerning "it" rarely appear in institutional discourse.

For example, University I (UI) encountered legal difficulties in 1987 when its sexual harassment policy was in court and declared unconstitutional. Representatives of University I are careful to explain that they "are currently writing" their policy and "procedures and are still under development." They have been currently writing their policy for five years now. This type of communication exemplifies both strategic ambiguity and exclusionary discourse that is often used to promote the interests of the dominant group.

Similarly, University E wrote that University E's "policy on sexual harassment is currently being drafted" and forwarded a 22–page document, single-spaced, front and back, about sexual harassment that they referred to as a "brochure." This rather lengthy "brochure is also being revised." Length is not its only problem. It relies on definitions of sexual harassment produced in the 1970s rather than the definition supplied by the EEOC. For example, "sexual harassment is best described as unsolicited nonreciprocal male behavior that asserts a woman's sex role over function as a worker" (Farley, 1978). This definition fails to see that men can be harassed, and that people can be harassed by peers and even subordinates (i.e., peer harassment, contraharassment, and consensual relationship harassment are not defined). Similarly, University B relied on a rather vague definition of harassment that combines both racial and sexual harassment under the same definition. Combining the two under the same guidelines amounts to ambiguity through what Daly (1973) called "universalization." Crocker (1983) addresses the problematic nature of definitions that are either too ambiguous or overly technical.

Furthermore, "report it" is an example of exclusionary discourse.

At first, one might be inclined to believe that nothing is excluded (i.e, either the victim reports the harassment or he or she does not report the harassment). This all-or-nothing view of reporting harassment fails to address several other options. For example, the university could encourage third party intervention and make it clear in the sexual harassment brochure that once the university or any agent of the university is made aware in any form of the harassment, they are responsible to take action. Furthermore, victims might find reassurance in information about class action suits.

"Report it" focuses on the role of the victim; and with or without a clear definition of sexual harassment, victims who wish to follow the advice of "report it" need to know to whom they report. University B established a sexual harassment policy in 1982 and officials are making efforts to update that policy. However, one of the procedural statements in the 1982 policy explains the role of the AAO in the following way: "The Affirmative Action Office of each campus is available to employees who may have need for information or guidance toward the proper complaint channels."

This recommendation would not seem so odd if the AAO representative had not written that University B has no brochure about sexual harassment "because of confusion on the procedures—who would be responsible for handling compliants [sic]." Thus a policy exists on paper, but is virtually meaningless to targets of sexual harassment. Ironically, the office that is supposed to help victims of sexual harassment is confused by the existing policy and procedures—another example of strategic ambiguity.

Most universities suggested only formal organizational channels by which to file a complaint. This discourse is exclusionary in terms of leaving out viable options including seeking help from the EEOC, other government agencies, lawyers, and women's groups to name a few. Two universities stood out as exceptions with respect to the use of strategic ambiguity and exclusionary discourse.

First, University D offers clear guidelines to organizational members on how or whom to contact in case of sexual harassment. University D offers over 89 contact persons ("trained to hear the concerns of sexual harassment"), representing 12 colleges, 21 administrative units, located at 21 campuses, plus the AAO, which is prepared to refer formal complaints to appropriate deans or supervisors. The AAO also handled referrals of complainants who were not satisfied with the outcome provided by a dean or supervisor by forwarding the complaint to the Equal Employment Opportunity Discrimination Review Committee (i.e., a state agency). University E also supplied victims with the names of government agencies that could assist in the formal complaint process.

Sexual harassment is infused with bureaucracy when victims are told to "report it" and are directed toward formal organizational channels. Only two exceptions exist among the Big Ten universities with respect to encouraging victims of harassment to file complaints outside of the university. This recommendation may sound like organizational suicide, but is one of the stronger statements that a university can make about sexual harassment (i.e., the university condemns sexual harassment on the grounds of its oppressive nature and is willing to support victims in their right to sue the university by freely disclosing information about whom they should talk to in a government agency).

In most cases, to "report it" is to situate sexual harassment within bureaucratic discourse. For example, no university encouraged student targets of sexual harassment to boycott the classes of professorial perpetrators. Nor did the university encourage students, faculty, or staff to name the harasser through a grapevine, to the campus or local newspapers with the story, confront or expose harassers in groups, or have a speak-out, protest, or march as proposed by Biaggio, Watts, and Brownell (1990). Nor did the administration encourage targets of sexual harassment to write the name of the harasser on the bathroom wall as Sandler (1988) has mentioned. Instead, sexual harassment is treated as a bureaucratized issue; controlled through layers of hierarchical discourse.

Not only does "report it" bureaucratize sexual harassment but also commodifies sexual harassment. Oddly enough, "report it" seems to be the end of the story for most universities. The exchange has been completed. Yet the damages of sexual harassment are enduring, with some women exhibiting signs of posttraumatic stress disorder long after the incidents have occurred (Castaneda, 1992; Conrad & Taylor, 1994). "Report it," relegated to the role of commodity, promotes the idea that once the incident is reported (i.e., exchanged) the victim is rid of its pernicious effects.

Reporting the situation as recommended in most of the university brochures privatizes sexual harassment by placing the victim in a one-on-one situation with the person in authority. Confidentiality is promised for both the victim and the accused. The charge is handled primarily behind "closed doors" as former President Bush has encouraged. One can appreciate that this protects the privacy of the victim and the accused, but one must also recognize that this keeps the abuse at the secretive level or as Cockburn (1991) described it: "Women's oppression takes the form of an open secret that is continually exposed to view yet remains forever unseeable and unsayable" (p. 170). Some universities are keeping no permanent records of sexual harassment. Subsequently, repeat offenders are always viewed as first-time offenders and patterns are difficult to detect. Universities often protect "the identities of repeat offenders" while placing "gag orders" on successful complainants (Conrad & Taylor, 1994). The university that offers silent solutions fails to voice a loud commitment against the abusive behavior of sexual harassment.

Thus "say no," "keep a record," and "report it" each act to bureaucratize, commodify, and privatize sexual harassment. Occasionally, universities offered recourses that were less limiting in nature; however, for the most part, sexual harassment is efficiently reduced and simplified into a bureaucratized, commodified, and privatized exchange.

Exemplifying what Baudrillard (1982/1988) calls the "political economy of the sign," the discourse itself takes on an exchangeable value similar to use value and exchange value of commodities in economic theory. The theory of the political economy of the sign has been instrumental in guiding this analysis in terms of the commodification of sexual harassment. Foucault's (1978) work on the history of sexuality and especially his elaboration of "confession" provided a framework for addressing the privatization of sexual harassment through "report it." Finally, poststructuralist/feminist theories provided the avenue by which sexual harassment could be viewed as "bureaucratized."

CONCLUSION

Institutional discourse on sexual harassment provided by the Big Ten universities invokes both oppressive and emancipatory conditions surrounding sexual harassment. Strategic ambiguity, exclusionary discourse, and taken-for-granted discourse have been used to privilege the interests of the dominant group by encouraging the bureaucratization, commodification, and privatization of sexual harassment. This has been exemplified in the critique of the Big Ten's discourse on sexual harassment. However, exceptions do exist in which some universities reduced exclusionary discourse by providing a wide range of recourses, clear definitions, and well-thought-out advice.

Although this study has been limited in scope, both in terms of a small sample size and an exclusive sample population (i.e., the Big Ten universities), the results are beneficial on several counts. First, increasing awareness of alternative recourses to sexual harassment should free the target from "institutional only" recourses. Second, this study reveals how the "say no" approach is not as neutral, innocuous, or simplistic as it seems. "Say no" may be harmful to unprepared individuals; "say no" privatizes sexual harassment, subsequently relieving the university of accountability; and "say no" commodifies sexual harassment as an exchange process rather than as oppressive displays of patriarchy. Finally, "say no" is reductionistic. This simplification plays into the bureaucratization of sexual harassment by treating it as an easily manipulated, rational phenomenon, rather than as an emotional, complex problem. Third, the requirement of documentation perpetuates the stereotype that women lack credibility; that sexual harassment without witnesses, times, dates, and so on also lacks credibility; and that written codes (i.e., documentation) create a false reality that action is being taken. Furthermore, universities must take stock of what happens to a sexual harassment complaint. In some cases, victims are turned away by inept or ignorant AAO representatives, are confused by the procedures, or assume that their options are limited to formal channels. "Reporting it" requires a clear definition of "it," information on places and people to turn to, and follow-up procedures. Bureaucratization results in a limited list of options generally secured through formal channels.

The results of this study do not support earlier contentions that policies and procedures are already in effect and are offering satisfactory solutions to the problem of sexual harassment. Therefore, the results of this study may promote further investigation into how other American universities are writing their policies, procedures, and brochures and how they follow through with the complaints that are voiced.

HIGHLIGHTING CHOICES

Thus far I have focused on the constraining factors of the institutional discourse supplied by the Big Ten universities. It is appropriate to highlight some of the more emancipatory discourses as well. First, I define emancipatory discourse as that discourse that promotes dialogue rather than closure. As such, I cannot offer the practitioner or the victim of sexual harassment specific recommendations that will result in "the best way" to handle sexual harassment.[10] What I can provide at this point is a summary of those discourses that seem most to open dialogue, increase awareness of the problem, and discourage the privileged from dominating at the expense of human dignity and justice.

Supplying clear and up-to-date policy, procedures, and brochures encourages visibility of the problem. Pointing out and condemning the role of the harasser (as Universities D, E, and F have done) reminds people who is to blame and who should be accountable for these actions, including the role of the university. With respect to advising victims or targets of sexual harassment, victims may appreciate a less authoritarian tone telling them what to do and what not to do. In regard to "say no," victims should be warned that face-to-face confrontation may bring on further harassment. They may consider writing a certified letter to the harasser, as recommended by Sandler (1992), or the university may suggest they see a trained counselor before deciding what to do next (see Universities D and G).

Documenting harassment is not a bad idea; however, it must not become a panacea for action or rely on frequency for validating sexual harassment. No incident should be considered trivial if it affects the victim. When addressing the concept of "report it," universities should not necessarily limit the reporting choices. Universities D and E both offered the names, addresses, and phone numbers of government agencies. It may also be helpful to add such contacts as the Rape Crisis Center, women's advocacy groups, and the nearest EEOC, as a few universities have done. Procedures are often vague and, in fairness to universities, many cases of sexual harassment must be dealt with individually. However, the procedures need to protect the victim (many universities seem to be concerned with protecting the innocence of the accused, but give little attention to the situation of the harassed). For example, the procedures are made to seem neutral, when in fact more often than not, the female victim is faced with reporting and pleading her case to members of the dominant group (i.e., the majority of professors, police officers, and administrators are male). Universities that support the training of contact persons who will stay with the victim at each stage of the process are offering a commendable service of support. Some victims of sexual harassment do not intend to file charges, but do want some reassurance that the harassment will end and that no backlash will follow. Third-party mediators may be helpful in such cases. Other victims of harassment may be too intimidated to come forward at all. When this is the case, the university should encourage others to come forward for the victim, as University H has done. There is nothing wrong with warning harassers that their actions are so insidious that the university recommends third-party intervention, class action suits, and a supportive system for victims. Furthermore, records should be kept. A great deal of documentation is encouraged for the victim, yet no documentation remains when the case is settled. This allows offenders to repeat their actions. These are just a few ways in which emancipatory discourse in policies, procedures, and brochures can open dialogue rather than close it.

The preceding discussion has focused on discourses surrounding the "harasser," the "victim," and surrounding institutional discourse. It is important to point out that we cannot "neatly divide the world into *victims, harasser,* and *everyone else,* as though *everyone else* were not responsible in some way" (Clair, 1996b, p. 325). All members of society engage in the production and reproduction or the creation and alteration of cultural structures and practices; thus sexual harassment affects all of us.

Finally, the present chapter has described three ironic elements in the organizational response to sexual harassment. It is ironic that a patriarchal means of organizing (bureaucracy), which has marginalized and subjected women and minorities, is used to frame the solution of the problem. It is ironic that sexual harassment recourses are often framed in the exchange process, because it is the objectification of women and minorities that supported sexual harassment. Finally, it is ironic that much of the public discourse surrounding sexual harassment acts to privatize or silence the issue. In the future, researchers should devote efforts toward revealing and clarifying the role that taken-for-granted meanings, strategic ambiguity, and exclusionary discourse play in perpetuating patriarchal practices. Not only are bureaucratization, commodification, and privatization worthy of further study in relation to sexual harassment, so are other problems of discrimination. Highlighting how discourse frames events and experiences as well as how experiences can be reframed offers both victims and managers an opportunity to review previously marginalized options and to make more informed choices. Finally, if we are to understand the relationship between discourse, sexuality, and domination, it is paramount that research continues to address how patriarchal practices demonstrate *institutional irony*.[11]

CHAPTER 6

Resistance and Oppression as a Self-Contained Opposite: An Organizational Communication Analysis of One Man's Story of Sexual Harassment

Not comprehending, they hear like the deaf. The saying is their witness: absent while present.

—Heraclitus

A recent call for organizational communication researchers to investigate the complex and contradictory aspects of organizational life (Deetz, 1992; Dervin, 1993; Grossberg, 1987; Mumby, 1993) provided the impetus for the present chapter. Focusing on the intersection of organizational communication, sexuality, and domination, this analysis addresses how resistance and oppression act as a self-contained opposite that contributes to hegemony. Specifically, the present chapter investigates how one man's story of sexual harassment reveals the gender structuring of organizations through discursive practices and how these practices contribute to resistance/\oppression. Examining how discursive practices perpetuate the gender structuring of organizations, especially through sexual harassment, can shed light on how oppression is maintained or resisted.

SEXUAL HARASSMENT AND THE GENDERING OF ORGANIZATIONS

Sexual harassment is an expression of gender discrimination and the abuse of power (Strine, 1992; Taylor & Conrad, 1992; Wood, 1992). Harassment is problematic in terms of its impact on the victims, organizations, and society at large. Affecting both men and women, sexual harassment is so pervasive that it can be considered "normalized" in our society. Numerous studies demonstrate the frequency of sexual harass-ment (Clair, 1993a; Gutek, 1985; Gutek & Cohen, 1987; Lafontaine & Tredeau, 1986; Loy & Stewart, 1984; McKinney & Maroules, 1991; U.S. Merit Systems Protection Board, 1981, 1988) as well as the emo-tional, physical, and economic effects of sexual harassment (Castaneda, 1992; Loy & Stewart, 1984; MacKinnon, 1979, McKinney & Maroules, 1991; "Our Stories," 1992; Strine, 1992; Taylor & Conrad, 1992; Wood, 1992).

Although women are more frequently victimized and more vulnera-ble to the economic repercussions of sexual harassment, men are also targets of sexual harassment. As Daly (1973) maintains, patriarchy is deeply embedded within our social structure. Both men and women pro-duce and reproduce the existing social order. Men may perpetuate the system through acts of harassment against others, through their silence or failure to support victims, or by accepting their own victimage. Women may perpetuate the current system by hegemonically accepting an inferior role in society, one that condones abuse. Women have been known to abandon other victims (Clair, 1993b; "Our Stories," 1992; Taylor & Conrad, 1992) and on rare occasions have been positioned as the harassers.[1] Thus, people perpetuate oppression through their own participation in the system. This hegemonic complicity is achieved through communicative actions (Clair, 1993a; Cockburn, 1991; Fergu-son, 1984; Strine, 1992; Taylor & Conrad, 1992; Weedon, 1987; Wood, 1992).

Although sexual harassment is a serious problem in its own right, it can also be perceived as a symptom of another problem, the gendering of organizations (Hearn, Sheppard, Tancred-Sheriff, & Burrell, 1989). Although most organizations attempt to present a gender-neutral image (Ferguson, 1984; Mumby & Putnam, 1992; Pringle, 1989), no organi-zation is free from sexual politics (e.g., see Cockburn, 1991; Collinson & Collinson, 1989; Daly, 1973; DiTomaso, 1989; Parkin, 1989). The gender structuring of organizations typically results in women receiving lower pay, lower-status positions (Epstein, 1988; Kanter, 1977), less prestigious positions (Coser, 1981), and positions adjunct in authority (Tancred-Sheriff, 1989).

Gender structuring is a social construction, which is subject to eco-nomic and historical contextual factors (Burrell & Hearn, 1989). Gen-dering, then can be understood as a discursive creation that has histor-ically promoted a sexist and oppressive society. As such, an investigation of the role that discursive practices play in the ironic and hegemonic aspects of oppression and resistance may provide some use-ful insights.

DISCURSIVE PRACTICES AND HEGEMONY

Relying on Ferguson's (1984) work, *discursive practices* can be defined as "the characteristic ways of speaking and writing that both constitute and reflect our experiences" (p. 6). These practices may include acts, as well. Deetz (1992) draws from the work of Foucault to explain that *discursive fields* exist contributing to an overall *enunciation* or an *articulation* of social relations. Specifically, "a discursive field consists of alternative ways of structuring the world and organizing social practice" (Deetz, 1992, p. 263). In other words, there exist numerous choices with regard to how we talk, act, and react to our everyday experiences. How we choose to format our discourse reflects and creates social reality. A discursive formation is selected from the alternatives, not always apparent, and both develops and is developed around certain notions of social reality. These discursive formations may in turn limit one's ability to see other discursive alternatives (Deetz, 1992; Laclau & Mouffe, 1985; Weedon, 1987). Discursive formations can become dominant, coexistent, or marginalized.

For example and with respect to sexual harassment, chapter 4 provides illustrations of how women talk about their reactions to situations of sexual harassment. Recall that one female nurse reported that a male doctor "came up to me a couple of days ago and said he gets turned on by pregnant women [the respondent was pregnant at the time]. I told him I felt sorry for him. . . . It was really an injustice to his wife" (p. 130). This woman has selected a discursive format in which she retells the story and describes her response to sexual harassment. She has selected a personalizing framework or format. In other words, although the woman could have discussed how this was an injustice to all women or all pregnant women, she does not. Instead, she enacts a personalizing discourse and one that claims the injustice has been perpetrated upon, not herself, but the man's wife. Thus, she has chosen a discursive formation from a wide variety of discourses.

Discursive practices that perpetuate the status quo in terms of the oppression of marginalized groups, especially women, have been countered by some individuals and actively supported by others (see chapter 4 for example). At times, subjugated groups are complicit in their own domination, although as discussed earlier this is not a simple matter.

In the previous example of the nurse who told the doctor that his remarks were an injustice to his wife, we see that the nurse frames the harassment as a personal and moral issue rather than a public and political issue. By doing this, the woman may on the one hand protect herself from further abusive comments, but she also perpetuates the image of sexual harassment as a personal concern rather than an injustice to all women. Thus, she has allowed the dominant interests (i.e., keeping harassment sequestered to the personal domain) to prevail.

Foucault (1977/1979) explains these complex discursive relations of force in the following way:

> this power is not exercised simply as an obligation or a prohibition on those "who do not have it"; it invests them, is transmitted by them and through them; it exerts pressure upon them just as they themselves in their struggle against it, resist the grip it has on them. (Foucault, 1977/1979, p. 27)

Thus, discursive practices and formations are inextricably linked with the complex matter of hegemony. At times, subjugated individuals actively participate in the discursive practices that sustain and intensify their own oppression.

Acts of resistance, like someone struggling in quicksand, often times perpetuate the current oppression. With respect to sexual harassment, it is possible that forms of resistance are oppressive and that forms of oppression are articulations of resistance (Clair, 1993b). The current investigation addresses the following premise: Do discursive situations, where resistance and oppression are self-contained, articulate a hegemonic condition that perpetuates the status quo?[2] Dervin (1993) calls for communication researchers to investigate "where hegemony and resistance meet" (p. 52). This study illustrates a discursive meeting of resistance and oppression.

The theoretical premise that opposites are self-contained can be traced to the ancient Greek writings of Heraclitus (see Kahn, 1979; Lloyd, 1966; Marcovich, 1967; Schiappa, 1991). Although Heraclitean thought offers a base for understanding self-contained opposites,[3] the theoretical and practical implications of this insight were left largely unexplored until postmodern writers resurrected the premise.

Current theoretical developments in the understanding of self-contained opposites, especially related to domination and resistance, are generally credited to Foucault. Foucault's work (1961/1973a, 1966/1973b, 1976/1978, 1977/1979, 1981/1991) clearly articulates the role of discursive practices in the perpetuation of resistance and oppression via the self-contained opposite.[4] However, Burawoy's (1979, 1985) work also provides an excellent theoretical framework for understanding resistance and oppression as a self-contained opposite. Burawoy (1979) suggests that the forms of resistance (i.e., games of making out) employed by shop workers are actually means of *manufacturing consent* in an exploitive system. "Alternatives [to capitalism] are eliminated or cast as utopian" (Burawoy, 1979, p. 93). This generates a consent to capitalist choices that produces "an unrealistically static image of society" (Burawoy, 1979, p. 94).

In short, the following interpretive analysis is guided by the notion that quasi-forms of resistance and oppression merge into a self-contained opposite that is expressed through discursive practices. These quasi-forms of resistance/\oppression create, perpetuate, and sustain current organizational order.

The following analysis of one man's story of sexual harassment represents a tentative step toward understanding resistance/\oppression as a discursive practice. The analysis is centered on the coexistence of opposites in unity (i.e., oppression as resistance and resistance as oppression) with emphasis placed upon how the micro-level practices are constituted and reinforced in macro-level power relations.

ONE MAN'S STORY

The following account provides a brief background about the published story of one man's encounter with sexual harassment, an explanation of the procedures used in order to procure additional information about the story, a summary of the published story, and an abridged description of the interviews conducted. These preliminary reports are followed by a critical interpretation of resistance/\oppression using the concept of self-contained opposites as a guiding theoretical premise.

The rationale to explore a case study of one man's account of sexual harassment via his own published text including follow-up interviews rests on two notions. First, it is not the intention of this chapter to prove the truth or falsity of the man's story, rather, it is to illustrate a set of discursive moves in a complex and tense situation that gives way to unexpected outcomes. Second, the case study approach is especially beneficial for understanding macro-level social constructions because the "micro is viewed as an expression of the macro, the particular an expression of the general" (Burawoy, 1991, p. 272). The approach used here follows Burawoy's (1991) premise "that micro and macro are discrete and causally related levels of reality and that generalizations can be derived from the comparison of particular social situations" (pp. 273–274).

Of particular interest is that the following story represents the rarest form of sexual harassment with respect to gender and role (i.e., women believed to be sexually harassing a man). It thus represents the most extreme case of micro-relations, yet as the interpretive case method promises even the most molecular of situations can provide significant information "about society as a whole" (Burawoy, 1991, p. 281). The following background information sets the stage for an interpretive analysis of resistance/\oppression as a self-contained opposite.

Background and Procedures

"Men Suffer, Too: A Story of Sexual Harassment" was published in a local newspaper, April 1992. Michael Gray,[5] the author of the article, recounts his experiences of sexual harassment at a midwestern medical facility. Although the text itself is worthy of deconstruction, a serious concern exists in the fact that the story could have been mediated by the editor of the newspaper. Therefore, I contacted Michael and requested an interview, and several subsequent interviews followed. The interviews were not taperecorded but copious notes were taken, nor was anonymity offered. These conditions were more than acceptable to Michael, as he informed me that he sent his story to the *Chicago Tribune, Indianapolis Star, New York Times, Wall Street Journal*, and *Washington Post*.[6] I questioned him concerning payment for his story from any of the newspapers. Michael said that his intention was not to gain money. The story was submitted in the form of a "letter to the editor," giving the newspaper all rights to publish without his approval or remuneration (see appendix A for a complete copy of the published article). In short, he received no payment.

The semistructured interview lasted over two hours. Prior to the interview, a schedule of approximately twenty-one questions was developed based on a reading of the published story that dealt with his experience at the medical facility (see appendix B). Michael freely volunteered information beyond what was asked. At the end of the interview, I promised to send Michael the completed analysis based on the published article.

Summary of the Published Story

The published article, "Men Suffer, Too: A Story of Sexual Harassment" (abbreviated as MST), describes Michael's work orientation at the medical facility. He claims that everything he learned in school became "superfluous" (MST). He claims that his coworkers continually rejected his efforts to be enthusiastic about his work. Specifically, Michael wrote that they told him "that doesn't need to be done," or "I want to do that later" (MST). Michael recalls being faced with an "inquisition" (MST) by his peers, all of whom were female nurses or nursing assistants. Michael describes how he was assaulted in the following conversation as he sat at the lunch table with his colleagues:

They demanded to know if I was a virgin, if I had ever had oral sex, if I had ever been with a black woman, and so on. I found this line of questioning inappropriate, since it had nothing to do with our work responsibilities. I asked that the subject be dropped. Eventually it was, when the women decided to get up and do some work.

In the published article, Michael notes that he reported this incident to the head nurse (a male), who told Michael to "get used to such things because they happen all the time in such situations" (MST). Michael's published article continues to tell the reader that he felt he had "no choice" (MST) but to accept his superior's definition of this reality. Nevertheless, Michael reports being fired from his job following his first evaluation. According to the published article, although Michael filed a suit with the Equal Employment Opportunity Commission (EEOC), he never felt satisfied by the outcome. He suggests that his frustration was further compounded by more information he learned from a former coworker. The published article continues, following Michael's termination, a former coworker at the medical facility encountered Michael "at a local restaurant" (MST). According to the informant, the head nurse told the staff at an impromptu floor meeting that Michael was schizophrenic.

In the published article, Michael writes that he "added this information to my initial charge with the EEOC" (MST). However, according to Michael, the EEOC seemed to feel this information was irrelevant. The published article continues to report that the female nursing assistants had sexually harassed Michael, but after being counseled not to do it again sexual harassment stopped. According to Michael's newspaper article, the EEOC ruled that his termination was due to "poor work performance" (MST) regardless of whether he was "affected by the hostile environment" (MST).

As Michael explains in the article, he felt frustrated by the way the EEOC handled the case, but discovered that neither lawyers nor the American Civil Liberties Union (ACLU) were interested in pursuing his allegations of defamation. Michael describes his frustration in the following way: "All I expected were my human and civil rights. What I received was inhuman" (MST).

The published account of Michael Gray's experience at the medical facility is intriguing on several counts. First, it provides a story of a man who is sexually harassed, a rare occurrence, or at least an occurrence rarely reported. The sexual harassment of men has been consistently neglected in scholarly literature even though approximately 15% of men report encountering some form of sexual harassment (Cammaert, 1985; Gutek, 1985; Gutek & Cohen, 1987; U.S. Merit Systems Protection Board, 1981, 1988). The published story indicates that Michael chose to report the sexual harassment, not only to the head nurse, but also to the EEOC. The disparity between individuals who experience sexual harassment and those who file formal charges with the EEOC is quite distinct. Formal complaints filed with the EEOC are much lower than reports of sexual harassment provided to researchers; women's formal complaints have been estimated at between 0% (Cammaert, 1985; Ukens, 1991) and 5% (Tangri, Burt & Johnson, 1982). The general dearth of formal complaints might lead one to suspect that this is a genuine account, albeit a rare scenario, or the published story is fiction (see Hyde, 1993). After reading the article, I was inclined to believe that it was based on actual events for several reasons. First, Michael acknowledged ownership of the article by signing his name rather than supplying the tag 'anonymous author.' Second, the description of the sexual harassment does not fit the stereotypical heterosexual male fantasy of an unwanted seduction scenario; rather, it fits with the more commonly reported descriptions of sexual harassment that act to embarrass and isolate the victim. Third, the responses that Michael reports receiving from the head nurse are similar to those reported by female victims of sexual harassment (Clair, 1993a; MacKinnon, 1979). Although the story seemed an accurate account of Michael's perception of the experience, editorial liberties may have been taken with the published article. For these reasons, an interview was requested.

Description of the Interview

Michael Gray agreed to meet me for lunch and discuss both the published account of his experiences as well as offer more detail about his experience with sexual harassment. Several telephone interviews were conducted with Michael following an initial meeting to gain more detail and verify information. The additional information gathered from follow-up discussions is included within the following description of Michael's interview.

During this interview, Michael was asked what he felt "prompted the nurses to act in a sexually harassing manner" toward him. Michael suggested that his gender "had a lot to do with it." Secondly, he claimed that the nurses seemed "curious" about his "sexual preferences." He was asked to elaborate upon the sexual harassment incident (see item 5, appendix B).

Michael again noted the incident where the assistant nurses questioned him about his sex life, while the supervisor (a female nurse) looked on. Referring to when the women asked if he was a virgin, Michael said: "I told them I wasn't a virgin. Then I started wondering what was going on here. I was laughing, too, nervously, trying to get out of it." In addition to being asked if he was a virgin, whether he had ever had oral sex, and whether he had ever slept with a black woman, questions that are all reported in Michael's published article, the nurses also asked him: "Have you ever had sex with another man? Have you ever given head? I think it was meant to entertain them. It didn't entertain me." These questions were not reported in Michael's published account. Yet they may play a critical role in understanding the discursive tensions that are at work here.

Michael explained that sexual harassment was common in the medical field. It is Michael's opinion that nurses, especially female nurses, encounter a great deal of sexual harassment. Michael reported that there were numerous occasions when assistant nurses were sexually harassed by the patients. The most common experience for the assistant nurses is male patients grabbing the nurses' breasts. Michael explained that the female nursing assistants: "accepted what was done to them in order to get through. They turned it into a game." According to Michael, this even happened to him once.

Flirting was especially tolerated "because it seemed to pacify the patients," said Michael, making them easier to handle. Supervisors not only seemed to condone such handling, but encouraged it, from Michael's view. Furthermore, Michael felt that his supervisor engaged in sexual orientation discrimination as well. For example, Michael related that one elderly female patient often requested certain nurses give her a back rub or bathe her. The shift supervisor (female) thought the patient might be a lesbian and makes jokes about her to other staff members.

Michael's comment reflects his own subjective awareness of harassment occurring both in regard to gender as well as sexual orientation. He informed me that these certain things were not discussed in the published article, nor did he feel that his sexual orientation was of anyone's concern. He filed a complaint concerning the sexual harassment, and reiterated "I was sexually harassed."

Frustrated by the working conditions with the assistant nurses and his shift supervisor, Michael told me that he reported the sexual harassment to his head nurse. According to Michael, the head nurse, who is hierarchically positioned above the shift supervisor, also encouraged tolerance of sexual harassment. He told Michael to "make up stories" that would satisfy the curiosity of the nurses. He suggested that Michael could "lie" to them to "cajole" them. Michael explained that he thought the supervisor was telling him "not to react to it so strongly." Michael seemed dissatisfied with this advice since he pursued his case further by contacting the EEOC.

Inquiring further as to why the nurses would harass Michael, I asked him if he knew whether the female assistant nurses harassed any other male assistant nurses. There were no other male nurses or male assistant nurses on his floor during his shift. It was his opinion that turnover of male assistant nurses, in general, is high. Michael did not assume any relationship, he merely observed this point. For whatever reasons, Michael did not speculate further about the turnover. Rather, he returned to our discussion of why the female nursing assistants may have harassed him. He summarized what he thought provoked the nurses into harassing him. In short, Michael said: "They were protective of what they did." When I asked Michael exactly what he meant by this, he answered:

> An old girl type network. Instead of boys, they happen to be girls. And you had to pass the muster. . . . I was the only man on the shift. I don't know what a man would do to gain entrance to the inner circle. And they didn't like me. And I think they didn't like me because they were afraid I would be smart enough to catch onto what they were doing and snitch.

I asked Michael to clarify what things he might *catch on to*. He answered:

> They would take naps and [pause]. And, oh, [pause] they would cut corners wherever they could [his voice changes indicating that he is mimicking the assistant nurses as he says] "Well, we're third shift and we can get away with what others, on other shifts, can't."

Michael's answer indicates, that in his opinion, two reasons were at the heart of the nurses being "protective of what they did." The assistant nurses are protective of the female monopoly they have on the third shift and they are protective of the work style they have developed. The first notion (i.e., a female-dominated work group will pressure a male to leave) has received little attention by researchers. However, the second proposition (i.e., work group norms are protected fiercely by the group) has a rich history of scholarly exploration beginning as early as the 1920s with the Hawthorne studies (Roethlisberger & Dickson, 1939) and continuing through to the work of Burawoy (1979). Early studies investigated work norms from a managerial perspective by asking why workers do not work harder (Mayo, 1947). Challenges to the managerial approach claimed that it was manipulative (Carey, 1967; Franke & Kaul, 1978; Redding, 1979). Burawoy's analyses suggest that work group norms restricting quota outputs are part of a sophisticated "game" of resistance and oppression that should lead scholars to ask why do workers work as hard as they do.

Burawoy (1979) suggests that "one cannot both play the game and at the same time question the rules" (p. 81). In Michael's case, two interconnected games are played. They are the politics of production relations and the politics of gender relations. A new worker to the group who represents both a challenge to the female solidarity as well as the work norm may encounter hostility from coworkers, which could result in frustration.

Michael described the most frustrating aspect of the experience in the following way:

> No one in any official capacity, well no one actually came out and said that what happened to me was wrong. I was wronged. I hadn't particularly done anything wrong. It was not especially my fault. I did try to be a good employee, I guess.

The equivocality of the statement, "I did try to be a good employee, I guess" can be explained primarily by denotative confusion (i.e., a "good employee" by whose definition?). Michael may equivocate about whether he was a good employee or not based on conflicting perspectives of what constitutes a good employee. If he accepts a definition rooted in class resistance, then he was a good employee when he tried to do work for the other assistant nurses or when he covered for them while they were napping. Yet these efforts were not rewarded. In fact, Michael states that he is met with responses such as "that doesn't need to be done" or "I want to do that later" (MST). These responses indicate that Michael may have been surpassing the work quota norms.

Even if Michael had maintained the work norm, his "good employee" status may be questionable considering that he reports engaging in an argument with a coworker. Michael stated that he argued with one of his fellow assistant nurses. He made an abrasive comment, which he claims was said in a "half-kidding manner." Furthermore, he claims that several nurses were participating in this style of conversation and that he thought it was part of the organizational culture. Nevertheless, this episode suggests that Michael does make mistakes. The rationalization of his own shortcomings as part of the organizational culture could be applied to the sexual harassment he received. In other words, the nurses could claim that they were merely enacting the generally accepted organizational culture or that they were merely "hazing" Michael as a new employee.

Michael does not view the incident as "hazing." Nor does he feel that he has been treated fairly by the organizational members, management, or society. Michael's feelings became clearer when he explained how writing the article brought a sense of closure for him:

> The culmination of the experience. It was cathartic. . . . All the humiliation. . . . To put it in one concise piece did a lot for me personally . . . a degree of emotion with the facts fairly clear. . . . This should be the last thing I do before I put it into the past. . . . I do it for myself, do myself justice, if no one else would.

The point here is not to determine the judicial guilt or innocence of the assistant nurses or of Michael. Nor is the point to seek justice for Michael who feels that "no one else would." Instead the point is to illustrate the discursive tensions surrounding this claim of sexual harassment.

OPPRESSION/RESISTANCE: A CRITICAL INTERPRETATION

The following passages provide a critical interpretation of the discursive practices surrounding Michael's experience. The interpretation is guided by the premise that oppression and resistance constitute a self-contained opposite that reflects the complex aspects of hegemony. Specifically, the micro-level discursive practices of oppression and resistance are explored in order to demonstrate their connection with macro-level structures.

Oppressive Resistance

Discursive acts, representing both oppression and resistance, are apparent in Michael's story of sexual harassment. The most obvious is that the female assistant nurses "resist the infiltration of men into a field that they dominate and in which these men often rise to high level administrative posts" (see Clair, 1993b, p. 38). In Michael's story, the highest authority figure mentioned within the organization is the head nurse, who is male. The resistance of the female nursing assistants is rooted in the idea that women must protect an inferior status within a patriarchal institution, as Michael notes, "they were protective of what they did." Expressing a complex form of hegemony (see Clair, 1993b), the nurses oppress the symbol of the oppressor to maintain their own oppression. Women, such as nurses, have suffered the indignities of sexual harassment, lower pay, fewer promotions, and less respect in the medical hierarchy (Fottler, 1984; Gans, 1984; Williams, 1989). Nevertheless, many female nurses support the recruitment of males into nursing (Fottler, 1984; Gans, 1984; Snavely & Fairhurst, 1984). Possible explanations for this support include: (1) that male nurses hold a higher-status position in society due to their gender encountering less resistance; (2) that women nurses enact a more nurturing role toward male nurses, who represent a minority group among female nurses (Snavely & Fairhurst, 1984); (3) that males will bring more prestige to the occupation and with it higher salaries for all nurses.

In this particular case as it is reported by Michael, the nurses resist Michael's entrance into the nursing field by sexually harassing him. This is a tactic commonly employed to keep nurses in their inferior position within the medical hierarchy and typically implemented in male-dominated fields (Cockburn, 1991; Ferguson, 1984; Gutek, 1985; "Our Stories," 1992). In essence, the nurses oppress Michael in order to resist further oppression. Yet, as further analysis shows, by oppressing Michael the assistant nurses reify the current system of privilege. Thus, oppression and resistance exist simultaneously, touching each other in tension, articulating a hegemonic moment. Furthermore, the nurses, like the bank-wiring workers of the Hawthorne studies, establish their own work norms, possibly as a form of resistance to managerially established work norms that are enacted on the first and second shifts. Michael's story suggests that he represents a challenge to this resistance. Thus, the assistant nurses must resist/\oppress Michael in order to maintain their current form of resistance.

In Resistance Lies Domination

There is much evidence to support the fact that female nurses are clearly sexually harassed by male doctors and administrators (Clair, 1993a; Parkin, 1989; Williams, 1989). Michael's story suggests that female nurses are also sexually harassed by the patients. Ironically, the nurses tolerate this behavior because as Michael noted, "it seemed to pacify the patients." Once again resistance and oppression coexist. In this case, the assistant nurses are led to believe that they must oppose the notion of resistance itself in order to control the patients. They are expected to succumb to their own degradation in order to dominate others. The message seems to be that they should ignore harassment but use it to control others. The self-contained opposite of resistance and oppression surfaces as an articulation of hegemony; the nurses seem to be expected to tolerate sexual harassment from the patients in order to control the patients. By doing so the nursing assistants actively participate in the domination of the patients as well as their own domination. The interests being served here seem complex. Although the assistant nurses may be able to control the patients through the strategy of tolerance, the strategy of tolerance defines the nurses as individuals who actively subject themselves to oppressive conditions. Thus, the story appears to suggest that assistant nurses are being used as adjunct labor, which maintains the status quo and serves the interests of organizational management (Tancred-Sheriff, 1989).

Similarly, Michael reported that he was counseled to "lie" about his sex life when he is harassed by the female nursing assistants. From his point of view, he is expected to appease them in order to promote the current system. In other words, the head nurse promotes a form of resistance for Michael to enact, one that appears to discourage metacommunication. Like the nurses, he is told to resist the temptation to resist. As Deetz (1992) has noted, the suppression of conflict in organizations allows the dominant group to maintain the current system. The self-contained opposite in this instance is intended to promote hegemony (i.e., Michael believes that by accepting his own domination he will be supporting the system). Based upon Michael's story, those guiding the system fail to acknowledge that the system itself is rooted in privilege for some and oppression for others.

Deception would present him with a sense of control, but that form of control at best would be a quasi form of empowerment. There are two reasons this is true. First, Michael's deceptive actions would be equivalent to that of the nurses who tolerate "flirting" and having their breasts grabbed in order to control the patients. Michael is expected to accept his degradation in order to survive the system. Secondly, it was not Michael who conceived of the lie as a form of resistance. Consequently, to lie would further disempower him in the sense that he would be enacting a form of resistance that is supplied to him by an authority figure and one that he is probably expected to comply with although it is not his choice to engage with the assistant nurses in either deception or honesty. He believes the questions themselves are inappropriate. However, should he choose the avenue suggested by the head nurse, he would be complying with a male in a position of authority, a fate not as submissive as complying with female assistant nurses, based upon notions of both organizational hierarchy as well as general male privilege in society; yet Michael is reluctant to choose either course of action.

In this situation Michael's discursive alternatives seem limited, if not a double-bind (see Bateson, 1972; Watzlawick, Beavin & Jackson, 1967; Wood & Conrad, 1983). Neither choice allows Michael to step out of the paradox and both choices illustrate the complex nature of resistance/\oppression. If Michael tells the truth to the nurses, they have succeeded in invading his personal life, making public what he preferred remain private. Thus, his resistance through truth sediments his oppression. If he lies to the assistant nurses, he allows the harassment to exist and possibly persist. Although he may feel that he has successfully fooled them, he would fail to resist the discursive act of harassment that initiated the need for such a lie. Suggesting Michael lie is similar to asking him to play a game "in order to get through" as female assistant nurses do when the patients harass them as described in Michael's story.

Burawoy (1979) suggests that supervisors and managers participate in the game-playing and thus permit a certain amount of resistance to exist. Game-playing, according to Burawoy, "first, obscures the relations of production in response to which the game is originally constructed; second, game-playing generates consent to the social relations in production that define the rules of the game" (p. 82). When the head nurse suggests that Michael lie to the nurses, he is, in essence, telling Michael not to challenge the game. He even offers him a means of handling the situation that will protect the established game-playing (i.e., the social relations of work).

Establishing frames around sexual harassment that make it seem trivial or gamelike is not uncommon (Clair, 1993a; Daly, 1973; Duncan, Smeltzer, & Leap, 1990; Gutek, 1985; MacKinnon, 1979). Accepting sexual harassment as a game or sport where the prey and predator articulate complex shifting relations of domination and oppression represent a hegemonic condition that fails to counter the patriarchal system. Furthermore, making a game of sexual harassment entangles patriarchy with capitalist production, thus complicating the issues of coercion and hegemony.

Resistance/\Oppression: The Game Goes On

Michael, however, refuses to frame the harassment in a gamelike way. Instead, Michael challenges the system by filing a complaint with the EEOC. The EEOC representative, according to Michael, would rather take the issue of his work abilities to court than the "fact" that he was sexually harassed. Michael continually resisted this option. He believes that what happened to him was sexual harassment. According to Michael, everyone agrees with this (e.g., "no one even attempted to deny it" [MST]). However, his case is mysteriously transferred to an out-of-state investigator. Although Michael could call collect to his representative in order to continue his case, he found it cumbersome. The representative wanted him to change his complaint. He repeatedly asked Michael to prove that he "was not a substandard employee." Michael said, "he didn't seem to understand my position." Eventually, Michael gave up when repeated efforts to entice the EEOC, the state ACLU, and private attorneys into taking his case failed.

Michael's ordeal, like that of most female victims of sexual harassment, is depicted as a bureaucratic nightmare. Bureaucratic discourse surrounding the proposed solutions to sexual harassment often leaves victims of harassment feeling victimized twice over as they are regulated into a patriarchal discourse (Clair, 1993c).

Although Michael's story carries similarities to those stories of other victims of sexual harassment, it is also unique in several ways that may complicate his relations with the EEOC. The general purpose of the EEOC is to provide an equal opportunity for individuals to enter and achieve progress or promotion within capitalist organizations. As Burawoy (1979) suggests, both unions and government agencies must be strong enough to command respect and allegiance from workers, but not so strong that they would challenge the current labor process.

Michael represents an anomaly to the capitalist system. Women or other marginalized members of society who attempt entrance into largely white, male-dominated arenas are at least professing a desire to play within the capitalist system. They are seeking equal opportunity to participate in the current 'games' of production. Michael's entrance into a largely female-dominated field of low status and low pay challenges both the internal and external labor market. In other words, he not only challenges the internal system that generally hires women, but he also challenges the external system that expects white males to seek higher-paying, higher-status jobs.

The EEOC is faced, in a manner of speaking, with a conflict of interests. It is not the charge of the EEOC to protect the interests of white males; thus Michael, in order to be supported by the EEOC, must supply a marginalized status. For example, if Michael claimed that his age or a disability provoked the assistant nurses to treat him as they did, then the EEOC could pursue the case without jeopardizing their own relationship with capitalist structures and practices. Michael is neither of sufficient age to argue age discrimination nor does he have a disability. The EEOC offers him an angle that would maintain the capitalist status quo; fired without just cause. Like the head nurse, the EEOC representative offers Michael a means to resist. Again it is not the solution that Michael seeks. Therefore, this form of resistance is once again a quasi form of resistance.

Michael's story depicts himself as both antagonist to working class solidarity as well as to a form of female solidarity. Thus, he seems to represent a challenge to sociopolitical relations (i.e., patriarchy) and to production relations (i.e., he does not attempt to get ahead in a capitalist system). Subsequently, the EEOC seems reluctant to represent his case as sexual harassment. In addition, the nurses center their resistance to Michael around social relations (i.e., the issues of race and sexual orientation) since they seem to have consented to production relations.

Sexual Orientation and Race Discrimination

Both sexual orientation and race play a role in the experiences Michael retells. Although Burawoy (1979) purports that social relations have little impact on production relations (i.e., black or white, male or female, workers participate in limited forms of resistance and similar forms of 'making out'), both social relations and labor relations are grounded in principles of privilege. Burawoy (1979) reports that his findings with regard to the relationship between social and production relations are "very tentative conclusions, based on flimsy data" (p. 156). Yet he notes that these findings do converge with earlier findings which suggest that social relations have little impact upon production.

Burawoy's (1985) later work provides an overview of production and social relations as founded in patriarchy, which he claims gave way to paternalism and eventually developed into monopoly capitalism. A thorough review of this claim is beyond the scope of the current project. Furthermore, it is beyond the scope of this project to determine whether patriarchy supports capitalism or whether capitalism supports patriarchy, or both. However, a partial interpretation is offered of the relationship between social and production relations. The analysis is limited to how the social relations of race, gender, and sexual orientation, as defined by patriarchy, are discursively practiced by the assistant nurses. These practices illustrate a complex relationship between resistance and oppression, which ultimately protect patriarchy within a capitalist context.

Although the racial implication is important in and of itself (West, 1993), in Michael's story the racial aspect is entangled with sexual orientation, also an issue in its own right (Hall, 1989).

> Racial and sexual harassment, separately and together, promote inequality, violate oppressed groups, work to destroy their social standing and repute, and target them for discrimination from contempt to genocide. Yet each also has a particular history, occupies its own ground, and works in its own way, both as expression and as inequality. (MacKinnon, 1993, p. 56)

According to Michael's story, after the nurses questioned his status as a virgin or not, they demanded to know if he had ever slept with a black woman. The nurses are not curious about just any woman, but a *black* woman.

Michael was asked why he thought the nurses inquired about sleeping with a black woman. He explained that in a "conservative" area interracial sexual relationships are frowned upon. Yet he said he was not sure why they had used a racial image to harass him. Michael admitted that this is the question that silenced him. He did not know how to answer the nurses.

Possibly the assistant nurses were testing his 'manhood,' noting that the nurses' first comment addresses his male sexual identity (i.e., Is he a virgin?). Because Michael's answer assures the nurses that he is not a virgin, the test of heterosexual masculinity escalates to the second question (i.e., Has he ever slept with a black woman?). Society has created several stereotypes of black females, some of these stereotypes are related to white male heterosexuality. One specifically describes the "black female as wild sexual [and] savage" (hooks, 1992, p. 67). The image has generated an increased competitive search on the part of white males to get "a bit of the other" (hooks, 1992, p. 23). To sexually possess a black female has become a disgusting game of white male supremacy (hooks, 1992). Michael may not be a virgin, but the question now raised by the assistant nurses' is whether Michael is "man enough" to have slept with a black woman.

Although Michael may have been trapped by the paradox of interracial relations and masculine identity, he was unable to voice what was happening to him. If he were to reply "no" to the question of having slept with a black woman, he would have faltered in his heterosexual prowess (i.e., the great white male who has failed to conquer the most sexual and savage of creatures). If, on the other hand, Michael answers "yes" he is placing himself into a precarious interracial situation.

Michael's silence is followed by a barrage of questions about whether Michael has slept with men or given them "head." The nurses, according to Michael, were desperate to label him, to define him, and to categorize him. They were angry that he refused to answer.

The nurses, according to Michael's story, seemed overly preoccupied with Michael's sexual orientation, wondering if he has "had sex with another man." The nurses seem intent on being able to categorize Michael's sexual preferences and orientation or to harass him by attacking his "masculinity" as defined by heterosexuality. In either case, this form of harassment reifies gender distinctions and the inferiority of feminine attributes. By harassing Michael in this way, the nurses are contributing once again to their own inferior status within a patriarchal/heterosexual system. They seem to place heterosexual women in a more privileged position than homosexual or bisexual men. The reason that a patriarchal society confers low status on homosexual men is because they are perceived as being similar to women, thus these men are placed in an inferior category (Daly, 1973). Supporting a system of privilege that is grounded in the male heterosexual narrative only reifies the status quo. When heterosexual women privilege themselves above gays and lesbians, they are participating in a subtle form of hegemony (Clair, 1993b). That is to say, the nurses actively participate in promoting the concept of privilege (see Gramsci, 1971, for a reference to hegemony through privilege as discussed in chapter 3). Participating in an ironic and hegemonic practice, the female nurses sediment patriarchal definitions of themselves, women, as inferior.

Race, gender, and sexual orientation are the focus of the assistant nurses' interrogation of Michael. According to Michael's story, the assistant nurses question Michael's status as a virgin, rely on racial stereotypes of black women, and ask pointed questions about Michael's sexual orientation. In doing so, the assistant nurses express resistance to Michael entering their work circle; yet concomitantly the nurses engage in discursive practices that reinforce their own oppression. They seem to accept the notion that some people are privileged over others, especially in terms of race, gender, and sexual orientation.

CONCLUSION

Michael's experience, like any "experience[,] is at once always already an interpretation *and* something that needs to be interpreted. What counts as experience is neither self-evident nor straightforward: it is always contested, and always therefore political" (Scott, 1991, p. 797).[7] The present interpretation of Michael's experience relies on the theoretical premise that opposites are self-contained. Self-contained opposites exposed in this analysis directly exemplify Heraclitus's notion of *coincidentia oppositorum* (i.e., opposites coincide). Furthermore, they reflect the complex nature of oppression and resistance that Foucault has perceived in society and explicated in his writings. Oppression becomes resistance when the female nurses *oppress* Michael through sexual harassment in order to *resist* being infiltrated by a male. Resistance becomes oppression when the nurses accept sexual harassment from the patients in order to dominate them. Furthermore, the female nurses contribute to their own oppression through their reliance on and use of sexual orientation as well as racism to taunt Michael.

Michael's resistance to sexual harassment extends from micro-level interventions to federal and state agencies. Michael is offered strategies of resistance by the head nurse, but recognizes that oppression is embedded in these quasi forms of resistance. The head nurse suggests that Michael appease the nurses and accept his oppression as a "normal" state of affairs. These discursive practices are common in scenes of sexual harassment (Clair, 1993a; Gutek, 1985; MacKinnon, 1979). As Michael invokes the help of the EEOC, his efforts are undermined by bureaucratic discourse that supports rather than rejects oppression (Ferguson, 1984). According to Burawoy (1979, 1985), the state, both directly and indirectly, supports the current mode of production. Michael's complaint to the EEOC challenges the current capitalist system. Challenging the capitalist system is not the charge of the EEOC. Thus, Michael resists macro-level opportunities for quasi resistance, too. Foucault explains that the micro-level discursive practices are entangled with macro-level discursive formations of domination. As Foucault (1977/1979) suggests, "these [hegemonic] relations go right down into the depths of society" (p. 27).

The nurses support a system of patriarchal privilege by invoking strategies of harassment that are grounded in gender, race, and sexual orientation discrimination. Although attempting to set forth a sense of superiority for themselves, the nurses unwittingly advance principles that discursively define their own subjectivity as well as other marginalized members of society as inferior, creating discursive moments that contribute to the hegemonic imposition by supporting a gender structuring of organization.

The limitations of this study are similar to those found in many other studies of sexual harassment. I wrote in chapter 4 that "methodological procedures focusing on recall of sexual harassment" (p. 132) may raise concerns over the respondents ability to clearly recall the events without "distortion" (p. 132). Nor does an interview approach address the "temporal character of how respondents came to understand their experience" (Clair, 1993a, p. 132). In addition, this analysis relies on a story as depicted by one participant, Michael Gray. Future studies might seek out situations more conducive to obtaining several viewpoints of the events. Furthermore, this analysis addresses a rare occurrence (i.e., women believed to be sexually harassing men), and is not intended to be generalizable; rather it is intended to open dialogue about issues that are often silenced.

The implications of this study for future work in organizational communication theory are threefold. First, the results of this study suggest that the gender structuring of organizations is a communicative phenomenon. Specifically, in this case, the discursive exchanges between organizational members reinforce organizational structure. This finding contributes to the growing number of studies that suggest that organizational structure has been reified when in essence, it is a discursive creation (Deetz, 1992; Giddens, 1979; Mumby, 1987, 1988). Second, the findings from this study support complex renderings of power as opposed to reductionist views that suggest power can be described in dualistic terms. By accepting a decentered view of power, researchers acknowledge that the notions of victim and victimizer exist in a complicated tension. Nor can we reduce the actors to victims and victimizers (see Clair, 1996b). This invokes a simplistic and bifurcated view of the situation and the actors involved. Third, this study addresses the discursive practices that allow us to see how "communicating is where the micro becomes the macro, the macro the micro . . . where hegemony and resistance meet" (Dervin, 1993, p. 52). Based upon this knowledge, future studies will be able to develop richer conceptualizations of hegemony and coercion than what is currently provided.

In addition, future studies in organizational communication may address the specific discursive framing devices invoked during communicative exchanges of a hegemonic nature (see chapter 4). For example, Michael Gray's story suggests that he was labeled a schizophrenic. This particular framing device may be similar to devices used by men to justify or rationalize the sexual harassment of women. For example, Anita Hill was accused of living a fantasy (Williams, 1995). As noted in chapter 4, some women were told they "misunderstood" the actions or intentions of the harasser. This supposed inability on the part of the victim to correctly define reality is similar to what Michael experienced (i.e., schizophrenics are supposedly unable to define reality).

Furthermore, future studies may reconceptualize resistance/\oppression as a discursive exchange process, one that allows for quasi forms of both resistance and oppression. By using the term *quasi forms* to describe aspects of resistance and oppression, rather than *pseudo forms*, this research suggests that no "true" or "false" discursive forms of resistance/\oppression exist, but, rather, that there are a variety of discursive forms of resistance/\oppression. Thus, some forms of resistance are not necessarily more "real" than others; rather, some forms of resistance may support oppression more than others and some forms of oppression may be articulations of resistance. Further research is needed to unravel the nature of these different discursive forms of resistance/\oppression.

The study of oppression/\resistance is not restricted to analyses of women's lives, although studies in this area can assist in illuminating resistance/\oppression.[8] In addition, resistance/\oppression has been investigated in terms of race, class, and occupation through ethnographic methodology.[9] These works can heuristically inform each other, thus contributing to an organizational communication theory of discourse and resistance/\oppression.

One man's story may be an everyday encounter within organizational life, which seems hardly worthy of critical acknowledgment; yet it describes discursive practices that create and reflect the intensity and complexity of power relations. As Weedon (1987) points out "it is only by looking at a discourse *in operation*, in a specific historical context, that it is possible to see whose interests it serves at a particular moment" (p. 111). Foucault (1977/1979) summarizes the situation in the following way:

> The overthrow of these "micro-powers" does not, then, obey the law of all or nothing; it is not acquired once and for all by a new control of the apparatuses nor by a new functioning or a destruction of the institutions; on the other hand, none of its localized episodes may be inscribed in history except by the effects that it induces on the entire network in which it is caught up. (p. 27)

The current study inscribed a localized episode of domination into history by presenting one man's story of sexual harassment. This undertaking illustrated the complexity of discursive practices surrounding and supporting the self-contained opposite of resistance∧oppression. Further research endeavors are needed to clarify the complex relationship of resistance∧oppression and communication. Answering this challenge may provide greater insight concerning the gender structuring of organizing of society into a gender-oppressive system. The present interpretation of one man's story of sexual harassment grants a mere glimpse into what needs to be investigated and what can be revealed about how the organizing of sexuality is achieved and maintained through discursive practices.

In the following chapters, I extend discussions of resistance and oppression, as well as silence and expression. Recently, scholars have asked challenging questions concerning what counts as resistance and how silence can speak. In Part III, I address these concerns and suggest that an alternative aesthetic perspective might provide guidance for further exploration into how silence is organized.

PART III

CHAPTER 7

When Silence Speaks:
A Discussion of
Self-Contained Opposites

We can only grasp silence in the moment in which it is breaking.
—Sheila Rowbothom

A woman remained silent. Long after the imposed silence associated with the mourning period was lifted, a widow from the Warramunga society chose to remain silent. Although the "mourning silence" is imposed on the women for a period of two years, this woman remained silent for twenty-four years. Her silence speaks to us. It speaks of oppression; it enunciates defiance; it articulates resistance. Furthermore, it evidences creativity; it demonstrates control; it languishes in frustration; and it isolates the woman while simultaneously joining her to others who have known or know of the imposed silence. Her silence speaks at the local level to the Warramunga community; the stories of her silence speak to generations of Warramunga people and beyond to you and me. It is both a local story and the collective story of all women.

For me, there was an immediate and intuitive interpretation of the woman's actions as a form of resistance. Maybe I was reminded of the child sent to their[1] room for misbehavior, who on being allowed to come out of the room refuses to do so. This is resistance, but a form of resistance that simultaneously imposes restrictions on the individual. For me, the story was of silence and expression. The silence speaks not only of the injustice, but also of the brave defiance against that injustice. For me, the story of the Warramunga woman was an episode in the life of one woman in a land far from my own home, in a culture very different from the culture in which I participate. Yet, simultaneously, the story of the woman who remained silent echoes the silences of many women, of many minorities, of marginalized people across cultures and throughout generations. Her silence is what McGuire (1985) calls an *open silence*; a silence pregnant with meaning and open to interpretation.

The story as told by Daly (1973) suggests that this woman was not alone in her silent resistance. Other women also chose to remain silent after the ban on speaking had been lifted. Yet one woman stands out based on the duration of her silence—twenty-four years. What if the continued silence had only been for one year, or one week, or one day, or even less, maybe for just one hour. Would we still consider the self-imposed silence to be a form of resistance? Would its meaning of resistance seem too ambiguous for us to accept. Maybe she simply was not used to speaking. Maybe it takes time for the vocal chords to respond. Maybe her continued silence is not a political statement, but a simple physiological response. On the other hand, I can imagine a continued silence of only one second that could speak volumes when combined with other nonverbal expressions. The point I am making is that *we* determine what counts as resistance.

Cooper (1995) provides a story of resistance where resistance seems to be simultaneously enveloped with oppression and which provokes the question: What constitutes resistance? The resistance is at times somewhat ambiguous, which leads Cooper to question taken-for-granted conceptualizations of resistance. Cooper's story is "about a 'middle aged African American' woman . . . [who] was erroneously sentenced to 15 hours' community service for a traffic crime for which she was subsequently acquitted" (p. 127). The woman fulfills her community service by working for a church where she already is a volunteer and thus effectively usurps the control of the courts, or so it would seem. Cooper questions whether or not this is resistance. She wonders whether if the courts were to know about the woman's choice would they care? She questions whether this act in any way disrupts the dominant ideology. "Does resistance simply depend on the subjective interpretation of the resister? . . . Does it require recognition on the part of the other actor or institution? Or does it necessitate *actual* resistance—the obstruction of dominant projects—hence (possible multiple) 'external' readings to determine whether it has taken place?" (p. 127).

The ambiguity of the term *resistance* and its current status as a profoundly popular expression has resulted in its overzealous use as an ambiguous umbrella term (Cooper, 1995). Cooper asserts that too many scholars are positioning resistance in opposition to power and relegating social relations back to a simplistic mode of dominated versus dominant. They are failing to search out the subtle nuances of how resistance is powerful. Nor does Cooper approve of a view of resistance that ascribes to it the status of *oppositional* (see, e.g., Fraser, 1989). Oppositional discourses highlight what varied marginalized groups share in common (i.e., their opposition to a central dominant ideology). Cooper believes that this terminology points us toward coalition building, yet paradoxically marginalizes our differences. It is a discourse of unity, one that Cooper describes as counterhegemonic, which she distinguishes from antihegemonic discourses. Specifically, "advocates of counter-hegemony argue that difference should be articulated to form a common, united front, anti-hegemonic supporters stress the benefits of frag-mentation" (p. 135). Cooper explains counterhegemonic projects as developing out of the work of Gramsci (1971) and culminating more recently in the works of Laclau and Mouffe (1985), who encourage us to see a plurality of subject positions that can be linked in their social struggles through a radical democracy. The antihegemonic position praises fragmentation and shies away from the privileging of new polit-ical projects as the answer.

Two feminist works, each published in 1989, provide overviews of these two approaches. Fraser's (1989) book, *Unruly Practices*, can be described as counterhegemonic according to Cooper's (1995) definition. Aptheker's (1989) book, *Tapestries of Life*, demonstrates the qualities most associated with the antihegemonic perspective. Reviewing each of these books for their focus on how the authors deal with silence/\expres-sion, resistance/\oppression, local micro episodes/\global macro events, and the plurality and shifting nature of subject positions will help us to generate new questions concerning the complexity of social relations that at the very least allow us to step outside of a traditional framework concerning the study of oppression, expression, and emancipation.

UNRULY PRACTICES

Fraser (1989) describes resistance through three forms of "needs talk" that occur at a variety of levels. First, Fraser explains *oppositional dis-course*, which serve to reinterpret the needs of a group and voice these needs as distinct from the previous interpretation of the group's needs. Fraser explains that "coining terms like 'sexism' or 'sexual harassment'" (p. 172) constitute a vocabulary that opposes previous interpretations of women's needs. This, in turn, creates "new social identities on the part of the subordinated group" (p. 171). It is this oppositional discourse that is viewed as breaking the silence of sexism "by speaking publicly the heretofore unspeakable" (p. 172).

The second form of discourse discussed by Fraser, is the *"reprivati-zation" discourse*. This discourse attempts to redefine the oppositional discourse as a private matter. For example, arguing that sexual issues (e.g., domestic violence) should not become the purview of the state demonstrates reprivatization. More often than not reprivatization dis-course functions in contradictory ways. As it attempts to silence the oppositional discourse, it at the same time legitimates it by invoking its terminology. Sexual harassment is another example. Since it has been named, those people who would attempt to reprivatize the issue cannot, for the most part, do so without invoking its new-found name. Thus, we see once again the self-contained opposite of silence and discourses acting in concert to articulate messages that are ironically in opposition to each other and yet very much dependent upon each other. Yet, this time, we see the discourse, with respect to the marginalized group, leaning toward an emancipatory possibility—possibilities that will be further explored in the following chapter.

Finally, Fraser comments on a third form of discourse that she labels *"expert" discourse*. This discourse is intended to link the social movement with the state. But before reaching this point, numerous interpretations are made surrounding the issue. "As they collide, we see a struggle to shape the hegemonic understanding" (p. 173), which usually leads to state involvement. A similar view of hegemony is taken up by Condit (1994), who explores the rhetorical choices and strategies that are invoked in the process of developing concordance among groups who might benefit from a mutually clarified position on the issue, but these rhetorical choices do not necessarily dictate a dominant ideology. Fraser suggests that "when expert needs discourses are institutionalized in state apparatuses, they tend to become normalizing" (p. 174), thus reducing human agency. In essence, we are trapped once again as the "normalized" individual is apt to reproduce the hegemonic order.

Fraser's unique feminist combination of what she refers to as quasi-Gramscian theory with a Foucauldian focus on discourse also describes resistance as occurring at several levels within society. Specifically, she states that they range from "the individual, cultural, and informal to the collective, political, and formally organized" (p. 177). These forms of resistance exist to counter the established system. One example that she relies on is drawn from the work of Rains (1971), who explored how black and white teenage females either internalized or resisted therapeutic constructions of their sexual actions and future choices. She suggests that white females internalized the system's therapeutic values, while the black teenagers resisted this construction of themselves and yet were still able to use the program for other services that they deemed helpful.

Finally, Fraser (1989) suggests that we should not give up the hope of achieving an emancipatory state. Our struggle is not in vain. Nor does she believe that it is beyond our ability to name the needs of marginalized people. She believes that although Habermas's ideal speech act may have some limitations, it is in essence still a healthy model that we should strive to attain. The possibility for a just and democratic society exists where all voices can be heard and not silenced.

TAPESTRIES OF LIFE

Resistance, Aptheker (1989) claims, is a term that "is freighted with historical interpretation and nuance. We bring many assumptions to this word because of the way in which it has been defined in general (by men) in society. When we look at it from the point of view of women's lives, however, the meaning of the word changes" (p. 169). Aptheker argues that her own and other feminists' reliance on male-oriented theories of resistance and emancipation have failed to address women's potential in terms of resistance and change. Drawing on the work of Harding (1986), Aptheker argues that a reliance on Marxist and neo-Marxist theories requires an altering of these theories in order to fit women into them, which in essence deforms the original theory. More specifically, she proposes that privileging theory itself may be at the heart of the problem.

An understanding of women's oppression and resistance requires starting with as little theoretical baggage as possible and must be flexible enough to hold a wide variety of women's experiences, not as the universal experience but as distinct experiences that share commonalties (Aptheker, 1989). The search for an understanding of women's experiences, for Aptheker, rests on "two factors, the sexual division of labor and the institutionalized subordination of women to men" (p. 13). These two factors lead to a shared consciousness of women that is played out in their everyday experiences. Aptheker argues that she is not inventing yet another theory of women's oppression; rather, she is suggesting a new way of representing women, of giving them voice and providing alternative ways of knowing. This, she argues, must be done on women's terms not male terms. Specifically, Aptheker writes:

> The strategies women employ in their daily lives are relative to their conditions. . . . Women's strategies have pivoted from different centers and different priorities [than have men]. . . . [Their resistance has often been] outside the boundaries of conventional politics. They cannot be judged or their critical effectiveness assessed by the designations employed in conventional social theory about the relations of power in the society. (p. 180)

Drawing on the work of Griffin (1978), Aptheker (1989) considers naming to be situated in a fundamental relationship with silence and explores how women name themselves and their experiences (also see MacKinnon, 1979; Wood, 1992). Yet one silence is never separate from other silences. Women hold a plurality of subject positions. Class, race, religion, ethnicity, age, sexual orientation, and other positions influence women's forms of resistance as they are situated in complex forms of oppressions. For example, Aptheker provides the stories of Japanese American women who survived internment camps during World War II. Although internment was indeed an oppressive condition, at the same time Japanese American women experienced liberating aspects during their confinement. Specifically, they were freed from much of the domestic labor that they had been burdened with, which gave them time to learn new crafts. Within the camp, they were able to work for wages equal to their male counterparts. In addition, the practice of arranged marriages was abandoned. Their oppression coexisted with liberation. Their resistances would have to be equally complex as they juggled the role of protecting their Japanese heritage, teaching the American cultural ways, and dealing with Japanese American males whose experiences of internment differed from their own.

According to Matsumoto (1984), Japanese American women in the internment camps would beautify small gardens and send away for fashionable clothes advertised in catalogues. These actions are interpreted as forms of resistance, which helped to create an image of normality that was meant to improve daily life by increasing morale. These acts of resistance are not judged for their effectiveness or their ability to challenge the social conditions. They are simply stated as examples of resistance that are often marginalized in the scholarly literature for not meeting heroic "male" standards of resistance. In addition to highlighting these often marginalized forms of resistance because they fail to meet the male standards, we need to dive into the eddies of irony that surround these forms of resistance. Concomitantly, this particular form of resistance further erodes the Japanese traditions while promoting the artifacts of American fashion. Furthermore, it defies the oppressive aspects of camp life while promoting patriarchal practices that place women in the position of being the emotional keepers, especially through flower gardens and fashion. The whirling discursive and material practices simultaneously speak of defiance and domination. The everyday micro practices seem to be fractals of a more global macro world. The complexity wells up from the plurality and shifting subject positions that multiple discourses and material practices churn up.

Aptheker (1989) presents a compelling representation of women's resistance through poetry, fiction, art, networking, and the narratives of women's everyday experiences as well as the more dramatic moments of their lives. She claims that by rendering women's experiences visible, we can come to a unique female understanding of resistance.

Furthermore, and like Fraser (1989), she believes that boundaries between public and private must be dislodged in order to understand the complexities of resistance. Yet, unlike Fraser, her focus is primarily on the private life of women as they cope with the day-to-day ramifications of a political and patriarchal system that creates poverty and pain for marginalized members of society. Drawing from the work of Adrienne Rich (1978, as cited in Aptheker, 1989), Aptheker sees the private struggles of women to survive as coping mechanisms that are, indeed, forms of resistance. Stories passed on from generation to generation demonstrate a practice of resistance that culminates over the years to create the collective story of a particular group of women. These collective stories represent a form of resistance that moves beyond the individual's experience.

Marxist-oriented models of resistance tend to judge resistance as to its ability to move to the state level. The effectiveness of the strategies is linked to whether or not they hold promise for creating a revolutionary change. Aptheker (1989) argues that men have had "the power to name what is collaborative, what is accommodation, what is resistance, what is progressive, as though the only viable and correct perspective was theirs" (p. 180). Aptheker views any form of coping and surviving as resistance. This position has serious implications for the study of hegemony, coercion, and resistance, which are taken up in the following section.

THE PARADOX OF HEGEMONY AND RESISTANCE

Aptheker's (1989) suggestion that all forms of coping are resistance brings into question whether any practices enacted by the marginalized members of society can also be labeled as promoting the hegemonic condition. For example, Foss and Rogers (1994) discuss two stories of women's responses to sexual harassment that are included in chapter 4 of this text. In presenting these stories, Foss and Rogers (1994) relied on an abbreviated version of the article that was published in an edited collection (see Bingham, 1994). The first narrative that Foss and Rogers select to discuss is the story of the nurse who was accosted by a doctor. The nurse, who was pregnant at the time, tells of the experience in the following way: "He came up to me a couple of days ago and said he gets turned on by pregnant women. I told him I felt sorry for him . . . it was really an injustice to his wife." In chapter 4, I concentrated my analysis on how this response might perpetuate patriarchy. In particular, I viewed it as a means of accepting the dominant ideological definitions of men's and women's relationship as heterosexual and private. The woman does not tell the interviewer that it was an injustice to her, to other pregnant women, or to women in general, but rather that he treated his wife unjustly by making advances toward another woman. Foss and Rogers contend that by focusing on the hegemonic possibilities,

I failed to recognize the message as a form of resistance. As they read it, the nurse was belittling the harasser, "thereby potentially avoiding negative feelings of blame and guilt on the part of the woman" (p. 169). I am not sure where Foss and Rogers pick up the discursive clues that this woman in any way feels guilty or blames herself thereby needing to relieve such guilt, but I do believe they are right in pointing out that in that particular version of the study, I focused on how this discursive practice supported rather than challenged patriarchy.

The second narrative that Foss and Rogers (1994) reinterpret is one where a woman trivializes what may have been very serious to her:

> Well, if it's subtle and it's jokingly, and it's not hurting me or my position, I'm okay with it, because it's not harming me. And it's nothing really direct. But then it annoys you and you want to do something about it. You almost want to dish it back really bad.

Foss and Rogers assert that although this response may perpetuate sexual harassment, it can also be read as "practical decision making" (p. 169). In other words, like Aptheker (1989) the authors see coping strategies as forms of resistance. While I recognize these tactics as forms of coping and asserted such in the original version of this article (see chapter 4), I did not define coping as resistance.

Aptheker (1989) would probably explain my lack of seeing coping as resistance as due to my embeddness in male definitions of resistance and my use of overarching theoretical models rather than a focus on the everyday practices. Foss and Rogers (1994) are in agreement that overarching models tend to globalize the everyday and promote solutions to everyday exchanges at institutional or state levels that neglect the individual's personal experience.

Ironically, prior to Foss and Rogers's (1994) critique I had written a book chapter with Michael McGoun and Melissa Spirek (Clair, McGoun, & Spirek, 1993) that focused on how women's responses to sexual harassment could be viewed as resistance. I relied on the same set of stories that were collected for the first study and are discussed in chapter 4.

The following excerpt from Clair, McGoun, and Spirek (1993) indicates that very similar interpretations of what Foss and Rogers (1994) believe to be new and crucial insights had been previously discussed. The excerpt follows:

> Although she said "You almost want to dish it back, really bad," she controlled that urge and instead used face-saving techniques or diplomatic negotiation by saying, "I know it's joking. . . . And I know you're just kidding around, but there's a limit. . . . Look, it makes me look bad." This employee allowed the harasser to save face by sug-

gesting that his intentions were not harmful, but that he had clearly crossed the line in terms of the "limit." The respondent reported that this technique worked well for her so far, but that she recognized that she might need to change her tactics if the harassment was more serious. . . . This passage . . . redefines the situation, persuades the harasser to stop, and maintains the work relationship. (Clair, McGoun, & Spirek, 1993, p. 225)

Once again, with respect to the narrative of the pregnant nurse, Foss and Rogers (1994) draw similar conclusions to the ones that we (i.e., Clair et al., 1993) discussed in 1993, as the following excerpt indicates:

Another form of negotiation is to threaten indirectly to expose the individual so as to cause him embarrassment or more serious sanctions. . . . A second respondent said, "I just told him, individually, that it was pretty rude considering that he was married. And it really was an injustice to his wife." These statements are similar to what Bingham and Burleson (1989) refer to as a conventional unifunctional message: "It issues a directive for the harasser to stop" and supplies a reason for the harasser to comply (p. 192). The directive to stop is not clearly stated, but rather implied (Clair, McGoun, & Spirek, 1993, p. 226)

Obviously, I was aware that the messages contained both aspects of resistance and aspects that could be considered hegemonic. Yet I chose to develop these two aspects separately. Foss and Rogers (1994) encourage researchers to focus on the local episodes of resistance and to minimize their reliance on global theoretical perspectives. This is in keeping with Aptheker's (1989) view.

For myself, I found that separating discussions of resistance and discussions of how people perpetuated the system, while useful in their own right, failed to capture the complexity of social relations. By the time I wrote "One Man's Story of Sexual Harassment," I was attempting to deal with both issues within the same interpretive space. Resistance can be oppressive and acts of oppression may be emancipatory. Yet this approach, whether driven by a critical focus or by a Foucauldian perspective, leans toward understanding how the system is perpetuated rather than how it is challenged or changed. For critical scholars like Willis (1977) and Burawoy (1979), the focus of this dialectic seems to be on how resistance, enacted at the micro-level, can be deceptively oppressive. In Willis's (1977) insightful study, working-class lads hegemonically invoke their own oppression by resisting the authority of high school experts and accepting that working in the factory is in their best interests. In Burawoy's (1979) analysis of factory workers' subtle games of "making out," resistance is ultimately seen as a means to manufacturing consent for the capitalist system. Foucault's version of resistance does little to move us beyond this dark outcome. Foucault's version tends to allow for an accumulated effect, but never a coordinated unity (Cocks, 1989).

Returning now to the works of Fraser (1989) and Aptheker (1989) that I reviewed earlier in this chapter, we see that these feminist insights have both illuminated and complicated the issues. Fraser (1989) sees the self-contained opposite (although she does not call it a self-contained opposite) as existing within a complex movement of relations. Recall that the oppositional voices (e.g., feminists' development of the term *sexual harassment* to name previously unspeakable conditions) were legitimated by those who attempted to privatize the issue of sexual harassment.

Aptheker (1989) discusses the emancipatory possibilities found in the oppressive situation of the Japanese American women forced into the internment camps during World War II. Aptheker also notes that women's increased use of divorce is not necessarily the end of "traditional values" as some have argued, but rather is the beginning of a new era of emancipated women. Thus, both authors in their own way are expressing how the micro is the macro, how hegemony and resistance meet, how expression is silenced, and how silence is turned into expression. Furthermore, Aptheker (1989) at times, provides a picture of the plurality of subject positions that women hold in society and how those multiple subject positions play a paramount role in the practices of both oppression and resistance. Both authors note the existence of multiple axes of power.

Nevertheless, we cannot dismiss the appearance that Fraser (1989) and Aptheker (1989) leave many of us longing for the moments of upsurgence. Fraser concludes that "social welfare programs perpetuate the subordination of women" (p. 12) and Aptheker's forms of resistance seem wanting as they often barely raise the condition of women above survival, and in one case surviving is the ultimate resistance when a woman manages not to commit suicide due to her life situation. This resistance, at times, seems pitiful.

Of course, Aptheker (1989) clearly tells us that we cannot judge resistance in the male terms of effectiveness if we are to reveal the multiple means of resisting. I agree that we must be open to multiple practices as resistance, but we may also need to look at practices that provide alternatives in addition to survival, which convert oppression into expression and hold the potential for change. In order to do this, we need to maintain the complex aspects of the self-contained opposite. We cannot limit our analyses to one side of the issue or the other (as many scholars, including myself, have done in the past). Nor can we limit our discussion only to class and gender, which has been so prevalent among feminist, critical, and postmodern scholars. Furthermore, we must be willing to engage any site, not just business organizations or state bureaucracies, in order to uncover how silence is organized.

CURRENT APPROACHES TO THE
SELF-CONTAINED OPPOSITE

I will not endeavor to unravel the history of the self-contained opposite.[2] Suffice it to say that, without a doubt, the existence of a perspective that sees the unfolding of events in a series of dialectical and self-contained oppositional practices is not new. Despite its rich historical past, this perspective has been underutilized in academic writing. Only recently are we seeing a concerted effort by scholars to understand social relations through the self-contained opposite. I believe this increased focus on the self-contained opposite can be credited to three influences. First, critical scholars like Burawoy (1979) and Willis (1977) have explored how resistance is oppressive. Second, Foucault has passionately and articulately argued on behalf of viewing reality as a series of discursive practices that contain both elements of resistance and oppression within the same moments. Third, feminists have made it quite clear that women's lives have been especially hurt by a sustained and unrelenting philosophy that supports the dichotomous separation of spaces, of bodies, of issues, of identities, and of interests. To recognize the self-contained opposite is to recognize that the personal is political, the micro is the macro, that resistance can be oppressive, and that communication can be silencing and silence can be expressive.

In the same year that I first published "One Man's Story of Sexual Harassment," several other works were also advanced on the topic of resistance and oppression. In an edited collection of essays, entitled *Resistance and Power in Organizations* (Jermier, Knights, & Nord, 1994), several authors promote the self-contained opposite as a way of understanding resistance and oppression that has been underdeveloped in labor process theories of the past.

Reacting to the recent focus on hegemony and the manufacturing of consent, Collinson (1994) questions the primacy of consent as the topic of investigation for labor theorists. He suggests that overstating either consent or resistance may contribute to a polarized view of social-labor relations. He argues that:

> Resistance and consent are rarely polarized extremes on a continuum of possible worker discursive practices. Rather, they are usually inextricably and simultaneously linked, often in contradictory ways within particular organizational cultures, discourses and practices. Resistance frequently contains elements of consent and consent often incorporates aspects of resistance. (p. 29)

Collinson (1994) focuses on two strategies of resistance—resistance through distance and resistance through persistence. Each of these strategies are discussed in light of how they contain elements of oppression. Each strategy is discovered within different case studies. The first is a case study of men working on a shopfloor of a manufacturing company. The men resist the oppressive conditions by distancing themselves from management. For example, they shun the notion of promotion into the managerial ranks because they are not, and do not want to become, like managers. Thus, they distance themselves in terms of subjectivity. The men also distance themselves in terms of space (e.g., the bathrooms become safe places). This strategy of resistance is deemed fairly weak by Collinson, who sees it as too easily converted into consent. As the men separate themselves, they instantiate their position as exploited labor.

The second case study reported by Collinson (1994) is that of a woman who has been denied a promotion without just cause. The woman suspected that the promotion was denied because she was pregnant at the time. Her resistance to this treatment takes on the strategy of persistence. She persistently seeks information about her denied promotion through hierarchical channels and through her union representative. Collinson suggests that her persistence to gain information and her solidarity with the union steward (who is female) helps her to establish a more effective means of resistance than did the men who invoked resistance through distance. This may be true, but it leaves us wondering how we are to determine what is resistance? Should we judge resistance for its efficacy? Can situations unfolding in different contexts be compared as easily as Collinson implies they can be? As Collinson briefly notes, it could be that the woman who resists being denied a promotion is only further buying into the system of hierarchical control by seeking the promotion. The male shopfloor workers, on the other hand, who demonstrate what Collinson believes is a weaker form of resistance may, gain advantages or prestige as "men" in their resistance through distance. It would seem that labor is not the only power axis at work here and judging the effectiveness of resistance is a tricky business.

O'Connell Davidson (1994) also finds paradox rooted in the labor relations of British workers at a utility company. The company institutes a new computerized system in conjunction with a team approach for handling customer relations. The computerized system and team practices are expected to reduce management's need for the current number of clerks. The system would make clerks redundant, who could in turn be dismissed. Ironically, the computer software is inadequate to the task. It becomes all too clear to the clerks just how important human skills are to the processing of customer services. Thus, what was intended to make the clerks redundant only emphasizes their unique abilities. They are not expendable. Recognizing this, they resist the computerized system as well as the team approach, which is intended to make them easily replaceable. In addition, the clerks, who are primarily female, find themselves faced with male-dominated hierarchies in both the company and the union. Thus, they too face more than one power axis. Their resistance takes on varied forms, ranging from the official (both formal and informal) to unofficial acts of sabotage. Because the workers see the company as providing a service, they are especially resistant to the company's overemphasis on profit-making and the failure of the new computerized system to offer quality services to the customer. Here, the workers' resistance promotes the former system, which was not necessarily free of exploitation.

To use the "control-resistance couplet," as O'Connell Davidson (1994) calls it, is to raise numerous questions. How are we to define resistance? What kinds of resistance elicit what kinds of responses from management? How can anyone possibly judge the effectiveness of resistance outside of the sociohistorical, political, and economic context in which it occurs? For example, O'Connell Davidson reminds us that we currently may not think of quitting one's job as an effective means of resistance, yet in the 1800s, even passive forms of resistance, like quitting, were considered criminal offenses. O'Connell Davidson summarizes the point in the following way:

> The broader implications of all this is simply that any theory of resistance or subjectivity which does not locate the subject firmly in the context of historical and objective constraints is more likely to intensify the "crisis" of labor process theory than to revitalize it. (p. 97)

Gottfried (1994) also investigates issues of control and resistance from a dynamic and dialectical perspective in her study of temporary workers. Relying on socialist-feminist theory, Gottfried explores the local resistances that temporary workers invoke. Temporary workers are perceived to be at a distinct disadvantage, in terms of resistance, because they do not have access to company resources, nor do they have a union. Furthermore, they are separated from one another spatially and temporally. However, it is also possible that because they are not housed under one institutional roof, these workers may be more difficult to control than traditional, permanent "in-house" workers.

Gottfried (1994) goes 'undercover' as a temporary worker in order to explore the forms of resistance available to temporary workers. She suggests that control is launched on two power axes—patriarchy and capitalism. Female workers are defined in gendered terms that are meant to support the gender and class structure of organizations. The organization providing temporary workers to other businesses initiates the control process by defining and promoting certain dress codes for women, encouraging certain emotional labor practices, and encouraging the image of temporary work as flexible and advantageous to a mother who needs to be home. Gottfried describes the control process enacted at the hiring organization as well. While working as a typist, she notes an error in a manuscript and reports the error to the supervisor who tells her not to read for content, "just type it" (p. 199). Gottfried resists this form of control by invoking what she calls "work-to-rule" (p. 119). That is, she types exactly what she sees and refuses to make even minor corrections that would normally be corrected by a typist. She enforces the rule to the disadvantage of the institution. Thus, Gottfried notes then that even the most marginalized individuals who have few resources at hand can still invoke local strategies of resistance. According to Gottfried, these forms of resistance do little to change the overall rules of the capitalist game. She suggests that

> accommodation is not without resistance but resistance often produces accommodation as well. Workers' adaptation games can disrupt production as well as promote capitalist objectives, but resistance remains accommodative as long as workers continue to play by the rules of the game. (p. 120)

I will provide one final example from *Resistance and Power in Organizations* that focuses on the simultaneous existence of control and resistance, before discussing some of the implications of these studies. Rothschild and Miethe (1994) also employ a dialectical analysis of organizational resistance and control. The authors explore whistleblowing as a means of resistance and challenge to exploitative practices. The authors provide the case of Anne, a thirty-seven-year-old woman who works for a production facility. Her job requires exposure to unlabeled chemicals. Although she notices some physical ailments early in her tenure, she presumes at first that the company would not purposefully place her in a dangerous situation. Considering herself a responsible employee, she reports that labels are missing from some of the chemical containers. This action is enough to result in her prompt dismissal from the company. She learns that the company has treated other employees in the same manner, and that her exposure to the chemicals has resulted in permanent liver damage, tumors growing in her mouth, and other serious physical maladies. Anne discovers that the company is forwarding sick employees to doctors who downplay the seriousness of the symptoms. She blows the whistle, files charges against the company, exposes the laxity of OSHA, and plans to tell her story on *60 Minutes*.

Rothschild and Miethe (1994) argue that Anne's case sets a dialectical process into motion. They explain it in the following way:

> Management chooses harsh measures no doubt to quieten the potential whistleblower and anyone else who may be harboring similar incli-

nations. But instead the reprisals only serve to confirm to the whistle-blower just how morally bankrupt and lacking in integrity their superiors are. (p. 266)

In short, the authors charge that attempts to silence the individual reaffirms the individual's commitment to voicing complaints.

Each of these articles draws upon either the self-contained opposite or the dialectical process or both to reflect upon social relations related to control and resistance in organizations. Of course, focusing on the labor process will surely invite interpretations that are heavy with criticism of class exploitation. Nevertheless, a few of the articles also develop another axis of power—patriarchy. None, however, develop other power axes, with regard to the plurality of subject positions. Although each chapter can be criticized for weaknesses and praised for individual strengths, I will not address the individual chapters in any further detail, rather what they provide as a whole is of more importance to understanding the organizing of silence.

In the final chapter of *Resistance and Power in Organizations*, Clegg (1994b) raises a serious issue concerning future directions for the study of resistance and power, but supplies a questionable answer. The purpose of Clegg's (1994) chapter "is to bring some preliminary theoretical order to the specifics of the case studies that comprise this volume [*Resistance and Power in Organizations*]" (pp. 287–288). Clegg argues that empirical case studies have demonstrated and supported Foucault's notion "that a general theory of power and resistance is neither desirable nor possible" (p. 316). Yet, if researchers totally abandon the search for theory, their efforts will end in an "infinite iteration of case studies of an extremely elastic concept of resistance [which] is also somewhat aimless" (p. 316). Rather than challenge the seemingly infallible insights of Foucault, Clegg accepts the collection of case studies, but not without some hesitation. "But what do we do with an endless number of case studies?" Clegg asks (p. 317). His answer is that we need to codify power relations, focus on strategies of resistance, and use "case-based knowledge of conditions most facilitative of resistance" (p. 317). In short, Clegg recommends creating a typology of resistance that is grounded in the notions of structure and agency (e.g., based upon how aware the subject is of their condition, how capable the subject is of connecting with local networks of resistance, and the subject's ability to link with larger-scale organizations that provide assistance). The typology is based on the subject's level of "consciousness" and how the strategy of resistance can be more or less extensive in relating to organizations (e.g., the most extensive organization is a solidaristic one). The goal of the typology is to categorize forms of resistance in order to single out those that are most effective.

Clegg chooses the typology as a neutral, middle-ground between theory and case studies. Yet, according to Foucault's (1973/1966) position, typologies are inherently biased and therefore limit "the conditions under which it is possible to know them" (p. 70). Drawing from Foucault, Gathercoal (1997) insists that classification systems are powerful analytic tools that "affect even our most basic understandings of the world, . . . silently shape our inquiries and influence apriori resulting methods, theories and observations" (p. 10). "Taxonomies are too easily dismissed as being atheoretical . . . [when they] may be ideological and hegemonic" (Clair, McGoun, & Spirek, 1993, p. 211). Thus, to assume that typologies either free us from theory or promote unbiased categorical schemes is probably erroneous, at best. Furthermore, we must ask ourselves if classification is what we want. As Rawlins (1998) reminds us, "we are seeking conversation, not classification" (p. 361).

A typology is one alternative, but one that is heavily weighted with ideological assumptions. Allowing individual stories to stand on their own is another alternative, but one that fails to give us theoretical guidance. Developing a theory is another alternative, but I believe it is a bit premature to suggest a theory of resistance/\control, oppression/\expression, micro/\macro exchanges. We have just begun to uncover the complexity of the shifting subject position of individuals as they are categorized into groups, and as they privilege and abandon each other and themselves. We have just started to explore oppression as resistance and resistance as oppression. We have barely begun to see how the micro is macro. We are only now beginning to recognize how silence is organized simultaneously as oppression and as expression. Finally, we have not explored the possible interconnections between these discursive and material practices. The self-contained opposites may be connected dialectically to each other. We need to explore the rich complexity of the self-contained opposite, the simultaneous aspects of incongruencies, the oppositional couplets, and the dialectical exchange.

We need desperately to render visible the oxymoronic aspects of social relations. We need to see how the self-contained opposite moves into a dialectical exchange. We need to explore how the silence of expression and the expression of silence inhabit the local as well as the global. We need to explore hegemonic discourses, like privilege and abandonment, but we also need to explore how these very practices throw off defeating discourses and turn privilege and abandonment into support and, at times, solidarity. As Alonso (1992) notes, "popular culture should attempt to recuperate this dialectic of reproduction and transfer-motion, accommodation and resistance—what Hall calls the *dialectic of cultural struggle*" (p. 418).

Bartky (1988) insists, it is in paradox that we find "pockets of resistance" (p. 83). Even more compelling is the possibility that a center of the self-contained opposite exists like the eye of a hurricane. There we may find alternatives that have not yet been explored.

There are alternatives to setting forth a complete finalized Truth discourse; there are alternatives to compiling story upon story of resistance; there are alternatives to typologies. The possibilities for research are endless. And these possibilities need not exclude the possibilities already in use. There is value in theory, in the stories, and in the typologies that we create. By viewing our own approaches to research as discourses, or as creations, we can choose to follow a rhetoric of possibility, a rhetoric of the aesthetic, a rhetoric of truth, or a rhetoric of the dialectic to name just a few. We must allow ourselves the imagination to not only appreciate, but also to move beyond grand theories, beyond simple stories, beyond typologies. The potential exists. The possibilities are there. The actualities are unfolding before us.

Researchers are not forced to explore and or render social relations according to either a counterhegemonic or an antihegemonic perspective. Cooper (1995) reminds us that "while counter-hegemonic projects encourage the transformation of structures on the basis of aspirational future, anti-hegemony reminds us that such a future can only remain a strategic narrative" (p. 141). Yet the two may meet, wrapping themselves around each other in a self-contained embrace.

I encourage a more in-depth exploration of how the self-contained opposites dialectically unfold, how the self-contained opposites reach out to incorporate and simultaneously disengage other alternative practices. I do not want to question only what is the most effective form of resistance, but rather how resistance intermingles with oppression to create new and unique discourses. For example, it is a wonder that one woman's story has moved from the Warramunga tribe—across time and space—to become a collective narrative—a symbol of silence as both oppression and resistance.

CHAPTER 8

Artful Practices and the Aesthetic Perspective

Depending upon one's definition of reality, silences woven into the fabric of a woman's text can be an absence or presence.
—Patricia Lawrence, 1994

At both the beginning and the end of chapter 7, I shared the story of the Warrummuga woman's silence and suggested that this particular story about silence has grown into a collectively shared narrative (Clair, Chapman, & Kunkel, 1996; Richardson, 1995). The movement of this story and its presentation to a different time and culture demonstrates not only how oppressive practices can be consumed in ways that challenge their intended effect, but also how a response to oppression may demonstrate an aesthetic creation with the ability to *move* others. In the current chapter, I discuss forms of appropriation, as well as consumption, and their relationship to aesthetic theory.

THE CONSUMPTION OF EVERYDAY PRACTICES

Although de Certeau (1984) dedicates his book to "the ordinary man," whom he views as "a multitude of quantified heroes who lose names and faces as they become the ciphered river of the streets," I am only deterred momentarily by this sexist language that forgets that women were made invisible, faceless, and nameless long before the *quantification of our heroes* through a positivist approach to knowledge. I am willing to read on, partly because I am the "other" who has learned to read beyond the prejudice; and partly because I did not start the book on page one. Disregarding any etiquette for reading in an orderly manner, I picked up the book and flipped through the pages, reading brief sections here and there as a word or heading caught my eye. It was intriguing enough for me to start seriously at the very beginning. And so I did.

Michel de Certeau (1984) argues that discursive practices are produced and consumed. However, this production need not be consumed or utilized in the way that the dominant group intended it to be consumed. In other words, communication is co-optable and the communiqués can be altered from oppressive practices to expressions of resistance. Michel de Certeau suggests then that we are not passive receivers. We can convert or co-opt or appropriate discursive practices to a variety of ends. Giving ethnomethodology a postmodern twist, de Certeau argues that resistance is made possible through the everyday practices of our making use of the original production for the purpose of resistance. This concept is not new among feminists.

De Certeau (1984) challenges the assumption that people are passive users or consumers of dominant ideology. Drawing on the failure of Spanish colonizers to "successfully" impose their culture on native "Indian" people, de Certeau describes how the subjugated "Indians" accept the conqueror's rituals, but *make* something quite different from them. When the subjugated group is unable to assert direct challenges to the dominant and oppressive powerholders, they may instead *consume* the practices and products of the predominant group in ways that *reappropriate* the intended meanings. Thus, the marginalized group transforms the original practice or product so that it benefits their interests and deflects some of the control and colonization.

Drawing from the work of Foucault, especially *Discipline and Punish*, de Certeau (1984) reminds us of the apparatuses of control as panopticon in nature—invisible, silent forms of control—that invade our institutional practices. De Certeau suggests that as the invisible and silent forms of control construct a discipline, an antidiscipline is set into motion. This antidiscipline or resistance is also a silent and nearly invisible practice, which he argues may have a logic of its own. De Certeau draws from historians, anthropologists, and sociologists, especially those from the school of ethnomethodology, to help him sort out the poetics of everyday practices that appropriate and reappropriate, make use of and make do (bricolage), manipulate, alter, transform, deflect, and twist the meanings of dominant discourses of discipline into "tactics of consumption, the ingenious ways in which the weak make use of the strong" (p. xvii).

De Certeau (1984) tells us that these everyday practices are then political events with trajectories, tactics, and rhetorics. Trajectories are paths that the "unrecognized producers, . . . the silent discoverers" (p. xviii) trace out as they enact or produce what was consumed in their own way and by their own standards. The trajectories can be read backwards or forwards; they twist and turn in a fragmentary fashion; and they "trace out the ruses of other interests and desires that are neither determined nor captured by the system in which they develop" (p. xviii). Tactics are everyday practices that instantiate themselves "into the other's place, fragmentarily, without taking it over in its entirety" (p.

xix). A tactic "does not have a place, a tactic depends on time—it is always on the watch for opportunities" (p. xix). Finally, de Certeau draws from the ancient archives of sophistic rhetoric to explore how the tactics work. Here, he argues that tactics must seduce, persuade, and make use of the ability "to make the weaker position seem the stronger" (p. xx).

Several forms of silent resistance exist. De Certeau (1984) describes two of them—*la perruque* and *bricolage*. La perruque, which is "the worker's own work disguised as work for the employer . . . differs from absenteeism in that the worker is officially on the job" (p. 25) or pilfers from the organization without stealing. Collinson's (1994) article, which was discussed in chapter 7, provides an example of *la perruque*. When laborers appropriate tools in order to work on each others' cars, rather than bringing them into the shop on official notice, they surreptitiously resist the capitalist system.

Gottfried's (1994) chapter, also discussed in chapter 7, might demonstrate a form of *bricolage*. Gottfried, enacting the role of a temporary secretary, makes a form of resistance out of what she has. She types according to the rules, typing in mistakes that normally would be edited out by a secretary, but after being told not to question things and merely to type what is there, she does exactly that. *Bricolage* is also evident among the restaurant workers that Crang (1994) studied. As he tells the story, one young server challenged the authority of a supervisor who insisted that she wear matching socks. Defying his authority, she pinned two matching socks to the back of her uniform and continued to wear colorful mismatches on her feet. Her *bricolage* was a sarcastic and silent statement of resistance. Her actions are a *trick*, a *bricolage* of making do with what little she has to resist the dominant forces that try to control her. Thus, de Certeau surmises that the consumers are not passive, but their resistances are often as silent and as invisible as the discipline explained by Foucault.

Another example of how the disenfranchised "make use" of the dominant discourse is by playing it *to excess*, which is exemplified in the following story. One of my undergraduate students shared with the class how she was treated as an employee of a Fortune 500 company, in terms of gender maintenance. She was hired as a receptionist. One day, early in her tenure, she wore pants rather than a skirt or dress to work. She was immediately notified by the supervisor that this was inappropriate dress for the office. Her protests were met with a dogmatic command that she, as a woman, must wear a skirt not pants. The student wore a skirt to work the next day. It was a shiny leather mini-skirt and she added large hoop earrings and a few other accessories. When the supervisor seemed shocked by her attire, she responded with a simple, "Well, all you said was that I have to wear a skirt." She finished her story by telling us that he never reproached her for wearing pants again.

This silent form of resistance makes a clear statement. Its surface level intent is to embarrass the supervisor into changing the dress-code restrictions. However, it should be noted that the resistance of following the rules to excess, in this case, ironically play off of the stereotypical image of a prostitute. We must be sensitive to what our resistances are saying at multiple levels.

Waggoner (1997) investigated a similar phenomenon at Mary Kay Cosmetics. Waggoner describes the Mary Kay saleswomen as invoking an "aesthetics of excess." Specifically, they "perform" femininity to the extreme. Their performances include working for prizes like the pink Cadillac, fur coats, and diamond rings. Furthermore, they design their business meetings like beauty pageants and crown a queen of sales at the annual meeting. Waggoner argues that this aesthetic performance is played out at such an extreme level as to act as a parody of patriarchal expectations of businesswomen. The parody then acts as a form of resistance.

Another example of silent resistance comes to us through Shannon Faulkner's story, as the following description illustrates. Shannon Faulkner sent her application to the Citadel in 1993. Although Bruce Smith (1996) reports that Faulkner deleted all references to her gender status on the application, Faulkner (1995) suggests that the all-male military academy simply made a mistake by assuming that she was male. At any rate, she was accepted. However, when the Citadel realized that they had accepted a woman, they were quick to rescind their offer of acceptance. Faulkner took her case to court and was allowed to enter the program in August of 1995. After meeting with oppressive acts that ranged from vandalism of her parents' home to death threats, Shannon embarked on some artful and silent practices of resistance herself. A pro-Citadel organization had T-shirts printed that read: *The Citadel: 1,952 Bulldogs and 1 Bitch.* In a silent show of resistance, Shannon donned one of the shirts herself. Thus, she consumed the dominant groups' rhetoric with a strategic and rhetorical tactic of her own.

In telling her own story, Shannon Faulkner (1995) is quick to remember those who were kind to her. She remembered that only one cadet demonstrated the bravery necessary to speak not only for her, but for what was right and just. This cadet was an African American who told Faulkner that, in the past, blacks had been barred from the Citadel. Furthermore, he told Faulkner, that it was time to end the discrimination against women. Faulkner tells us that this man suffered for his brave defense of women at the hands of other cadets.

Marginalized groups, as I indicated in chapter 3, far too often privilege themselves and abandon each other. However, Faulkner's case points us in another direction and calls for a theory grounded in possi-bilities for future change. As the members of Developments Alternatives with Women for a New Era (DAWN) (1985) tell us, "we tend to look with suspicion upon any political force or body that is not of our own making: [But] a process of dialogue and working on joint programmes is the only way to begin to build mutual respect" (p. 88). Mutual respect seems evident in Faulkner's anecdote *and* in the telling (and retelling) of the anecdote.

It has often been suggested that we will find our future in our chil-dren. In the same year that Shannon Faulkner struggled with the Citadel, a group of little girls developed their own forms of resistance.

One day during that summer, I sat watching my then 10-year-old daughter play baseball. She and her teammates suddenly launched into a cheer that cracked the patriarchal code:[1]

> Mirror, Mirror on the wall,
> Pretty girls don't play ball.
> So
> LET'S   GET   UGLY!

The girls were cheering for themselves as they played baseball. (By the way I have on more than one occasion been chastised for saying that my daughter plays baseball. The comment that follows is "You mean softball, not baseball." To which I respond, "You mean hardball or soft-ball. Obviously, they are both baseball." This never fails to anger the person who has given me reproach, as if girls and women have no right to play baseball. They must continually be reminded that they are not playing baseball, they are playing softball. I refuse this definition of what my daughter does.)

I listen to the girls cheer. They scream it over and over.

> Mirror, Mirror, on the wall,
> Pretty girls don't play ball.
> So
> LET'S   GET   UGLY!

This noisy activity is a silent form of resistance. They have challenged their position in baseball. They have challenged definitions of themselves with regard to femininity. They have even challenged the fairytales they were told as young children.

Ironically, as this form of resistance played itself out at the *girl's softball* field, a little girl was resisting in a different way just a mile or so away at the "baseball" field. This little ten-year-old and her parents threatened to sue the sports league that had refused to allow their daughter to play "hardball" with the boys.

Resistance comes in many forms, and the link between resistances is worthy of attention. In the same year that Shannon Faulkner was finally admitted to the Citadel, in the same year that a little girl made the "hardball" all-star team, another group of little girls playing softball continued their cheers. They chanted to the rhythm of "Sound Off," making use of a military march:

> We don't play with Barbie dolls!
> We play with our bats and balls!
> We don't wear no mini-skirts!
> We wear dirty socks and shirts!
> We don't care about our hair!
> Softball is our only care!
> We don't worry about our faces!
> We're too busy stealin' bases!
>   Sound Off! 1, 2,
>   Sound Off! 3, 4
>   Bring it on home
>   1, 2, 3, 4,
>   1,2. 3,4!

These silent forms of resistance may at times seem quite noisy yet we must question the role they play in silence and expression. How are they produced? What do they express? How are these artful practices consumed? Do they break through the edges of political or patriarchal silence? And how can these noisy practices be designated as silent forms of resistance? Can theory help to answer these questions?

How, de Certeau (1984) wonders, is one to explain these practices in terms of theory? He puts it most eloquently when he writes:

> A particular problem arises when, instead of being a discourse on other discourses, as is usually the case, theory has to advance over an area where there are no longer any discourses. (p. 61)

It was this very kind of postmodern revelation that allowed drastically different perspectives to surface. What was once articulated through a dominant discourse (e.g., What is Truth?), was now envisioned as the consequences of discourse itself. The first discourse had defined the world, but the second discourse argued that the first had no inherent authority to do so. Discourses upon discourses and truths upon truths were set free by a postmodern perspective. The leading theories (if we can call them theories) of the postmodern perspective necessarily had to be grounded in *discursive* genres.

According to de Certeau (1984), narrative may be the best guiding theory and practice of a postmodern approach to exploring the world. Narrativity, according to de Certeau, may reflect reality, but more than that it "exercises itself" (p. 79). For de Certeau, "*a theory of narration is indissociable from a theory of practices, as its condition as well as its production*" (p. 78 emphasis in original). This theory of narrativity has been well developed by scholars from a variety of disciplines (e.g., see Boje, 1991; Fisher, 1984; Mumby, 1988; Personal Narratives Group, 1989; Richardson, 1995) and has served us well. I do not intend to diminish its import in any way, but I do suggest that an aesthetic perspective may provide an alternative perspective for viewing resistance/\oppression and silence/\expression. Postmodern narrativity undoubtedly will contribute to the aesthetic perspective, and narrative theory can be included within an aesthetic perspective. The point here is *not* to provide an all-encompassing perspective, an umbrella term that gathers all theories under it. To the contrary, I merely mean to open our options to include creative forms in addition to narrative and to remind us to explore the aesthetic aspects of narrative.

For example, Daly (1973, 1984) provides creative forms of appropriation that do not demand the narrative genre as a guide, yet they do not exclude narrative either. Daly playfully and politically reclaims language. She twists the dominant discourse into alternative ways of speaking or writing that grant us new ways of knowing and participating in our realities.

Not only does Daly (1973, 1984) develop the notion of reclaiming the man-made language in a theoretical sense, she also practices this form of resistance by providing women with new meanings for patriarchal discourse. She plays artistically with language. She creates new forms that resonate for many women, but of course not for all. Feminist writers are doing what they are preaching. They become what they say they are. Like postmodern art that both represents a reality and creates a reality, feminist writings are at the "cutting edge." If we compare feminist writings to Robert Indiana's art piece the *Target,* which is both a rendering of a target and is in its own right a target, we see how feminist writing *represents* resistance and *is* resistance. Indiana's *Target* is both present and absent. He has achieved a statement that is itself. This is what feminists have achieved—the *pièce de résistance*—literally and figuratively. Feminist activities that both represent and create resistance epitomize the principles of postmodern theory with political purpose. These works sit at the center of the self-contained opposite.

Feminist works exist both as representation and as an actuality. For example, Tillie Olsen's dynamic book on silence and interruptions not only talks of resistance to the patriarchal practice of defining woman as interruptible, but also *is* an interruption. Olsen's book interrupts patriarchy by disrupting the dominant discourse. Her work is self-contained. It is an actuality that promises to open upon multiple possibilities for resistance. Its very existence is a discursive and material creation—an aesthetic achievement. Recognizing that feminist products and practices exist as aesthetic experiences, encouraged me to explore the possibilities of aesthetic theory in the explanation of resistance and oppression as well as silence and expression.

Feminist work in the area of aesthetic perspective lifts the shade and opens the window onto new and exciting theoretical vistas. Where postmodernism seems to paint us into the proverbial corner, with regard to theory, the aesthetic perspective celebrates walking across the freshly painted floor. Feminists can and do draw from postmodern work, but they must incorporate the materiality of their reality. Aesthetic theory, as developed most recently by feminist scholars, answers this need. As they recognized the unique aspects of aesthetics to help them explain the interconnections of resistance and oppression, silence as expression and expressions that are silenced, and the personal as political, they opened onto a new way of theoretically viewing and explaining the world.

THE PHILOSOPHY OF AESTHETICS

The aesthetic perspective was not developed overnight. Nor was it developed from a single discipline or a single theory. Neither is it cooked and ready to serve. An aesthetic perspective has been developing for centuries and will continue to develop, I expect, for some time to come. Several disciplines have contributed to a new view of aesthetics. This new view of aesthetics challenges the dogmatic and essentialist character of past perspectives of aesthetics; thus, it provides a new form of guidance that neither requires theory nor dismisses theory. It makes room for theories like that of Fraser (1989), as well as collections of story upon story as in Aptheker's (1989) work. In order to understand the new aesthetic perspective, it may help to review traditional aesthetic theory in the briefest of overviews before explaining current conceptualizations of aesthetics.

Traditional "Western" Aesthetics

The earliest written commentaries on the subject of aesthetics have been traced to ancient Greece (Hein, 1993). Art and aesthetic experience surely existed for other ancient cultures, but whether written critiques of art or aesthetics existed before classical Greece or in other more distant cultures is unclear. Regardless, Plato's discussion of art (e.g., poetry) as merely a reflection or imitation of reality influenced discussions of art and aesthetics for centuries to come (Dickie, Sclafani, & Roblin, 1989).

Plato makes strong claims against art in his *Poetic Inspiration: The Ion* and *The Quarrel between Philosophy and Poetry: From the Repub-*

lic, Book X (see Dickie et al., 1989, for a reprint). According to Plato, art fails to provide us with knowledge and is, generally speaking, a poor substitute for reality. More specifically, for Plato, art is an imitation of an imitation with little value of its own. Plato splits the arts from reason in a dichotomous fashion (Schaper, 1989). The arts for Plato are considered inferior to any rational form of logic. These disparaging comments were challenged by Aristotle.

Aristotle's defense of the arts argues that the aesthetic creation is more than an imitation. It speaks not only of what has passed, but also of what might be. For Aristotle, poetry provided an alternative form of philosophy. Aristotle continued his discussions of aesthetics via an essentialist position. That is, in addition to providing a philosophical vehicle, art can be defined according to certain ontological characteristics. For example, Aristotle explains the difference between the telling of a horrible monstrous event with the sole purpose of frightening the audience and the artistic development and recital of a tragedy. Art, for Aristotle, followed certain principles and demonstrated essential characteristics. This essentialist approach would come to dominate most discussions of art and the aesthetic experience for several centuries. Yet Schaper (1989) argues that Aristotle should not be interpreted as providing an essentialist definition, but rather a formalist definition that does not require every genre of art to follow the same means or modes of production. Nevertheless, debates about which characteristics were most essential to the definition of an aesthetic experience or to the creation of an art form varied from scholar to scholar. The idea that art or the aesthetic experience depended on some set criteria remained firm.

Tolstoy (1896/1960) defined art as an activity that *infected* others with emotion. He expected this emotion to move people to the highest moral good. Art did not require an objective tangible outcome (e.g., a painting, a poem). It could rest in a feeling, an experience, a phenomenon of varied sorts. The ultimate essential quality of art was to be found in its *infectiousness*, which could be achieved through *individuality*, *sincerity*, and *clarity*. Tolstoy's definition, then, seems to rely heavily on rhetorical forms of persuasion, although he does not reach this conclusion.

Others would contribute to the list of essential aspects of either an artistic creation or an aesthetic experience without necessarily drawing a clear distinction between the art product and the aesthetic experience. Based on the eighteenth-century, Kantian notion that the aesthetic is beyond and devoid of interest, Bullough (1912) argues that the aesthetic experience is achieved through *psychic distance*. He explains in a rather eloquent passage that we must suspend our everyday notions of a phenomenon in order to experience the aesthetic aspects of the phenomenon (see Battin, Fisher, Moore & Silvers, 1989, for a reprinting of the complete description of experiencing fog as an aesthetic experience). Bullough uses the experiencing of fog to show how the everyday can be transcended. At first, he suggests, we might be dismayed by a fog. A sense of dread or uneasiness may pervade our thoughts, but an aesthetic experience allows us to bracket out the associated fears or frustrations and experience the fog on its own terms. That is, we establish a psychic distance. This allows one to see:

> the veil surrounding you with an opaqueness as of transparent milk, . . . observe the carrying power of the air, . . . note the curious creamy smoothness of the water . . . strange solitude . . . concentrated poignancy and delight. (p. 44)

Bullough's notion of *psychic distance* is reminiscent of Husserl's *epoché*. We begin to see the connections between aesthetic theory and phenomenology. However, feminists interpret Bullough's psychic distance in a very different way.[2]

The list of criteria concerning an aesthetic experience was developed and refined over the years. Stolnitz (see Battin et al., 1989) argues that we need *disinterest* (i.e., psychic distance), *sympathy*, and *contemplation*. Aldrich (1963) suggests that the individual must be able to experience the phenomenon from several different perspectives. Beardsly (1969) adds that the creative activity must be rendered *unified, intense, complex,* and *pleasurable.* Clive Bell, Immanuel Kant, and others argue the significance of composition and form. What counts as an aesthetic experience, as art, and good art has been argued throughout the ages.

Each of these debates came to an abrupt, albeit temporary, halt when Morris Weitz (1977) defined art, art theory, and the aesthetic experience as an open concept. Weitz, a disciple of Wittgenstein, argues that art and its surrounding activities have never been static, and they can never be static. Art must challenge its own said boundaries because it is an inherently changeable, creative, open-textured activity. It is undefinable. Tilghman (1989) supports Weitz's view and adds that aesthetic theory has had little impact upon the arts or upon aesthetic experiences as a whole. Theory has little to do with artistic expression, Tilghman concludes.

However, Danto's (1964) work sits in stark contrast to Weitz's view by suggesting that we cannot have art without theory. Theory is at the heart of the artistic experience and its creation. He suggests that the "art world" helps to define art itself: "To see something as art requires something the eye cannot decry—an atmosphere of artistic theory, a knowledge of the history of art: an art world" (p. 177, as cited in Dickie et al., 1989). Art is based on interpretation and interpretations must come from the art world, according to Danto. Silvers (1989) argues that each historical period has provided distinctly different interpretations of art. Some artistic renderings have only been judged to be art many years after their initial conception. To argue that art depends on the art world is to render art into a continual flux that depends upon the whim of an elite social circle, which may be exactly what Danto wanted.

Dickie (1989), after several attempts, proposes that art exists in a circular system of relationships within the art world. He attempts to make these definitions collapse in on themselves. His institutional theory is designed to allow both the artists and the art audience (e.g., critics, curators, collectors, general public, etc.) to establish or co-produce each other. Stecker (1989) argues that Dickie "fails to show that existing in an institutional framework is a necessary condition for being art" (p. 124). It would seem that the "art world" itself could be considered a creation. Feminists have argued that Dickie's definition does little to escape from the elitist definitions of the past. Women's art has frequently been discussed, marginalized, or redefined as craft by the "serious" art world (Hein, 1993).

Discussions of art and aesthetics can be quite confusing as some scholars focus on the creation, others spotlight the spectator, and others highlight the artist. A few scholars address the aesthetic experience, while others address the politics of art.

Although I am tempted to simplify and summarize these aesthetic positions so that I can proceed to a more contemporary view, I realize that to do so would fail to provide a full picture of the theories that influence an alternative aesthetic perspective. Therefore I need to summarize briefly the aesthetic perspectives of Karl Marx and Fredrick Nietzsche as they relate to the organizing of social relations.[3]

Marx on Aesthetics

No discussion of the philosophy of aesthetics would be complete without addressing at least the early works of Karl Marx. Marx's theory of alienated labor is indeed one of the most powerful statements on the aesthetic nature of human kind.

Marx begins his 1844 manuscript, "Alienated Labor," with the argument that we have presupposed a particular political economy. "We have accepted its terminology and its laws. We presupposed private property; the separation of labor; . . . competition, the concept of exchange value, etc." (p. 131). In doing so, the worker sinks into a miserable existence that is reified and perpetuated. According to Marx, the political economy and the organization of labor are accepted as "apparently accidental conditions [that] are simply the expression of a necessary development" (p. 132).

Marx continues his discussion of 19th-century capitalism by explaining the role and the implications for the worker. The role of the worker is to produce, and the "more commodities the worker produces, the cheaper a commodity he [sic] becomes" (p. 133). This exploited laborer exists as an *alien being*. An explanation of this alien being follows.

First, Marx presumes the creative nature of human beings:

> The animal builds only according to the standard and the need of the species to which it belongs, while man [sic] knows how to produce according to the standard of every species. . . . Man [sic], therefore, creates according to the laws of beauty. (pp. 139–140)

Then Marx explains that our every activity is a creative extension of our being. He asserts that this creative being is present in both *praxis* and *product*, which he suggests are stolen from the laborer who must work for another's profit:

> This appropriation appears as alienation; the worker's spontaneous activity appears as the activity of another, living appears as a sacrifice of life, production of the object as loss of the object to an alien power, to an alien person. (p. 146)

In essence, Marx describes being human as a creative activity. Every activity is an expression of self, and the self exists in relation to others (see p. 141). This is how life is *affirmed*. According to Marx, when the individual is exploited, life cannot be affirmed, and the alienated individual denies him or herself (see p. 136). For Marx, the political economy that sustains capitalism is the expression of alienated labor.

Although Marx's 1844 manuscript trails off as an unfinished contribution, its implications for political economy were taken up and addressed in his later works. The implications for an aesthetic perspective where life is realized in expression, drew less attention at first, but today we see it realized in works, like that of de Certeau, which attribute everyday resistance with the characteristic of artful practices.

The idea that the ontological essence of being human was directly related to activities in its broadest sense (praxis) and the expressive outcomes of these activities (product) provided an insightful way of viewing our organizing practices. And although the aesthetic perspective faded into the background of Marx's critiques, it took center stage in Nietzsche's writings.

Neitzsche on Aesthetics

Over a century ago, philosopher Friedrich Nietzsche merged two areas of ancient Greek philosophy into a unique couplet. The 19th-century philosopher found Greek conceptions of aesthetics enchanting. Further, he found Heraclitus's philosophy of the self-contained opposite intriguing. Together, the two form the basis of Nietzsche's provocative, albeit controversial, thoughts on the human condition. To praise Nietzsche's insights is not a failure to recognize his shortcomings. I am not alone in finding Nietzsche's philosophy arrogant and misogynistic. Yet I think his work is of paramount importance for understanding the aesthetics of organizing.

Nietzsche's doctrine of *perspectivism* and the *aesthetic* calls into question traditional views of ontology and epistemology. His texts on Being and Becoming are directly related to his views of the aesthetic as well as the self-contained opposite. As suggested earlier, the self-contained opposite has been described by different names (e.g., *coincidentia oppositorum* by Heraclitus and the self-contained opposite by Nicholas of Cusa in the 15th century). Nietzsche called the experience of simultaneous opposites, *dialectical monism* (Howey, 1973). Dialectical monism guided Nietzsche's discussion of reality. Specifically, Howey (1973) writes:

> At first, it appears that Nietzsche totally rejects the classical metaphysical two-world view of Appearance and Reality, or Becoming and Being. However, on closer examination, it becomes clear that Nietzsche wishes to transform what has been traditionally regarded as a dualism into a "dialectical monism," thus achieving a synthesis of Heraclitus and Parmenides. (p. 49)

For Nietzsche, what is usually taken as a permanent or fixed reality by everyday perception is nothing more than an illusion. Thus, we have an illusion of *Being*. Because our realities are illusions, the best hope for reaching our potential is to recognize the illusive aspects of these realities. Once we recognize the illusion, we inevitably see that we are not *Being*; instead, we are *Becoming*. In other words, reality does not exist outside of the individual; rather, realities are *created*.

Postmodernists have taken Nietzsche's notions of Being and Becoming as creative endeavors that are achieved through discourses. They push discourse rather than creativity to center stage. Discourse is everything. "For Nietzsche, however, art is the fundamental ground for the revelation of Being" (Howey, 1973, p. 56). These two positions need not contradict each other since discourses can be viewed as creative endeavors. "Nietzsche is saying that a new kind of THOUGHT is necessary in order to grasp REALITY" (Howey, 1973, p. 58 emphasis in original). That new THOUGHT is dependent on the aesthetic perspective. Nietzsche writes: "Art and nothing but art! Is the great possibilizer of life, the great seductress to life, the great stimulant of life . . . art is *worth more* than truth" ([Nietzsche] *Will to Power*, 853, I and IV—an unused draft for a preface for a new edition of *The Birth of Tragedy*—as cited in Hollingdale, 1973, p. 155).

Nietzsche tells us that

> it is only as an *esthetic phenomenon* that existence and the world are eternally *justified*— . . . as knowing beings we are not one and identical with that Being who, as the sole author and spectator of this comedy of art, prepares a perpetual entertainment for himself . . . like the weird picture of the fairy-tale which can turn its eyes at will and behold itself; he is now at once subject and object, at once poet, actor, and spectator. (Nietzsche, 1872/1954, pp. 974–975)

Nietzsche's notion of the aesthetic is directly related to our creative capabilities. He tells the reader that

> form has merely been invented by us. One should not understand this compulsion to construct concepts . . . as if they enable us to fix the *real world*; but as a compulsion to arrange a world for ourselves in which our existence is made possible. (Nietzsche, 1901/1968, p. 521)

As we create our realities and live these illusions, we come to know them as given. Eventually, Nietzsche explains, we will forget that these realities are creations. They will become hardened and inflexible. We will then reify the illusion we live and "only insofar as man forgets himself as a subject, indeed as an artistically creative subject, does he live with some calm, security, and consistency" (Nietzsche, 1873/1989, p. 252, as cited in Whitson & Poulakos, 1993, p. 136). It is the aesthetic expression of life that allows for life. Whitson and Poulakos (1993) interpret Nietzsche to mean that aesthetics "makes it more hospitable, in effect turning the chaotic into the orderly, the dangerous into the safe, and the hostile into the amicable" (p. 137). But we must be careful in these interpretations, because Neitzsche's work allows for the creation to be tragic or even horrifying if it affirms life in some way. Allow me to provide an example of a situation where Nietzsche's concepts are stretched to understand horror and hostility through an aesthetic perspective.

Phillip Wander (1983) provides an analysis of the aesthetics of fascism through the medium of film. Wander implores us to "understand fascism as a potential response to crisis, instead of discredited doctrine or an example of German militarism and Italian gullibility" (p. 70). Wander argues that fascism is created as an attractive solution to problems through the glorification of violence, and that glorification is abundant in films.

War, or the threat of war, according to Wander (1983), is the quintessential example of violence and the fascist means of justifying authoritarian control. War is the ultimate test of the value of life and the glorification of death, according to fascist doctrine. Film, far too often, depicts war as "necessary and natural" (p. 71), and couches this premise in hauntingly beautiful or at least aesthetically powerful media images. The *Deerhunter*, *Patton*, *M*A*S*H*, and *Apocalypse Now* are each reviewed by Wander for their aesthetic ability to create an image that glorifies war.

Nietzsche was opposed to fascism, but he was also opposed to communism, democracy, and Christianity. Nietzsche's aesthetic was based on the glorification of man (and I do mean *man*). His affirmation of life and glorification of man rested in the concept of the "Superman" and his politics suggested an elite version of Aristotelian governance.

Nietzsche's aesthetic perspective was drawn from his obsession for Greek perfection. Although it demonstrates brilliance, it is also an arrogant, elitist, and separatist aesthetic, which he summarized in the following way:

> Nothing is beautiful; man alone is beautiful: all aesthetic rests on this piece of ingenuousness, it is the first axiom of this science . . . nothing is ugly save the degenerate man. (Nietzsche, 1888/1974, pp. 75–76)

Nietzsche sought the meaning of aesthetic in the "self-preservation and self-aggrandizement" of man. (Hollingdale, 1973) The degenerate man is equated with ugliness.

For Nietzsche, woman was the quintessential example of the degenerate male. His works suggest that woman should be defined and treated according to the ancient Greek dictum—that women are deformed males. Of course, there exists an aesthetic beauty about woman at the surface level for Nietzsche, but this beauty is meant only for man's pleasure. His writings on women are quite clear. The surface beauty is an instinct and, other than this seductive beauty, the only value women hold is to reproduce the species and possibly give birth to a "superman." Their quest for equality disgusts him, and he reiterates the call for women to be silent in church, silent in politics, and silent on the topic of woman herself (see Mahowald, 1983).

Nietzsche believed that the aesthetic justified life, affirmed existence, brought order to chaos and glorified *man*. Nietzsche praised those cultures that were "severe . . . against women," and suggested that the move for equality was deplorable and dangerous. As woman "unlearns her *fear* of man," she demands equality and thus becomes tasteless and degenerate (see Mahowald, 1983, p. 77). How life affirming can a perspective be that relegates half the human race to the role of servitude?

Here, I recognize Nietzsche as a man who certainly comes up short of understanding the possibilities of some of his own insights! Woman's presumed *beauty* and *inferiority* are an illusion; a reality created by those, like Nietzsche, who fell prey to their very own creations. The images were set, hardened in stone, reified so that even Nietzsche failed to see that the everyday creations that organize sexism are illusions. Or, perhaps, he recognized the aesthetic creation for what it is, but feared losing his own privileged position. Power can be seductive and the seductive may be entangled with yet another form of the aesthetic. Equality for women challenged the *illusion* Nietzsche had created within his own social reality. An alternative aesthetic perspective calls for a more inclusive form of aesthetics. It leaves behind arrogance, I hope, and revels in the creative, the paradoxical, the simple, the stunning, and the glimmering moments of life that give meaning to our experiences. It addresses the mundane as art, the hostile as an aesthetic resolution, and organizing practices as aesthetic expressions.

Feminists on Aesthetics

In a provocative collection of essays, several feminists challenge traditional aesthetic theory. Korsmeyer (1993) suggests that "for all the feminist analyses of art, literature, and philosophy that have appeared in the course of the last twenty-five years, philosophical aesthetics has remained relatively untouched until recently" (p. vii). It is true that feminist critiques have consistently challenged the evaluation of women's art, but it has usually leaned on the shoulders of formalist theory. In other words, feminists are outraged, and rightly so, that George Elliot had to hide her gender behind a masculine pseudonym in order to be recognized as a great writer or that Virginia Woolf is considered an exception among women. Feminists are angry that works like *Life in the Iron Mills* are lost or forgotten to future generations, largely because the author was a woman (see Olsen, 1978). Furthermore, feminists decry the use of an "aesthetic criteria to silence the radical potential of texts by denying them a place in the canon" (Weedon, 1987, p. 146). Weedon provides the example of Charlotte Brontë's *Shirley* as being condemned by critics as "artistically flawed" because it resorts to incorporating passages about "the rights of women to self-determination" (p. 146).

Elaine Showalter (1985) develops a gyncentric model of aesthetics intended to "focus on the newly visible world of female culture" (p. 28). She believes that women's art, especially literary works, must be judged according to the cultural position and constraints that surround the creative endeavor. Weedon (1987) argues that a feminist poststructuralist aesthetics must recognize the plurality of subject positions (e.g., class and race in addition to gender), as well as the patriarchal constraints of the times in which the work was written. Doing so allows us to see how women could access certain forms of aesthetic avenues and shed light on the historical conditions under patriarchy.

Although each of the above approaches challenge the place of women in aesthetic evaluations, they have barely begun to challenge and or "make use" of the central concept of aesthetic theory. Nevertheless, it is these very challenges that help others to recognize "masculine bias as an integral structural element of the historic concepts of creativity, excellence, and artistic purpose" (Korsmeyer, 1993, p. viii). These past contributions encouraged feminists to rethink aesthetic theory.

Hein (1993) argues that:

> Aesthetic theory, though motivated by the same drive to bring about order and unity that dominates all conventional theorizing, is bound by the peculiarities of the domain it covers to be uniquely open-ended and to preserve the diverse and the disorderly. (p. 4)

Like the postmodern perspective, then, aesthetic theory is "grounded in paradox" (p. 4). The nature of creativity resists the doctrines that impose order or rules or laws. Reminiscent of Weitz's open-textured theory of art, Hein argues that aesthetics and aesthetic theory are rooted in paradox. Creativity depends on challenging its own definitions. An aesthetic perspective is self-contained; it not only allows one to resist and challenge the current conceptualizations of aesthetics, but quite nearly demands it. An aesthetic perspective encourages itself and disposes of itself simultaneously. Unlike postmodern disciples who expect postmodernism to be the final discourse on the discourse of theory, the new aesthetic theory relishes a creative companion to its own existence. The postmodern perspective argues that there are truths, but no one Truth. Similarly, and speaking figuratively and literally, an aesthetic perspective would accept the old school of realism as well as the new school of the abstract or the surreal as valid renderings or truth. Yet the aesthetic perspective would not position itself as the ultimate rendering. It would, in fact, celebrate the next movement in theorizing. Like postmodernism, it traps the user in a paradox of ultimate explanation, but simultaneously encourages the user to both appreciate its subtle nuances and create yet another theory that steps beyond itself. An aesthetic view is not afraid to say of itself, I am an art form. However, postmodern works rarely if ever pronounce themselves as just another discourse or as artistic expressions (see Baudrillard, 1987, for an exception).

The alternative aesthetic perspective is situated at the center of the self-contained opposite as it sets forth closure through each iteration and concomitantly laughs at the very idea of closure. Drawing on Hein's (1993) work, Clair and Kunkel (in press) suggest that "aesthetic theory provides a unique philosophy as it is grounded in paradox, defies closure, acts as resistance, and intensifies plurality and confusion."

Viewing the world aesthetically opens onto a world of possibilities.

For example, the new aesthetic allows us to view marginalized forms of writing or writing by marginalized and silenced people in a unique way. We can explore their ability to speak of a condition and to be that condition. A variety of feminist writings also both represent and act as forms of resistance. Each volume given to exposing patriarchy not only speaks of resistance within the pages, but is in and of itself a form of resistance. Every work published "makes use" of the dominant medium. Publishing an article or a book that speaks of feminist resistance *poaches* on the past means of silencing women. Both writers and readers "make use" of an organization in ways that may not have been intended. That is, they are using the artful practices of resistance that de Certeau mentions. Writers and readers of feminist works resist patriarchy by existing. Their books not only *speak of* resistance, they *are* resistance. An alternative aesthetic perspective allows us to see not only the artful practices of resistance as tactics, strategies, or techniques, but also as artistic, creative expressions of being. In keeping with Marx and Nietzsche, expressiveness is being.

As discussed earlier, like Robert Indiana's artwork, which both represents a target and is a target, writing on resistance by marginalized and silenced members of society both *represents* resistance and *is* resistance. This expression of self-containment is worthy of serious investigation. Keeping in mind the plurality of subject positions and their shifting nature, we need to explore this phenomenon of self-contained expression as it exists for varied situations of domination, oppression, and silence for varied populations. Although I have described this alternative aesthetic perspective as something new, it is more likely that its philosophical underpinnings have waxed and waned throughout human history. For example, ancient Cherokee culture was embedded with an aesthetic philosophy of life, of organizing, and of silence as an integral aspect of expression. Exploring such a philosophy may contribute to the development of an alternative view of aesthetics that is grounded in ancient wisdom and which provides for future possibilities.

Traditional Cherokee Aesthetics

Veiled in a blue-gray mist, the Appalachian mountains arch into a starry darkness that is punctuated by the full round light of brother moon. It is here that Awiakta (1993) takes us with her on a "daydream at midnight" that is intended to explain the meaning of Native American aesthetics, especially Cherokee aesthetics. She has set the stage briefly with comments that are conveyed through a traditional western scholarly framework. For example, she discusses the psychology of Carl Jung and the phenomenology of Gaston Bachelard. Each employ the house as the metaphor for life. Jung's house is compartmentalized and must be "brought under control" (p. 171), Awiakta explains; and, Bachelard's house is devoid of women. It is a place where: "No woman speaks of her experience—not even in the cellar, much less in the attic. There is no bedroom and no kitchen in Bachelard's house (extraordinary omissions for a Frenchman) and no nursery—no comfortable space for the fecund and the regenerative" (p. 171). Although Bachelard fails to provide an inclusive perspective, he later expands his image of the house to an "airy structure that moves about on the breath of time" (Bachelard, 1969, pp. 51–54 as cited in Awiakta, p. 172). Here Awiakta credits Bachelard as finally beginning to dream the web that Native Americans have dreamt for centuries.

The Cherokee philosophy of aesthetics suggests that aesthetics is woven into every aspect of life and is inseparable from all creation. Awiakta explains this as the "habit of being" where patterns and rhythms sustain the heartbeat of humanity. A circular culture, rather than a linear one, that views life itself as an artistic creation.

Connections are crucial to this philosophy of the aesthetic. Bateson (1979) defined "aesthetic, . . . [as] the pattern which connects" (p. 8). And he argued that questions concerning relationships are aesthetic questions. For these insights, Bateson's ideas were described as "startling," "fascinating," "challenging," and "brilliant." Yet, when these same practices of thought, these same ways of being are presented by a marginalized sect of people, they are often demeaned, ignored or romanticized. Nevertheless, and once again, Awiakta probably would praise Bateson, as she praised Bachelard, for dreaming the web.

Simultaneous opposites are easily interwoven into the Cherokee aesthetics. Words, can capture the essence of opposites coexisting as in the case of nunda—the sun or moon, but which can be distinguished as dwelling in the night (nunda sunnayehi) or dwelling in the day (nunda igehi). And although brother moon is sometimes spoken of as male he also contains the spirit of woman—Geyaguga (Mooney, 1992/1891/1900). The same is true of sister sun who is also spoken of as male. Roles are exchanged without causing disruption to the Cherokee way of being. The essence of masculinity and femininity exist together in harmony and balance. Harmony and balance are central to the Cherokee habits of being. Understanding simultaneous opposites as dwelling together creates an aesthetic that allows the Cherokee to "inhabit all its parts simultaneously" (Awiakta, 1993, p. 176). Thus, ancient magic is juxtaposed to common logic or scientific wisdom without the usual tension that western philosophies associate with such couplings. The Cherokee way of being calls for one to move from "intellect to the intuitive and back again" (Awiakta,

p. 177). It celebrates the "power of change and transitoriness balanced with the power of continuance. . . . This is the Great Law, the Poem ensouled in the universe. The people sing it, dance it, live it" (p. 178).

Cherokee aesthetics, like most Native American aesthetics, wraps the universe around our shoulders like a beautiful blanket or a delicate shawl. Surrounded by all of the creations and recognizing their connections allows one to listen to the silence, to hear the rocks sing, to see the thunder of the waterfall, to feel the night stars, to smell the first days of winter, or to taste the wild roses. Cherokee aesthetics demonstrates that each reality is a creation that is dependent on silence (in this case, listening to the world around us) and on articulation (in this case, expressing the creation). The simplicity of silence is matched only by its complexity, which is also true of articulation (see Clair, 1997). Expression comes in many forms and is woven throughout daily life, which captures the essence of the universe. Aesthetics and communication are intricately woven together for the Cherokee who believe that reality is a rich interpretive process.

Keeping this aesthetic tradition in mind, Awiakta (1993) leaves behind the scholarly traditional writing style and takes us with her as she enters a "daydream at midnight." There we find the Cherokee aesthetic in the soft voices of distant relatives gathering around a ceremonial fire. "We sit among the Deer Clan but withdraw into our inner space . . . into a silence that allows the fire's image to deepen [as we listen to the shell shakers dance] . . .

SSH . . . ssh . . . SSH . . . ssh. . . . (Awiakta, 1993, p. 177)

AESTHETIC THEORY AND ORGANIZATIONAL STUDIES

As the preceding discussion suggests, the philosophy of aesthetics has been viewed from a variety of perspectives. Each of these philosophies purports that aesthetics is at the heart of the human experience. Recently a call for scholars to employ aesthetic theory as a means of understanding organizational life (Calas & Smircich, 1996; Ottensmeyer, 1996) has encouraged both further development of the theory and its application. Clair and Kunkel (in press) argue that some of the recent attempts to employ aesthetic theory have "floundered in traditional views by defining the organizational aesthetic experience as simply the relationship between worker satisfaction and producing a beautiful product (White, 1996), by limiting organizational aesthetics to the conceptualization of organizations as patrons of the arts (Jacobson, 1996 p. 6)," or investigating the relationship between aesthetic surroundings and organizational behavior (Maslow & Mintz, 1956; Mintz,

1956; also see Gagliardi, 1996, for an overview).[4] Instead, Clair and Kunkel promote the work of Antonio Strati (1996), who expands the definition of the aesthetic as "beautiful, ugly, kitsch, grotesque, tragic, sacred" organizational experiences (p. 209).

Drawing from this expanded definition of the aesthetic experience, Clair and Kunkel (in press) explore the narrative constructions of suspected child abuse as told by former elementary school teachers. The situation is filled with silenced people. The children search for a voice; the teachers seem to be silenced by bureaucratic discourse; and the onlookers stare with motionless lips. Their work reveals that the teachers, who have no viable, realistic solution, move the experience into an aesthetic experience through the use of narrative. The teachers create a place for the abused children in our hearts and in their hearts. Through the aesthetic resolution, the teacher provides a place to care for the child. The teacher creates a new aesthetic reality where the abused child "disappears as a person and reappears as the tragic character who represents the ironies of life." The circumstances exist at one level and yet at other levels of reality. Different realities are *woven* together. Finally, the teacher provides an aesthetic reality where the *tragic* becomes a *tragedy*, where a once silenced story is told.

Buie (1996) takes a different approach to incorporating aesthetic theory. Buie imagines the marketplace as an aesthetic experience that compels people to enter into a *rhythmic cycle* of "essential activity of all life" (p. 225). In addition, Ramirez (1996) takes yet another approach to aesthetic theory. He compares organizational life to the artwork of Christo. Thus, he explores how organizations are *wrapped* through activity and what *forms* emerge. Although each of these approaches are unique, they share similarities that are congruent with Native American aesthetics—weaving realities together, listening to silence, entering rhythmic cycles, and wrapping reality around us like a blanket. Traces of Marx's theory, Nietzche's theory, and other prominent scholars' theories of the aesthetic are also found in these approaches.

The varied approaches to applying an aesthetic perspective to life experiences is testament to the creative possibilities and varied forms that an aesthetic perspective might allow for. These varied interpretations of the aesthetic perspective allow us to ask questions of a different sort and explore organizational and social phenomenon in unique ways. In addition, each of the three organizational examples presented above draw from communicative expressions to guide the work.

Clair and Kunkel (in press) discover that narrative creations can stimulate an aesthetic experience that reflects reality and creates reality, that acts as resistance while demonstrating domination, and that speaks in a way never imagined by previous theories, such as narrative theory.

An aesthetic perspective allows and affords such insights. Furthermore, an aesthetic perspective does not constrain the practices or the study of these practices to a narrative approach. Both Buie (1996) and Ramirez (1996) rely on metaphor to develop their creative interpretations. Metaphor, imagery, irony, and other linguistic genres could all be used within an aesthetic creation. These articles demonstrate a link between aesthetic theory and communication theory.

Aesthetic theory suggests that discourses are creative experiences. Yet aesthetics does not rely solely on the word; it can cross expressive formats. It may be the exhilaration associated with discovery or the satisfaction associated with the freedom to express. Aesthetic experience might even be felt in the gentle lullaby, in the soft calming "sh" sound. Creative expression, aesthetics, can exist in silence and silence can be an artful form of expression. The postmodern perspective draws on the metaphor of discourse. Literally, the written and spoken word create our realities. Figuratively, material acts or products are described as discourses because they symbolically express meanings. The aesthetic perspective draws on the metaphor of art (visual, musical, lyrical, literary, performance, dramatic, and poetic to name a few); artistic metaphors encourage an exploration of the form and the function of the discourses described by the postmodern perspective. Discourse, as described by postmodernism, and aesthetics chase each other in a circular fashion; as discourse is creative and aesthetics is expressive. The aesthetic approach searches out our everyday practices as artful expressions, as crafts, as cartoons, as tragedies or comedies, as reflections, impressions, or expressions, and as symphonies as well as solos. The aesthetic perspective acknowledges the realistic renderings as well as the surrealistic experiences of social relations. It is the poetics and the performances of life.

Aesthetics combines praxis and product. It transcends the mundane through the mundane. An aesthetic perspective relishes creativity and encourages escape from the very boundaries and limitations it self-imposed. It is a vibrant pulsating perspective. It is philosophical, political, phenomenological, and spiritual.[5] It is often the expression of the unspoken; the language of silence; the image of the invisible. Aesthetics works hand in hand with the postmodern perspective, the feminist perspective, the critical perspective, the interpretive perspective, and the shared and overlapping combinations of these perspectives in order to provide us with a rhetoric of untold, unheard, unseen, and heretofore unimagined possibilities.

CHAPTER 9

From Whispers to . . .

Regardez moi.
Cela sufait;
je suis art.
—Ben Vautier,
1964

The title of this book, *Organizing Silence*, captures at least two unique and overlapping meanings. "It simultaneously refers to the ways in which interests, issues, and identities of marginalized people are silenced and to how those silenced voices can be organized in ways to be heard" (see Clair, 1997, p. 323).[1] In this sense, silence is organized. Whether one speaks of silence as oppression or as resistance, or as a self-contained opposite of oppression/\resistance, it is organized. Whether silence is institutionalized through the state or hidden in plain sight and explained away as forms of everyday random acts of violence, it does contribute to the organization of our social realities. Silence, as a form of defiance through grassroots movements or the seemingly spontaneous expressions of resistance, demonstrates organization. Silence takes on varied forms and fulfills a variety of functions. Silence participates in the creation of our lives.

In addition, "organizing silence," as an expression, is intended to represent the complex, dialectical, and sometimes paradoxical aspects of silence and voice" (Clair, 1997, p. 323; also see Crenshaw, 1997; Dervin, 1993; and Scott, 1993, in addition to the sources cited in chapter 2). The idea that silence and voice exist as simultaneous expressions suggests that bifurcating the two may leave us with a partial understanding of who we are and how we live our everyday social realities. This particular dialectical approach is based less on dialectical tension and more on the simultaneous aspects of opposites. For example, resistance shares a space with oppression; the personal is political; the micro meets the macro; communication can be silencing and silence can be deafening. Future moves in this area of study should give way to the possibility of viewing our social exchanges less as antagonistic opposites and more as an array of expressions that reflect and create our social realities.

I have attempted, for the most part, to look at organization in a verblike fashion by talking in terms of organizing practices. For example, sexual harassment, which is both a discursive and a material practice, organizes a gendered construction of the world. As important as it is to explore the *organizing of* certain realities, it is also important to see how *organizations*, which are part of that creation, perpetuate or challenge the created realities. In other words, organizations, especially when perceived as entities, act as accomplices in the organizing of everyday life.

Individual and local organizational responses, as well as societal institutions, can contribute to the organization of silence. For instance, legal institutions, which claim the role of prosecutor, defender, and judge, have a mixed record concerning the protection of marginalized people. In a specific case, in the state of Ohio, a judge sentenced a man to only nine months probation for physically assaulting the woman he was socially involved with. And the judge ordered the man to marry the woman that the man had allegedly abused. This was meant to teach him a lesson. Virtually silenced, the woman was sentenced to a life of domestic abuse. However, in a loud outcry, an alternative organization (i.e., different from corporations or government bureaucracies) rallied behind its spokesperson to counter the judge's discriminatory practice. Specifically, Patricia Ireland, president of the National Organization for Women (NOW) was outraged by the incident as well as the judge's edict ("Woman-beater," 1995). Her rage and the rage of others like her compelled the judge to retract his mandate of marriage. Yet the rulings original validity was drawn from the *organizational legitimacy of the law* (i.e., the legal system perceived as an organization). The alternative organization, also relying on a form of organizational legitimacy, created sparks that altered the course of a dominating and oppressive practice that could have destroyed the life of one woman.

There are organizations that speak on behalf of the silenced. Yet it would be unfair to make blanket generalizations about the abilities or inabilities of institutions to speak to the needs of silenced, marginalized people. It would be erroneous to think that alternative organizations can solve all our problems. Furthermore, to picture "legitimate" organizations as either dominating or emancipatory is likewise a simplification. Nevertheless, to challenge the taken-for-granted goodness of these institutions is to question and possibly to disrupt dominant discourses that are oppressive.

Certain organizations in society have achieved a sense of legitimacy that makes their existence seem indispensable to our lives. The rhetorical question might be asked: How could society function without the legal system, the medical community, the public and private educational systems, the churches and synagogues, and the military services? The current ideological design of society could not function well at all without these institutions. Yet the current design is not without serious flaws. Many scholars have and continue to address how these organizations are positioned in such a way as to perpetuate silence through their own sanctimonious legitimation. In the following section, I provide a few examples of scholarship that questions traditional organizations, some that I have mentioned previously.

Mary Daly (1973) tackles the misogynistic socializing of people through religion, especially the Catholic Church. Kathy E. Ferguson (1984) challenges bureaucracy from a feminist perspective. Catharine MacKinnon (1979) and others challenge the legal system for, far too often, being an institution of injustice. Ernesto Laclau and Chantal Mouffe (1985) question the current practices of democracy. Marxist scholars address the inequities of capitalism. Paul Willis (1977) questions how the public school system in England supports a class-based economy by leading working-class kids to get working-class jobs. Michelle Fine (1992) explores the educational system in the United States to procure information about sexist, racist, class elitist, and general discriminatory practices embedded in educational systems. Pam Chapman (1994), Michelle Violanti (1996), and others have investigated the role of the military with respect to silencing the victims of sexual harassment and discrimination, especially within the United States Navy. Dean Schiebel (1996), among others, questions the sexist traditions that are found within medical schools, and that more than likely seep into the everyday practices of the medical community. Teun van Dijk and associates (1997a & b) and others, explore the embeddedness of racism in language and society. George Cheney (1991) argues that we have become an organizational society and Stan Deetz (1992) questions the role of democracy in a society that has been colonized by the corporate world.

Without a doubt, we are beginning to see the bigger picture. We need to explore further how these institutions support each other with respect to silencing marginalized people. For example, in chapter 6, it became evident that the role of the EEOC could protect people only within the confines of a capitalist "bottom-line." How does the existence of one organization provide the legitimacy for another? Now that we have addressed these institutions individually, we need to juxtapose them to each other. We need to highlight the shadows of the practices that provide support for injustices from institution to institution and from one institutional practice to another. How does silencing people through certain institutional venues provide outlets for other institutions to marginalize different groups of people? If it is true that these macro-institutionalized practices create grand discourses (Lyotard, 1984) that are embedded within everyday talk and the everyday communication reinforces the current discourses of domination (see Clair, 1996a) how are we to untangle their relationship? What micro∧macro-level practices reinforce a detrimental cycle of resistance∧oppression rather than an emancipatory one? How are scholars who study phenomena as though it is confined to the *internal* workings of *the organization* (see Smith, 1990/1993, for a discussion of the container metaphor) ever to escape the micro-orientation? How can we understand the richness of these practices and how they create our social realities if we position the phenomenon as related *to* communication rather than *as* communication? How can we possibly improve the world unless we recognize that our realities are pliable, open, and malleable. They are creations. These creations may be dialectical, confusing, spinning, eddies of expressions that are difficult, at the very least, to discern. Nevertheless, if we are to discover anything new or vital concerning the complicated aspects of organizing our realities, then we must challenge ourselves to complicate our research. Furthermore, if we are to expose the silence of oppression, then we must challenge not only the obvious power-holders, but also ourselves and each other (see Fine, 1994).

African American feminists challenge the white middle-class values of the often well-educated, white feminists (hooks, 1984). Audre Lorde (1984) challenges not only the white middle-class value system of some feminists, but also the heterosexuality encouraged by certain representations of womanhood, of racial identity, and of sexual orientation as a heterosexual given. Ecofeminists challenge both African American and white feminists for the failure to recognize the plight of the Native American people and the land that they hold dear (e.g., see Gaard, 1993). Third World women challenge those who have assisted the colonizers (Development *DAWN*, 1985) or those who have been too quick to name and judge the silences of others (Barley, 1996; King-Kok Cheung, 1992; also see Adams, 1994, for her discussion of Anzaldua [1987], Moraga [1983], and Marmon Silco [1981] with respect to silence). Other challengers add their voices and concerns to the litany of problems that have plagued marginalized and silenced members of society. Each of these challenges, to each other and to systems of domination, are only a few of the ways in which silence is shattered as oppression and reorganized as resistance. We need to listen to the silences and let the silence speak.

Before I discuss ways of listening to silence and ways of encouraging the voices of others, I need to elaborate on the previous discussion of aesthetics (i.e., as found in chapter 8) and position the aesthetic perspective here as a means of exploring and researching social problems and communication issues. An aesthetic perspective may provide an alternative guide for studies of the complex interrelationships of subjectivity, resistance/\oppression, micro/\macro-level experiences, and the expressions of silence as well as the silencing of expression.

In chapter 8, I summarized select positions on the topic of aesthetics. That review moved from Plato and Aristotle to current feminist renderings. I cited an earlier work that I co-authored with Adrianne Kunkel (in press) to characterize the incredible potential of aesthetic theory to capture both the shifting and changing essences of silence/\expression, resistance/\oppression, micro/\macro-level episodes, and the positioning of people in systems of social order. Specifically, we stated that "aesthetic theory provides a unique philosophy as it is grounded in paradox, defies closure, acts as resistance, and intensifies plurality and confusion." Simultaneously, an aesthetic perspective calls for a poetic interpretation, an ability to see the spirit or soul of a phenomenon, a rendering that is both rich and veracious, and an expression of the phenomenon that recognizes and recapitulates obscure relationships. Aesthetic perspective provides for the juxtaposition of unexpected insights. It playfully captures the chiaroscuro of the life experience in both its vibrancy and its shadows without dismissing a sensuous and serious portrayal of the depths, the curves, the intricacies, and the interstices of life. The aesthetic perspective is ripe as a means for exploration and is rich in possibilities for expression.

Earlier, I supplied a series of examples of how an aesthetic perspective has been applied to organization and organizational communication studies, but I cannot urge strongly enough that this perspective be applied across a variety of fields of study and topics of inquiry. An aesthetic perspective offers innumerable ways in which we can listen to the silence and let voices speak.

AN AESTHETIC PERSPECTIVE AS ONTOLOGY, EPISTEMOLOGY, METHODOLOGY, AND EXPRESSIVENESS

To describe the aesthetic perspective as vibrant and pulsating, as philosophical, political, phenomenological, and spiritual, is to leave readers in a tentative position where they may still be grasping for a firm hold of the aesthetic perspective. In the following sections, I hope to make the aesthetic perspective more tangible. I frame this discussion of aesthetics in philosophical terms, that is, as a way of being (ontology), a way of knowing (epistemology), a way of approaching, interpreting, and analyzing (methodology), and a way of expressing (expressiveness). Expressiveness winds its way through ontology, epistemology, and methodology as the following sections reveal.

AESTHETICS AS ONTOLOGY

Marx, Nietzsche, and Awiakta each suggested that the aesthetic per-spective is an ontological explanation that describes our way of being in the world as the result of human creations. We create our realities. This is not to say that our realities are free of incumberances. There exists in each reality a *historicality*—a previously created reality of the past that impinges upon the creations of the future (Heidegger, 1926/1962). The creations, according to Nietzsche, are the ways that we arrange the world to make it, generally speaking, a hospitable place in which to live. The alternative aesthetic perspective that I provide here argues that the creations are simultaneously the ways in which we experience the world and the ways in which we come to know the world. Our knowing gives way to expression and the expression of our knowing once again becomes our being. An aesthetic perspective is circular, or possibly self-contained, but not necessarily limiting.

According to Heidegger, *Being* is dependent upon *interpretation*. He suggests that we take up residence or begin to dwell in the *interpretation* of reality. In accordance with both Marx and Nietzsche, Heidegger pro-poses that those realities often take on significance and concreteness so as to leave the individuals unaware of their creation. For Marx and Neitzsche, this meant that the world in which people live is reified. For Heidegger, this meant that the essence of being was disguised. His phe-nomenology called for discovering or uncovering the phenomenon in question, because what appears or seems to be may only be an illusion. In order to reveal the essence, *interpretation* is necessary. Discourse is required to uncover the illusion or appearance. It is *idle talk* that main-tains the illusion and *interpretation* that reveals it as an illusion. For Hei-degger, "signification is rooted in the ontology of Dasein (Being-in-the-world)" (p. 209), because it is through discourse that Being discloses itself and holds the possibility for "an articulated understanding" (p. 213).

Nietzschean aesthetics are driven by the goal to affirm life; Heidegger's phenomenology is predicated on the expression of care. Specifically, Hei-degger suggests that "no sooner has Dasein expressed anything about itself, than it has already interpreted itself as care (cura), even though it has done so only pre-ontologically" (p. 227). Thus, according to these views, we cre-ate realities to affirm life and care for ourselves. But I must add that it is also true that no sooner has Being expressed itself to itself or to others, or for itself or for others, than it has already created, expressed, and aestheti-cally experienced itself as creation, as an aesthetic reality. The following example is intended to demonstrate the alternative aesthetic perspective as it relates to Nietzsche's ontology of aesthetics, Marx's concept of alienation, Awiakta's habit of being, as well as Heidegger's phenomenology.

An Urban Ethnography

In a compelling ethnographic study, Conquergood (1994) introduces the reader to the street gangs of South Chicago. He immerses himself within the South Chicago neighborhood with the intention of exploring how communication creates and organizes the "communal ethos of gangs" (p. 24). Conquergood begins by pointing out that "the gang as a group is a way of being in the world" (p. 24). We are at once reminded of the philosophy of Nietzsche, as well as those of Awiakta and Heidegger.

Conquergood, however, draws from the work of anthropologist, Mary Douglas, who envisioned cultures as active voices, to guide his study. Douglas perceived the everyday life world as a series of negotiated exchanges that create culture. In addition, she was especially interested in the negotiation of individualism and communalism. She invested much of her energy in exploring the ideas of categorization, boundary-making, and in-group/out-group practices. Conquergood suspects these issues play a key role in determining the communal ethos of gangs. He explores them first through "nonverbal channels of communication: hand signs, color of clothing, tilt of a baseball cap, brand of tennis shoe and style of lacing, whistles, . . . and earrings" (p. 27). Conquergood also explores the murals, the graffiti, and even the tattoos used by gang members. Although not discussed specifically as such by Conquergood, these emblems can be perceived as aesthetic creations that enable culture. But the aesthetic is not limited to these "nonverbal" forms of expression. Conquergood is reminded of the work of Carey (1989, as cited in Conquergood, 1994), who suggests that we *"take up residence"* in the world that we create, and the work of de Certeau (1984), who talks about marginalized people using artful practices to create *safe dwelling places* in which to resist the dominant group. Without a doubt, we see here the influences of Nietzsche and Heidegger and possibly Bachelard.

In this study of gang culture, Conquergood first provides us with an interpretation of gangs according to mass media as troublemakers. Their graffiti is perceived as meaningless territorial markers. And their behavior is connoted as criminal defiance to an orderly world. Conquergood challenges this interpretation and after immersing himself in the neighborhood, he "uncovers" the essence of the gang as a form of resistance to an already forced reality. The gang members resist interpretations of themselves as low-life individuals. They garner respect within the neighborhood by creating images of themselves as belonging to an organized group, a gang, that commands respect. Second, according to Conquergood, the gang members watch out for one another. They vow to one another that they will not let each other go hungry or be humiliated.

Their existence as a gang is predicated on concern. Finally, Conquergood's rich portrayal of gang life highlights the poverty and struggle of these urban youths. His concluding arguments plea for economic and social reform.

Conquergood's work provides a critical ethnographic view of organizing that dips into phenomenology and lends itself to an aesthetic perspective. His ethnography provides voice for a silenced segment of society. Specifically, marginalized youth are made central to his study and an alternative organization (i.e., the gang) is viewed through a liberal and lenient lens. We come to understand that the gang members have created a place to dwell in that speaks of both resistance and care. Thus, one asks how might an alternative aesthetic perspective contribute to this already rich and compelling critical ethnography? I believe it might contribute additional insights in at least four ways, by:

1. Expressing hidden ironies
2. Exposing the silenced within the silenced
3. Looking for realities that are woven within realities
4. Exploring the role of the scholar as artist, who both renders and creates an image which both reflects and creates a reality where the artist is part of both the creation and the audience.

Hidden Ironies

Aesthetic theory revels in paradox and seeks out the ironies of life as though they are complementary colors that give depth to a painting. One way to discover these ironies is to juxtapose what seems to be opposite. In Conquergood's study, we see that the gang members create a world in which to live that justifies their existence and affirms life. In essence, they live an aesthetic reality. Furthermore, by interpreting their existence as care, the members of the gang are afforded the creative outlet to develop a living narrative of who they are, what they stand for, and how they will be treated or respected. Eventually, they come to dwell in this narrative (or performance as Conquergood, 1991, might describe it) that makes their world worth living in and resists ready-made interpretations of who they are. At the heart of this interpretative performance lies an irony. Allow me to explain.

Nietzsche tells us that we create realities that are reified so that we can bring a certain amount of order to chaos. However, we must keep in mind that the *new order* may have its own chaos. For street gangs, the newly created world where alienated poverty-stricken, immigrant urban teen-agers create a way of being, gives them a sense of belonging, dignity, and security (Conquergood, 1994). Yet that security, or care, as

Heidegger might describe it, is riddled with chaos and violence. The gangsters must continually watch each other's back. And, in a sense, this gives their creation a sense of adventure, dark as it may be, that takes on epic proportions and gives meaning and justification to their lived experience (also see Trujillo & Dionisopoulos, 1987 for a discussion of creating "unrelenting drama" in ordinary times among police officers). Ironically, as their realities become more embedded and more secure, the members face more danger. The self-contained opposite surfaces in the aesthetic creation—that which is intended to affirm life is that which threatens it the most. That is, the more dangerous a gang's aesthetic reality becomes, the more the gang members affirm and legitimate their existence and simultaneously jeopardize that existence. The reality conceived in care requires the development of a reality conceived in danger. Essentially, in this case, care commands and demands danger. In short, hidden ironies are at the core of this creation.

The Silenced within the Silenced

There are other obscure relationships embedded within the gang narrative that demonstrate a silence within the silence and that are subtly positioned within the creation. An alternative aesthetic perspective begs for the subtle nuances of the artistic form to be recognized. Like the mute but counted measures of a sonota, silences are subtly embedded within silences that give form to artistic creation. Using aesthetic feminist insights to listen to the silenced voices of women, it becomes clear that these male gang members have created a place for women within their reality that reeks of sexist patriarchy. The word 'pussy' is spray-painted across a brick wall and is used to demonstrate disrespect for a rival gang, which, of course, concomitantly demonstrates disrespect for women, but this is never discussed within the article. Specifically, the statement reads:

> This is King's world
> You're just living in it
> Pussy   Folk's was . . .
> (Conquergood,
> 1994, p. 38)

The rest of the message is hidden behind the shoulder of a gang member who is demonstrating ways to stand and posture in order to signify gang membership and privilege. Ironically, this blatant disrespect for women is countered by the members' macho insistence to fight if anyone disrespects their girlfriends. The reality they have created, it seems, has drawn heavily from the patriarchal world that surrounds them. We do not simply create alternative realities that act as resistance to oppressive grand realities, instead we are living in the midst of multiple creations that can impinge upon one another and that exist at multiple levels. The gang's aesthetic reality creates a place for girls and women that silences them. The gang reality claims a dwelling place that acts as resistance for the male gang members, but it inadvertantly acts as an oppressive reality for girls and women. There are silences hidden within silences.

Realities Woven within Realities

Creativity may be bounded in the sense that the male gang members here do not escape much beyond the world that they challenge, but it is also boundless in that the possibilities for resistant realities to be created are endless. There are realities woven within realities. I will discuss just one example. The gang reality has been described as an aesthetic creation. It acts as a form of resistance to a social reality that positions poor, urban, immigrant youths in a disadvantaged and disempowered position. The gang reality challenges that preconceived reality, but this does not mean that the capitalist reality that frames these youths into a situation of poverty is any more or less an aesthetic creation than the other. Remember that Marx argued that we accepted capitalism as a reified reality, rather than recognizing it as a created reality.

The conclusion of Conquergood's chapter on the South Chicago street gangs calls for us to make socioeconomic changes for these disadvantaged youths. Conquergood reminds us that we should not speak of gang reform unless we speak of jobs. Although well-intended and *realistic*, this call to action suggests only two realities exist: the capitalist/democratic socioeconomic system that thrives on images of the American dream and the gang's reality of resistance and care. The call for jobs gives little more than entry into a reality that has failed many working-class members of society.

The aesthetic perspective challenges us to search for other realities and their interrelationships. The aesthetic perspective challenges us to create new approaches for studying, analyzing, and expressing our realities. The aesthetic perspective challenges us to create new worlds.

Scholar as Artist, Art, and Audience

Nietzsche (1872/1954) explained aesthetics as an all-encompassing practice, like the fairytale that looked upon itself. Foucault (1966/1973) addressed the same principle in *The Order of Things*, where he holds up Valsquez's painting *The Maids of Honor* as an example of how the artist and the subject(s), the subject(s) and the audience, create each other and exchange places ad infinitum. Once again, using Conquergood's study of gang culture as an example, I will point to how Conquergood is engaged in the creation of a reality of realities that turn upon themselves. However, this way of being is also a way of knowing; therefore, I will discuss this aspect of the aesthetic perspective in the following section under the rubric of epistemology.

AESTHETICS AS EPISTEMOLOGY

Aesthetics is more than a way of being. It is also a way of knowing (Ottensmeyer, 1996). If what we experience is captured in some form of expressiveness then the ways in which *we know* are *aesthetic creative exchanges of experience*. Expression is merely experience exchanged and experience is an aesthetic expression. Heidegger described this expression as an *interpretation*. Recalling Bullough's (1912) description of the fog as a phenomenon that once incited fear but that can be moved to an aesthetic level, we have a clearer picture of what Heidegger means by interpretation. By *interpreting the fog* as creamy smoothness, the fear disappeared and the individual was left with a state of pleasure. Two things must be noted about how the person comes *to know* the fog. First, there is no reason to dismiss the initial experience as a nonaesthetic experience simply because it is less pleasurable. Second, the initial knowing of the fog is also an interpretation or expression of the fog. There is not necessarily any *natural* or *given* way of knowing fog. Knowing the fog is in itself a creative endeavor. The experience may be exchanged or reinterpreted from fear to pleasure; from pleasure to poetry or prose; from prose to scholarly statements; and so on. Thus, we come to know through our aesthetic creations.

In keeping with our earlier examples, Conquergood comes to know gangs as providers of care. Ironically, Conquergood embodies the notion of care. He becomes a caretaker or carekeeper, as he exchanges his experiences into a compelling ethnographic format. He continues to care, not only at the level of providing the gang members with his phone number (i.e., the individual members are cared for), but by publishing creative expressions of how he *knows* these gangs (i.e., the image of gangs as an organization is also cared for). He is the artist who presents us with his rendering of gang life. We, in turn, create a place for Conquergood's way of *knowing* and *expressing*. Eventually Conquergood becomes both artist and part of the rendering, as do we.

Aesthetics as epistemology is open to a variety of ways of knowing. Some people come to know according to the beauty and simplicity of mathematical formulas. They often leave behind myth and magic, narrative and poetry, dance and image as ways that interfere with their way of knowing, their way of expressing their being. They render a very different picture of the world than an ethnographer would. Nevertheless, they have created a way of knowing that perpetuates a way of being through a particular way of expressing. And the same is true of those who come to know through narrative, poetry, dance, and other creative forms. Their perspective speaks of their own aesthetic reality and their silences express the shadows in which they live. Thus, our ways of knowing are creations or expressions. Furthermore, our ways of knowing implicate how we approach the formal or informal methods by which we gather, explore, interpret, and express experience.

AESTHETICS AS METHODOLOGY

The perspective that we take influences the methods that we employ. I have suggested elsewhere that we need to

> study the phenomenon, not the *organization* or a *group of individuals*. Make visible, the invisible. Search out what is absent. Look for who is silenced and how this silencing is achieved. Explore the unique in order to shed light on the familiar and explore the familiar in an attempt to highlight the complexities of everyday life. (Clair, 1996c, p. 9)

Although it has been suggested that all methodology is part and parcel of someone's aesthetic reality, alternative forms of methodology may highlight the created characteristic as opposed to the reified assumptions of our lives. An aesthetic methodology highlights the created aspects of being and knowing while focusing on expressiveness. For instance, one might employ an

> ethnography of expression [that] shrugs off the constraints of place and time and embraces the communicative and expressive practices as central. Moving freely from place to place, ethnographies of expression 'displace' the practices that were once viewed as tied to a specific location. . . . Meanings and practices change, develop, disappear, and reappear as they strain, struggle, squeeze, slip and slide among the practices that create cultural meanings, and the meanings that create, sustain, and sometimes challenge the practices. (Clair, 1996c, pp. 9–10)

This postmodern perspective is not new (e.g., see Clifford & Marcus, 1986; Conquergood, 1991; and Rawlins, 1998 for a brief overview of alternative approaches to ethnography). For instance, the notion of sliding through history to capture the meaning of an event is deftly described in Trujillo's (1993) critical and postmodern ethnographic exploration of the mecca of individuals to the John F. Kennedy assassination site. Another interesting example is Aden's (1995) exploration of nostalgic communication about baseball in a specific documentary that draws from the past to create a "place" of security for workers. These and other alternative ethnographies suggest that culture does not stand still in time, that communicative creations extend beyond geographic and temporal restraints, and that ethnographies of expression or meaning contribute valuable insights about our social relations.

One of the most interesting examples of contemporary ethnography that I have come across recently was written by Bryan Taylor (1996). His article draws on the work of Bahktin to expose the dialogic construction of the meaning of Los Alamos (both the laboratory and the museum). Taylor employs traditional ethnographic methods with nontraditional forms of presentation that culminate in a new way of knowing the nuclear debate. He uses a variety of voices and expressive styles, including narrative, poetry, and conversational script, to develop a dialogue among his own collection of observations. The different voices "speak" to each other and grant new insights. This alternative approach highlights the created aspects of our realities.

Other alternative approaches exist that may in one form or another call upon aesthetic aspects. For example, feminist deconstructions force us to look at the world as it is turned upside down (Martin, 1990). Feminist postmodern ethnographies challenge us to question old concepts and explore new modes in terms of authorial stance, reflexivity, objectivity, and polyvocality (Wolf, 1992; also see Petronio, 1994, for a collection of essays on the dialogue of evidence). Rambo Ronoi's (1992) article sucks us into her world of the erotic dancer/researcher and speaks to the creation of a life world that demands self-reflexivity. In the same collection of essays, Richardson (1992) argues for the poetry of sociology and Neumann (1992) takes us on a journey of the recollections of travel. Neumann captures a moment where place and expressiveness meet (see Ellis and Flaherty, 1992, for other examples of alternative aesthetic approaches to researching the lived experience, and Fine, 1994, for other suggested readings). Trujillo's class (Communication Studies—298, forthcoming) playfully yet rigorously renders clear the cultural experience of the postmodern bar. Yet, on a more somber note, Krizek (1992) unveils the uniquely ordinary ways in which we come to say good-bye to those whom we have loved and have lost through death.

These alternative ethnographies are just one way in which to highlight the aesthetic perspective that encourages a creative expression of our created realities. I have offered only a few examples from an ever growing body of alternative approaches for exploring, creating, knowing, and expressing our social realities, (e.g., also see Clifford & Marcus, 1986, and Van Maanen, 1995). The aesthetic perspective is not only open to alternative ways of viewing phenomena, but encourages a variety of approaches, especially aesthetic ethnography. Other examples might be found in works that specifically focus on listening to silence.

LISTEN TO THE SILENCE AND LET THE VOICES SPEAK

Listening to Silences (Hedges & Fisher Fishkin, 1992) became the focus and title of a collection of edited essays that pays tribute to the work of Tillie Olsen. In her work, Olsen featured "unnatural silences" surrounding the creative endeavors of writers and would-be writers. These unnatural silences are defined as, "those [silences] that result from the *circumstances* of being born into the wrong class, race, or sex, being denied education, becoming numbed by economic struggle, muffled by censorship, or distracted or impeded by the demands of nurturing" (Hedges & Fisher Fishkin, 1992, p. 3). These unnatural silences have been camouflaged by a noisy set of discourses that intend to make them seem natural. Olsen highlighted story after story of the unnatural silencing of certain people. She pointed to the numerous ways in which people were silenced. Her examples range from the social expectations placed on women to be nurturing to the deeply embedded sexist traditions of academicians who deemed books written by women as superficial.

The essays that honor Tillie Olsen's contributions are divided into three parts. The first part dedicates itself to Olsen's work directly. The second part focuses on how contemporary feminists are exploring the ironic aspects of silence as "presence and absence, as inscribed in the text and as external to it, as both oppressive and as empowering" (Hedges & Fisher Fishkin, 1992, p. 6). This second part focuses on the poetry and prose of marginalized writers. Part three treats silence as an everyday matter by providing stories of how the authors, women of academe, find themselves and others silenced in their university setting.

Demonstrating what could be considered a literal (or literary) approach to an aesthetic perspective, these scholars critique the artistic endeavors of others to highlight silence. Furthermore, they create artistic narratives representing their own lived experiences. Each of these essays helps the reader to listen for the silences embedded within texts, within our everyday lives, and within the lives of others. These essays are culturally diverse, rich with examples, and both insightful and poignant renderings of silence. They can indeed help us to listen to the silences around us.

An additional collection of essays, entitled *Our Voices: Essays in Culture, Ethnicity and Communication* (Gonzalez, Houston, & Chen, 1994), provides a series of commentaries that let the words of marginalized members of society speak to issues of identity and silence. *Communication and Disenfranchisement* (Ray, 1996), *Courage of Conviction* (Perry & Geist, 1997) and *Interpreting Women's Lives* (The Personal Narratives Group, 1989) are all examples of books that speak to and of, for and by the silenced "others." Books like these produce creative outlets for voices to be heard and a way for us to listen.

In an unprecedented move, the *Journal of Applied Communication Research*, under the editorship of William F. Eadie, sponsored a space for people to tell their stories of sexual harassment ("Our Stories," 1992). The editor explained that he was encouraged to do so by Tom Brown, Julia Wood, and Gary Kreps. These scholars should be commended because the journal provided an outlet for the silenced to speak and be heard. Furthermore, scholars addressed these stories by applying theoretical insights to them. Practices like these answer Ferguson's (1994) call to add marginalized voices and political interpretations to our study of organizational life. Furthermore, it provides the virtually uncensored stories of marginalized people. This is what Aptheker (1989) called for and which follows an antihegemonic approach. But the journal is more than a collection of stories, it also supplies theoretical insight that lend themselves to a counter-hegemonic approach. Together, these approaches provide a unique way for knowing.

More recently, Leah Vande Berg provided space within the *Western Journal of Communication* for invited scholars to address issues of "voice." As journals devote space to previously silenced issues, interests, and people, we experience new possibilities to make silence known. These are brave moves that speak to the integrity and commitment of the editors and the organizations that sponsor them. These are new ways to listen, new ways to be heard. One might interpret these moves as providing a new way to orchestrate our realities, to envision our research, and to sculpt our humanity.

Of course, there are other ways to listen to silence and to express voices. An aesthetic perspective may be the impetus for broadening our views. Not only does it open new vista for study of organizations, organizational practices, and organizational communication, but it also encourages the study of alternative modes of organizing and expressing ourselves. For example, like Conquergood (1994), Fine (1992) recognizes and legitimizes the graffiti artist. Both Aptheker (1989) and Foss (1988) celebrate Judy Chicago's dinner party as an expression of women's creativity and resistance, as well as an alternative rhetorical means for women to voice who they are without relying on who men are in order to name themselves. An aesthetic perspective might contribute further to a growing number of studies that address the power of art forms to hold a people together. For example, discussions of the Ghost Dance reveal more than an exotic ritual (see Morris & Wander, 1991). Aesthetics may help to organize the insightful works exploring dialogues, performance, recollections, narrative, and poetry (see Ellis & Flaherty, 1992; also Pollock, 1994, on performance) as ways of knowing and telling our experiences. Aesthetics might further contribute to the already provocative articles that invoke music, lyrics, and jazz to study organizations, labor, and cultural practices and ideologies (Bastien & Hostager, 1988; Conrad, 1988; Eisenburg, 1990; Goodall, 1991; Grossberg, 1986; Weick, 1979). Aesthetic theory might contribute additional knowledge about common pasttimes as institutionalized expressions. From studies of the meaning of organized baseball (Trujillo, 1992) to the baseball cheers of little girls in a dugout, we can begin to see how creations are micro and macro, noisy and silent, dynamic and subtle, oppressive and resistant. From the legitimating of formal organizations to the institutionalizing of counterhegemonic organizations like Women's Equity Action League (WEAL) and NOW, the Rainbow Coalition, DAWN and Dignity, we see that silence is organized as oppression and as resistance. An alternative aesthetic perspective allows us to bring into relief the ironic relationships between these organizations and organizational communication practices.

From the image of a stone in a Japanese garden, a scholar can move to an understanding of organizational culture (Mitroff, 1987). From the telling of a tragic moment where people become symbolic characterizations of a society gone wrong, scholars can recognize how bureaucracy interrupts the life world (Clair & Kunkel, in press). From the images of draped figures, a scholar can expose the activities that wrap and form organizational life (Ramirez, 1996). The potentialities of an aesthetic perspective to make sense of the world are unlimited.

An aesthetic perspective encourages alternative and creative new ways of exploring our social relations. An alternative aesthetic perspective puts a positive spin on our ability to continually challenge previous theories. A traditional "western"[2] approach to social science tells us to challenge the preexisting theory for its flaws, dethrone the reigning principles, and crown a new royal theory to take its place. It is grounded in a rhetoric of argument, debate, and, more often than not, a rhetoric of antagonism. In contrast, aesthetic theory is pregnant with possibilities. An aesthetic perspective suggests that scholars might continue these debate-styled discourses just as traditional art and classical music continue to make expressive contributions; or they may find alternative ways of inserting novel notions into the dialogue of ideas. An aesthetic perspective encourages the possibility that we can provide new and compelling perspectives concerning social relations.

For example, the first chapter in this book *The First Word Was Silence*, attempted to create an alternative theory of the origin of language that would draw from the rich reserve of theories on the subject— from classical texts to postmodern discourses. In doing so, something new about language was unveiled—that something was that language and silence were born together of the same breath and that breath was not exclusive; rather, it was inclusive of marginalized and silenced people.

I would not want anyone to think that the aesthetic perspective intends to dismiss a rhetorical or discursive perspective. To the contrary, these theoretical positions provide balance for each other. Rhetoric is an aesthetic creation and aesthetics are persuasive. Rhetorical theories and aesthetic approaches exist as companions in the night, as the following vignette hopes to portray. I will let the vignette stand on its own merit, like a painting on an easel for your perusal, your pleasure, your critique, and your insights. I mean only to leave you with what was an aesthetic experience for me and one that speaks of silence.

FROM WHISPERS TO . . .

One quiet evening, the silence spoke to me. It was Sunday, November 24, 1996. My friend Rachel and I joined others who were attracted to a three-part special event sponsored by the Speech Communication Association (SCA) (now known as the National Communication Association, NCA). More specifically, it was sponsored by SCA's first vice president, Judith Trent, and hosted by James Chesebro and Sheron Dailey. This event began with what was described as a *silent march* that was guided by the glow from the *lighting of candles*. The half-mile march along the boardwalk, passed Seaport Village, and ended at the North Embarcadero Marina Park, where speakers mounted the steps to a dias and waited their turn to reflect on issues of *celebrating diversity and multiculturalism.*[3]

When Rachel and I entered the area where the silent march was to begin, we were greeted warmly and given a green strip of bandanna to tie around our arm to designate our inclusion as marchers. "Why green?" I asked. "No particular reason," I was told. Ah, something without symbolism, how refreshing, after days of being saturated with the symbolic aspects of nearly everything. And yet here I was participating in a symbolic statement in opposition to recent political activities in the state of California to abolish affirmative action.

People around us were chatting quietly and carrying candles as they walked along the dock. At first, that felt awkward to me. After all, wasn't this supposed to be a *silent* march? Were these people breaking their call to silence? Maybe my Irish-American Catholic upbringing was merely interfering with my judgments. Carrying candles and marching silently reminded me of past sacramental marches. It invoked a religious and authoritative image for me. I shook the image from my mind and realized that I was actually quite pleased to hear talking on this *silent march*. Rachel and I broke our silence, as well, by talking about how we came to enter the communication field. I spoke in whispers, at first.

I told Rachel that I had majored in art in high school. I had been more fortunate than most of my high school cohorts because I was able to attend the local community college to study art. Without a doubt, I was not the most talented among my peers. One other, in particular, was much more artistically skilled than I was. She came from a "broken" family, something she preferred not to discuss, but I remember being able to feel her pain. We became friends and eventually roommates. I loved her.

My friend took a job in a factory to help support her mother and siblings. When I eventually went away to a university to continue studying art, I missed her, and my family, and other friends. I told Rachel that I wrote to my ex-roommate commiserating my loneliness and homesickness. I told her that I wanted to come home. She wrote back saying that I was the only one she knew who was going to college and that I should stay. She added that I should stay for everyone who did not get to go to college. Rachel and I continued the dialogue, but my thoughts were elsewhere. I was imagining my longtime friend, her face, her hair, her smile. Rachel asked me something like, "Where is she today?"

"Working in a factory," I replied.

The silent march was ending. We spilled out of the narrow rows of marchers and into the seating arranged before the stage where the evening speakers would reflect on issues of diversity. Our candles sparkled in the night.

Introductions were made before the speakers began. The first speaker was Bruce Gronbeck. He paid tribute to the native people of this land who made room for Europeans without questioning whether they were citizens. This double-edged comment criticized California for its blatant rejection of people from other countries entering its boundaries and reminded all those who were listening of the history of the native people who were denied citizenship within the new America. I was reminded of my Cherokee ancestors.

My mother's great-great-grandmother was a Cherokee woman, who brought 12 children into this world. She hid her family deep in the mountains of Cherokee County, North Carolina, to avoid the forced removal, what is commonly referred to as the Trail of Tears. In later years, she watched from her own sick bed as her family, her children, and grandchildren were taken ill with smallpox after they wrapped themselves in blankets provided by soldiers from Civil War encampments. After burying her husband, one of her 12 children, and three of her grandchildren, she moved her family to Tennessee, where my mother grew up, and where we visited my grandparents. Professor Gronbeck continued his tribute to the native people. I continued to reminisce.

I thought of a friend, whose father recently died. She told me, some time after the funeral, that at the funeral a man approached her, saying that he was an old friend of the family and that he had something for her. He then supplied her with a picture of her great-great-grandmother, who was also Cherokee. My friend had never known that she was part Cherokee (although she had always felt it in her heart and reported that now she knew she was not a "wannabe," but was truly part Cherokee). The man explained that for varied reasons many families disguised their Cherokee heritage. He told her of her ancestry, which had been silenced for a lifetime and more.

Later, I sent a message to Bruce Gronbeck. I thanked him for his tribute to the native people's of this land. Wado, Tsogali (Thank you, friend).

It must be pointed out that an irony exists here. As I promote affirmative action, I am cognizant that many Native Americans do not seek equal access into the corporations or traditional universities of the United Sates. Many prefer their own schools and universities and work at their own pleasure. Instead, many seek an end to broken treaties and the continued destruction of Mother Earth as well as corporate and government encroachment on what little land they have left. As Morris and Wander summarize the situation, they [Native Americans] seek "to create a future by looking to the past" (p. 185) and affirmative action is not necessarily a part of this vision.

Furthermore, while affirmative action provides access, it does so within the constraints of a capitalist system. Affirmative action may be little more than a baby step in undoing past and present injustices. Although it provides positive action filled with choices for those who have been silenced and marginalized from equal access to jobs and education, it promotes a system that Marx describes as the expression of alienation and exploitation.

Fern Johnson followed Bruce Gronbeck with a strong statement opposing racism, sexism, and sexual orientation discrimination in corporate America. She called upon the members of SCA to use their talents to bring representation to marginalized people. Orlando Taylor echoed these sentiments and contributed his own voice to the dialogue on diversity. Alma Simounet-Geigel asserted that she could not "envision studying and practicing real-life communication within a framework that promotes the exclusion of cultural diversity." She added that, "This sense of overuniformity, encased in a cultural world with no challenges, breeds social decadence, boredom, and in certain instances death."

Carloyn Calloway-Thomas opened her remarks by sharing a quote from *The Axemaker's Gift*, a book by James Burke and Robert Ornstein:

> Our ancestors . . . never had to deal with all of humanity as a factor in their daily lives, because for most of history they only knew a small number of individuals going about their particular activities in a very small world. They could slash-and-burn a forest or wipe out many species and then move on, because there was plenty of Earth and few of us.

My Cherokee part took offense at being grouped with people who slashed and burned things, destroyed species and moved on, but I also must admit that my great-great-grandmother did marry a European, a British man to be specific. And family stories indicate that they hacked down a fair number of trees in their day. But I did get the point that Carolyn Calloway-Thomas was making. It is an important point. She continued:

> Today, however, humanity consists of more than scattered bands of people isolated in their own villages and towns. Today, ideas, people, and products flow easily across borders affecting us in ways that our Stone Age ancestors never, ever dreamed of. The persistent, messy conversations and debates about feminism, multiculturalism and gay and lesbianism that rage across the land . . . urge upon us serious questions about who we Americans truly are. . . . And what is at stake when we try to address the grievous wounds of women, African Americans, Latinos, Native Americans, gays and lesbians, Asian Americans, and others?

At this same conference, a friend and colleague, Cynthia Stohl, would later ask, "Who are these 'others'?" She wanted to know who would be included in the litany of marginalized people. It was not asked in a derogatory manner. I do not believe she meant—Where will it all end?—rather, I believe she meant—How are we to determine who is considered marginalized and who is not. Should we mention those who have suffered for their religious beliefs? How can we address the grievous wounds of a Jewish people whose history is synonymous with suffering? Who will speak for the children? Where are the homeless? How do we listen to the people of far-off lands? It is a question whose answer, I believe, should remain open. It is a question that cannot be answered without listening to the silences that surround us and the stories that are sequestered.

Tom Nakayama spoke of his family's history, of his people's history through poignant anecdotes. He brought a part of the past into the present as he reached backward to speak of life in California for emigrants.

Jeffrey Woodyard took us deep into ancestral caverns as he asked:

What of those ancestors whose centuries of labor, defense of American freedoms, and investments in the nation's political economy; whose children's children who—because of ancestry—have been systematically marginalized from access and opportunity throughout the cultural history of the American experience?

I was reminded of my ancestors, mixed bloods who fought for the North during the Civil War. I was reminded of my Irish ancestors who worked in factories, but eventually earned law degrees. I thought of other people's ancestors as they labored as slaves in the plantation fields. And I thought about the children, the children of the past, the children of today and the children of the future. Jeffrey continued:

Exclusivity in our research and in our knowledge base does not honor the faith of the ancestors.

Diversity is a given in American civil life.
American life is about communication
amongst diverse communities.
Diversity and communication are inseparable in the
American experience.
The ancestors knew this as truth.

My colleagues, let us place our belief in this truth at our alter of public faith. And leaving this alter, let us transform the work of this association. With the faith of the ancestors, we can disrupt our own traditions of exclusivity, so that when they speak of us as ancestors, they will honor us for the professional communities we will have built.

At the conclusion of the speeches, people applauded and they raised their candles high one last time before they extinguished them. Night fell darkly around us. The voices trailed off. But I would not forget that I heard the silence. And it was sponsored by an organization that is more than 4,000 voices strong. As I walked back along the dark promenade, I was reminded of the words of the novelist, Eva Figes (1987):

And the dark silence that surrounds me
is full of possibilities.

NOTES

CHAPTER ONE

1. In disagreement with these authors, Girard (1972/1977) argues that "It is foolhardy to condemn the search for a real origin simply because the search has not been successful so far" (p. 91).

2. Neurological discoveries, such as the function of the Broca's area (responsible for muscle movement and speech production) and the Wernicke's area (responsible for syntax, grammar, and language comprehension) as well as brain lateralization and cross-modality, encouraged a reexamination of language origin theories (Watzlawick, 1978). Advances in anthropology and primate studies further contributed to this activity, especially adding support for theories concerned with the origin of gestural language or both gestural and verbal languages (see Gardner & Gardner, 1969; Hewes, 1973; Hill, 1972; Hinde, 1982; Liska, 1984; Orr & Cappannari, 1964; Tanner, 1981). Finally, technological advances (e.g., sound spectrograph) spurred studies of chimpanzee vocal qualities (Snowdon, Brown, & Peterson, 1982).

3. See Revesz, 1956/1946, for a review of the Classical position on the verb that he attributes to the insights of J. G. Herder, a German linguist, in 1770.

4. Two debates raged during the Classical period concerning the compatibility of theories about the relationship of verbal and gestural languages and concerning the necessary and sufficient conditions for language development. Condillac did not confine designation to oral language (see Aarsleff, 1982; Kristeva, 1981/1989; Peaden, 1993). Gestural expressions are also capable of discursive activity; however, sound may have been the most conducive or at least "most convenient of all" forms (see Kristeva, 1981/1989, p. 178). Whether gestural or linguistic language came first or arose concomitantly is still debated today (Orr & Cappannari, 1964; Raffler-Engel, 1988).

5. Yet a debate of another sort surfaced during the 1800s concerning the antecedents of discourse. Condillac refutes theories that argue that language developed on the principle of reason and that, instead, needs motivated the development of language. Rousseau argues against both reason and needs as the impetus to language development and offers instead a principle of passion. It is Diderot who is credited with "a materialist conception of language" (see Kristeva, 1981/1989, pp. 181–182). He did not privilege the oral over other forms of discursive activity. Diderot investigated, in addition to oral language, both the language of the deaf and the language of artists' paintings. His arguments sug-

gest that once representation occurs, in whatever form, the representation becomes a reality in itself. Evolutionary, environmental, and ecological determinants for the development of language are still open to discussion (e.g., see Mortensen, 1991).

6. First, establishing paternity in a non-monogamous society would be difficult to say the least. Although gibbons pair-bond and share infant care, the lactating female acts as provider and takes on the role of primary caregiver. The face-to-face encounters of lactation may facilitate language development (Tanner & Zihlman, 1976) in the mother/\infant relationship, the "primary, most intense, and longest lasting social bond" (Fedigan, 1982, p. 181; also see Goodall, 1971). Studies support the idea that strong male/female bonds are rare. A few baboon troops have male caregivers who build stronger attachments to the infant than the mothers do (DeVore, 1963). However, this is not the norm among other primates, including chimpanzees. The expected behavior of the male ranges somewhere close to the center balance between affection and aggression, most likely within a protective context (Fedigan, 1982). Therefore, in some cases it may have been the father/\infant relationship that gave rise to the *propositional expression*, but it is unlikely. Based upon these findings I will take the liberty of describing the relationship as mother/\infant.

7. Lieberman (1975) and associates (Lieberman, Philip, Crelin, & Klatt, 1972) reconstructed a Neanderthal's vocal tract based upon a cast of a fossil skull. Using a computer simulation program they concluded that the sounds [a], [i], and [u] would have been impossible for Neanderthals to have enunciated.

8. Girard (1972/1977) suggests that "infanticide has its place among ritualistic practices; the practice is too well documented in too many cultures (including the Jewish and the ancient Greek) for us to exclude it from consideration" (pp. 9–10). Furthermore, gaining access to infants through varied practices is common among chimpanzees (Bernstein, 1970).

9. Girard (1972/1977) describes the mediator in the following way: "the mimetic model directs the disciple's desire to a particular object by desiring it himself [sic]. That is why we can say that mimetic desire is rooted neither in the subject nor in the object, but in a third party whose desire is imitated by the subject" (p. 170). I realize that I am taking some liberties with Girard's notion of the mediator. His analyses are more likely to lend themselves to an interpretation of one male mediator (e.g., the father) desiring the object (e.g., the mother) by the subject (e.g., the son). The son in turn imitates the father's desire. On the other hand, I describe the mother as the mediator who is attracted to and desires the infant, most likely in a nurturing way. Not only does she act as the first model of desire, but also as the first model of nonviolence through protecting the infant.

CHAPTER 2. SILENCING COMMUNICATION

1. The section entitled "Challenging Foucault" is drawn from an earlier unpublished version of Clair (1994a).

CHAPTER 3. ORGANIZING SILENCE

1. Therefore, at times my discussion may seem contrived and oversimplistic as it relies on old categorical techniques; yet at other times the discussion may seem a bit confused due to an attempt to address overlapping subject positions. These same limitations will be true of the discussion of between groups privileging. In other words, making use of terms like *within groups* and *between groups* are both useful and limiting. They provide a good example of *linguistic limitations* that influence how we think and even question the world around us. For now, I accept their limitations in hopes that their heuristic value will help to shed light on how marginalized groups, at times, privilege and abandon each other in a complex series of hegemonic and coercive functions.

CHAPTER 4. HEGEMONY AND HARASSMENT

1. The data for this study were collected prior to the Clarence Thomas nomination hearings, which raised public awareness and sensitivity to the issue of sexual harassment.

2. The names used in this study are pseudonyms. They have been listed in alphabetical order for the reader's convenience in determining when one woman's story is included under more than one framing technique.

CHAPTER 5. BUREAUCRATIZATION
OF SEXUAL HARASSMENT

1. The legal definitions of sexual harassment have been developing over the last decade. The current definition of sexual harassment, as supplied by the Equal Employment Opportunity Commission (EEOC) and upheld by the Supreme Court, is described on page 55 in chapter 3. It is a paraphrased construction of Konrad & Gutek's presentation (see Konrad and Gutek, 1986, p. 422). For further information on the definition of sexual harassment, also see Gutek (1985), Konsky et al. (1992), and McKinney and Maroules (1991). For a current review of the legal dimensions surrounding sexual harassment, see Paetzold and O'Leary-Kelly (1993). For an excellent interpretive analysis of sexual harassment definitions including those promoted by the National Advisory Council on Women's Education and the EEOC, see Crocker (1983). A reading of Crocker's work stimulates thought about the reification of the current EEOC definition.

2. Estimates indicate that 42% of female and 15% of male government workers face sexual harassment at work (U.S. Merit Systems Protection Board, 1981, 1988). With respect to women in private sector jobs, the figures vary from 48% (Clair, 1993) and 50% (Loy & Stewart, 1984) to 75% (LaFontaine & Tredeau, 1986). The situation is not better for students, staff, and faculty on college campuses. Campus harassment ranges from 21% of male students to between

30% and 89% of female students, approximately 11% of clerical and maintenance staff, and between 14% and 48% of faculty (McKinney & Maroules, 1991).

3. Patriarchy has been defined by several authors:

1. A perverted paradigm rooted in sadomasochism whose myths and institutions are responsible for war and oppression (Daly, 1984)

2. Cockburn (1991) offers a collection of definitions ranging from the "simplest . . . a system of social structures and practices in which men dominate, oppress and exploit women" (p. 7) to a complex view of patriarchy as a shifting system of control changing throughout history in an interrelated fashion with the modes of production yet not necessarily tied to those economic systems

3. Foucault (1978) relates patriarchy to *patria potesta*, the right of the father to kill his servants or children based on early Roman law. Engels (1884/1983) takes a similar perspective adding that the father also had the right to kill his wife. For a critique of Foucault, see Baudrillard (1977/1987, 1982/1988). For a critique of Engels and Foucault, see MacKinnon (1989, 1991, respectively).

4. The concept of framing has a rich history. Goffman (1974) credits Gregory Bateson as the first to develop the idea that communication is framed. Bateson drew from Whitehead, Russell, Whorf, and other philosophers to develop the notion that communication can be presented at more than one level. In short, the communication can comment on itself (i.e., metacommunication). Several scholars have used the concept of framing to understand such concepts as interpersonal relations (Rawlins, 1987), leader-member exchange (Fairhurst & Chandler, 1989), conflict and negotiation (Putnam & Holmer, 1992), the paradox of professional women (Wood & Conrad, 1983), and sexual harassment (Clair, 1991, 1993, 1994; Clair et al., 1993). Although not specifically addressing the notion of "framing," (Gutek 1985) and MacKinnon (1979) offer excellent examples of how victims and judges, respectively, frame sexual harassment.

5. I am using the term *bureaucracy* as defined by Ferguson (1984) as both a structure and process:

> As a structure it can be described as a fairly stable arrangement of roles and assignments of tasks: since individuals in their day-to-day interactions with bureaucracies tend to experience them as static and fixed authority structures, it is the established structural dimensions of bureaucracy that are most readily identified. Bureaucracy is also a process, however, a temporal ordering of human action that evolves out of certain historical conditions toward certain political ends. The maintenance of bureaucracy is an ongoing process that must be constantly attended to; its modes of domination must be reproduced and the opposition it generates must be located and suppressed. (pp. 6–7)

6. Several scholars have addressed the issue of the private/public realm as well as the private/public communication. For different perspectives, see Cox

and James (1987), Engels (1984/1983), Fraser (1989), MacKinnon (1989), and Sennett (1977). With regard to sexual harassment (see Clair, 1991, 1993, 1994), I am using privatization as a verb (i.e., as a discursive practice/activity used to frame issues). Drawing from all the above-mentioned authors, I define privatization as a discursive practice that is intended to sequester issues and interests, in this case, sexual harassment. Privatization acts to frame issues as "incontestable" as Fraser would describe it and as belonging in some "place" or "relation" that is "personal" and often labeled of less importance to society as a whole.

7. Although Engels's initial arguments are lauded by feminists, his contradictory commentaries are more than questioned. Specifically, his philosophy of women is criticized for failing to take into account a pervasive system of patriarchy, placing more attention on the public realm over the private, and using the argument that the proletariat family would benefit from the mother's staying at home when he discusses the exploitation of the proletariat by the bourgeoisie (Cox & James, 1987; see MacKinnon, 1989, for a more complete feminist review and critique of Engels).

8. See Culler (1982) for a detailed description of deconstruction as a methodology.

9. This information is based on interviews conducted by Kirsten Leysieffer at a state-level EEOC for an article in progress that has yet to be titled. Purdue University: Department of Communication, West Lafayette, Indiana.

10. Placing a section of recommendations into the text may be misleading to the practitioner, the victim or target of sexual harassment, as well as the scholarly reader. It is also important to note that my use of the terms *target, victim, survivor,* and *harasser* is not without sensitivity. The terms *target, victim,* and *survivor* carry intense connotative and denotative baggage as they are applied to individuals who have experienced sexual harassment. The use of these descriptions should not be taken lightly. See Clair (1996b) for a feminist deconstruction of the meaning and messages associated with each of these terms. Returning to the subject of recommendations, to simplify such a complex phenomenon rubs against the grain of critical feminist and postmodern endeavors. As Grossberg (1987) explains,

> the cornerstone of critical work is its committed opposition to any reductionism, its recognition that concrete reality is always more complex and contradictory than our intellectual schemes can represent. . . . The unfulfilled promise of critical work is to find ways of incorporating this fundamental insight into its most basic theoretic and analytic tools, to recognize that the truth is not always concrete. (p. 89)

In addition, Daly (1973) has argued that feminists do not wish to overthrow one dogmatic truth for another. However, critical feminist theorists walk a tightrope on this subject as they themselves are critical of those who "only" interpret and fail to act. I have resolved this dilemma for myself by highlighting discourse that may open and continue dialogue on prescriptive measures for dealing with sexual harassment. For readers interested in general recommendations, see Neugarten and Shafritz (1980) and Gutek (1985, 1989).

11. I believe I originated the expression *institutional irony*, but it came about as a direct result of my being influenced by Angela Trethewey's work. I would like to thank Angela for our conversations concerning institutional irony. (Also see Trethewey, 1992.)

CHAPTER 6. ONE MAN'S STORY OF SEXUAL HARASSMENT

1. During the fiscal year of 1993, the EEOC registered 11,908 sexual harassment complaints. Of these complaints 9% were brought by males. The EEOC tracks the gender of the complaining party, but not the accused. Therefore, the figure of 9% includes men who are charging both or either males or females as the harasser(s). It is also possible that women are harassing women. This information was gathered during an interview that I conducted with Michael Widomski, information specialist of the EEOC, Office of Communications and Legislative Affairs, Washington, D.C., July 20, 1994.

2. See Willis (1977) for a discussion of the hegemonic moment with respect to the oppressive socialization of working-class lads; see McRobbie (1981) for a feminist critique of Willis's work.

3. Marcovich (1967) presents a table of successive and simultaneous opposites as well as their reasons for unity based upon the fragments of Heraclitus's work.

4. For critiques of Foucault, see Best and Kellner (1991), Fraser (1989), MacKinnon (1991), Phelan (1990), Weedon (1987).

5. "Michael Gray" is a pseudonym. In addition, the title of the newspaper article has also been altered.

6. Although the author/respondent originally agreed to public disclosure, following the two successive interviews he requested that confidentially be maintained.

7. See Strine (1992) for an application of this concept to the sexual harassment of females.

8. See Fraser (1989) for a discussion of the four works concerning client resistance. Specifically, Fraser suggest that these examples of resistance range from "the individual, cultural, and informal to the collective, political, and formally organized" (p. 177). The works referred to include, but are not limited to those written by Fox, Piven & Cloward (1971, 1979), Rains (1971), and Stack (1974). Other works written by Crow Dog with Erdoes (1990), the Personal Narratives Group (1989), and Trethewey (1992) also provide descriptions and or discussions of women's resistance and oppression.

9. See Burawoy (1979), Burawoy et al., (1991), and Willis (1977) for discussions of resistance and oppression from class, race, or gender orientations.

CHAPTER 7. WHEN SILENCE SPEAKS

1. I invoke a certain amount of resistance by refusing to invoke "his/her" as the singular pronoun to follow "child." I let "their" act as singular or plural in rhythm with the word "you" as well as in rhythm with most English speak-

ers from America. "He/she," "his/her" has served its purpose to highlight the patriarchal leanings of language and a recovery of place for females. Maybe it is now time to introduce a third term.

2. My own work has been influenced by philosophers ranging from Heraclitus to Nicholas of Cusa, from Hegel and Marx to Foucault, from feminist theory and activism to cultural philosophies with a less dichotomous focus (e.g., Chinese and Native American).

CHAPTER 8. THE AESTHETIC PERSPECTIVE

1. Most texts written on the topic of breaking the patriarchal code (see, e.g., Daly, 1984; Penelope, 1990; etc.) focus on uncovering the hidden meanings embedded in our linguistic system. That is, philosophers, theorists, linguists, and other *experts* decipher the patriarchal code for us. In the example of the girl's baseball cheer, we see not only the *unauthorized* and *marginalized* break the code, but they assert their defiance in creative ways. Cracking the code implies both the deconstruction of patriarchal discourses and the creation of meaningful resistances.

2. Distance as a requirement for the aesthetic was first introduced by Kant and detailed later by Bullough. Nietzsche felt that disinterest was a ludicrous criteria for an aesthetic experience, as he suggested men would be hard pressed to prove disinterest in the female body as they viewed a nude statue. Feminists decry disinterest on similar yet less mysogonistic grounds. They claim that interest, especially in politics, can be the source of and give meaning to the creative endeavor (see Hein & Korsemeyer, 1993; also see Awiakta, 1993).

3. I have employed the "[sic]" symbol after male-dominated imagery of humanity for Karl Marx's quotes because his position on whether women exist as a part of humanity seems more a possibility than it did for Nietzsche. Nietzsche did not mean to include women within the term "man." Therefore, no "[sic]" symbol is used.

4. I do not mean to discredit these early or current traditional and functionalist approaches to aesthetics and organizational communication. My own master's thesis was devoted to the relationship of aesthetic surroundings and escapism (see Clair, 1986). But I do believe there exists a richer potential than what the traditional functionalist school implies.

5. Although I do not develop, in detail, a "spiritual" position in relation to the aesthetic perspective, works such as *The Reinvention of Work* (Fox, 1994) or *Centering* (Richards, 1962) might be of interest to readers searching for spiritual works on the topic. Furthermore, the Native American perspective of aesthetics weaves the spiritual aspect throughout our habits of being.

CHAPTER 9. FROM WHISPERS TO . . .

1. This sentence and others (citing Clair, 1997) may be direct quotes from my 1997 article, however, those quotes were simultaneously being written for the present book.

2. I set off the word "western" in quotes because it is another example of linguistic limitations that have been driven by a political and patriarchal agenda. This language functions to split the world in half—eastern from western. It then labels *western* as white European so that every time someone invokes "western tradition" as a description, it further erases Native Americans.

3. The speeches presented at the Speech Communication Association's annual meeting in San Diego in 1996 will be published in their entirety by the SCA/NCA.

REFERENCES

Aarsleff, H. (1982). *From Locke to Saussure: Essays on the study of language and intellectual history.* Minneapolis: University of Minnesota Press.

Adams, K. (1994). North American silences: History, identity, and witness, in the poetry of G. Anzaldia, C. Moraga, and L. M. Silko. In E. Hedges & S. Fisher Fishkin (Eds.), *Listening to silences: New essays in feminist criticism* (pp. 130–145). New York and Oxford: Oxford University Press.

Aden, R. C. (1995). Nostalgic communication as temporal escape: *When it was a game*'s re-construction of a baseball/work community. *Western Journal of Communication, 59,* 20–38.

Albrecht, T., & Hall, B. (1991). Facilitating talk about new ideas: The role of personal relationships in organizational innovation. *Communication Monographs, 58,* 273–289.

Aldrich, V. (1963). *The philosophy of art.* Englewood Cliffs, NJ: Prentice Hall.

Alonso, A. M. (1992). Gender, power, and historical memory: Discourses of Serrano resistance. In J. Butler & J. W. Scott (Eds.), *Feminists theorize the political* (pp. 404–425). London: Routledge.

Anonymous (1991). Masquerade: Organizational culture as metafiction. In P. J. Frost, L. F. Moore, M. R. Louis, C. C. Lundberg, & J. Martin (Eds.), *Reframing organizational culture* (pp. 311–326). Newbury Park, CA: Sage.

Anzaldúa, G. (1987). *Borderlands/La Frontera.* San Francisco: Spinsters/Aunt Lute.

Aptheker, B. (1989). *Tapestries of life: Women's work, women's consciousness, and the meaning of daily experience.* Amherst, MA: University of Massachusetts Press.

Aram, J. D., & Salipante, P. F. (1981). An evaluation of organizational due process in the resolution of employee/employer conflict. *Academy of Management, 6,* 197–204.

Ardener, R. (1975). *Perceiving women.* London: Malaby.

Awiakta, M. (1993). *Selu: Seeking the Corn-Mother's wisdom.* Golden, CO: Fulcrum.

Bachelard, G. (1969). *The poetics of space* (M. Jolas, Trans.). Boston: Beacon.

Banks, S. P., & Riley, P. (1993). Structuration theory as an ontology for communication research. In S. A. Deetz (Ed.), *Communication Yearbook 16* (pp. 167–208). Newbury Park, CA: Sage.

Banner, L. W. (1986). Act One. *Wilson Quarterly, 19,* 90–98.

Barley, L. L. (1997, May). *Speaking themselves: Palestinian women's views on feminism and their movement.* Paper presented at the annual meeting of the International Communication Association, Montreal, Quebec.

Bartky, S. L. (1988). Foucault, femininity, and the modernization of patriarchal power. In I. Diamond & L. Quinby (Eds.), *Feminism & Foucault*. Boston: Northeastern University Press.

Bastien, D. T., & Hostager, T. J. (1988). Jazz as a process of organizational innovation. *Communication Research, 15*, 582–602.

Bateson, G. (1972). *Steps to an ecology of the mind*. New York: Ballantine.

Bateson, G. (1979). *Mind and nature: A necessary unity*. New York: E. P. Dutton.

Battin, M. P., Fisher, J., Moore, R., & Silvers, A. (1989). *Puzzles about art: An aesthetics casebook*. New York: St. Martin's Press.

Baudrillard, J. (1987). *Forget Foucault*. New York: Semiotexte. (Original work published 1977)

Baudrillard, J. (1988a). *The ecstasy of communication* (B. Schutze & C. Schultz, Trans.; S. Lotringer, Ed.). New York: Semiotexte. (Original work published 1987)

Baudrillard, J. (1988b). For a critique of the political economy of the sign. In M. Poster (Ed.), *Jean Baudrillard: Selected writings*. Stanford, CA: Stanford University Press. (Original work published 1982)

Beardsley, M. (1969). Aesthetic experience regained. *Journal of Aesthetics and Art Criticism, 28*, 3–11.

Berger, P. L., & Luckmann, T. (1966). *The Social construction of reality: A treatise in the sociology of knowledge*. New York: Doubleday.

Bernstein, I. S. (1970). Primate status hierarchies. In L. A. Rosenblum (Ed.), *Primate behavior* (Vol. 1). New York: Academic Press.

Best, S., & Kellner, D. (1991). *Postmodern theory: Critical interrogations*. New York: Guilford Press.

Biaggio, M. K., Watts, D., & Brownell, A. (1990). Addressing sexual harassment: Strategies for prevention and change. In M. A. Paludi (Ed.), *Ivory power: Sexual harassment on campus* (pp. 213–230). Albany: State University of New York Press.

Bickerton, D. (1981). *Roots of language*. Ann Arbor, MI: Karoma.

Bingham, S. G. (1991). Communication strategies for managing sexual harassment in organizations: Understanding message options and their effects. *Journal of Applied Communication Research, 19*, 88–115.

Bingham, S. G. (Ed.). (1994). *Conceptualizing sexual harassment as discursive practice*. Westport, CT: Praeger.

Bingham, S. G., & Burleson, B. R. (1989). Multiple effects of messages with multiple goals: Some perceived outcomes of responses to sexual harassment. *Human Communication Research, 16*, 184–215.

Bishop, S. L., Feller, D. S., & Opaluch, R. E. (1982). Sexual harassment in the workplace as a function of initiator's status: The case of airline personnel. *Journal of Social Issues, 38*, 137–148.

Blair, C., Brown, J. R., & Baxter, L. A. (1994). Disciplining the feminine. *Quarterly Journal of Speech, 80*, 383–409.

Boje, D. M. (1991). The storytelling organization: A study of story performance in an office-supply firm. *Administrative Science Quarterly, 36*, 106–126.

Bollnow, O. F. (1982). On silence—findings of philosophico-pedagogical anthropology. *Universitas, 24*(1), 41–47.

Brown, N. O. (1966). *Love's body*. New York: Harper & Row.

Buie, S. (1996). Market as mandala: The erotic space of commerce. *Organization, 3*, 225–232.

Bullough, E. (1912). 'Psychical distance' as a factor in art and an aesthetic principle. *British Journal of Psychology, 5*, 87–118.

Burawoy, M. (1979). *Manufacturing consent: Changes in the labor process under monopoly capitalism*. Chicago: University of Chicago Press.

Burawoy, M. (1985). *The politics of production: Factory regimes under capitalism and socialism*. London: Verso.

Burawoy, M. (1991). The extended case method. In M. Buroway, A. Burton, A. Ferguson, K. J. Fox, J. Gameson, N. Gartrell, L. Hurst, C. Kurzman, L. Salzinger, J. Schiffman, & S. Ui (Eds.), *Ethnography unbound: Power and resistance in the modern metropolis*. Berkeley: University of California Press.

Bureau of National Affairs. (1988). Sexual harassment among civil servants. *Fair employment practices* (Vol. 7, pp. 82).

Burke, K. (1966). *Language as symbolic action*. Berkeley: University of California Press.

Burrell, G., & Hearn, J. (1989). The sexuality of organization. In J. Hearn, D. L. Sheppard, P. T. Sheriff, & G. Burrell (Eds.), *The sexuality of organization* (pp. 1–28). London: Sage.

Buzzanell, P. M. (1990). *Feminist approaches to organizational communication instruction*. Paper presented at the annual conference of the Organization for the Study of Communication, Language, and Gender, Reno, NV.

Buzzanell, P. M. (1995). Reframing the glass ceiling as a socially constructed process: Implications for understanding and change. *Communication Monographs, 62*, 327–354.

Calas, M. B., & Smircich, L. (1996). The journey to neo-disciplinarity. *Organization, 3*, 186–188.

Cammaert, L. (1985). How widespread is sexual harassment on campus? *International Journal of Women's Studies, 8*, 383–397.

Campbell, K. K. (1986). Style and content in the rhetoric of early Afro-American feminists. *Quarterly Journal of Speech, 72*, 434–445.

Carey, A. (1967). The Hawthorne studies: A radical criticism. *American Sociological Review, 30*, 403–416.

Carey, J. (1989). *Communication and culture: Essays on media and society*. Boston: Uwin Hyman.

Carini, L. (1970). On the origins of language. *Current Anthropology, 11*, 165–167.

Castaneda, C. J. (1992, August 3). Tailhook investigation "no help." Women go public, may file suit. *USA Today*, p. 3A.

Chapman, P. A. (1994). *Sexual harassment, bureaucratic silence: Implications for organizational communication*. Unpublished master's thesis, Purdue University, West Lafayette, IN.

Chase, S. (1938). *The tyranny of words*. New York: Harcourt, Brace and Company.

Cheney, G. (1991). *Rhetoric in an organizational society: Managing multiple identities*. Columbia: University of South Carolina Press.

Cheung, K. K. (1992). Attentive silence in Joy Kogawa's Obasan. In E. Hedges & S. Fisher Fishkin (Eds.), Listening to silences: New essays in feminist critique (pp. 113–129). New York and Oxford: Oxford University Press.

Chevalier-Sholnikoff, S. (1982). A cognitive analysis of facial behavior in Old World monkeys, apes, and human beings. In C. T. Snowdon, C. H. Brown, & R. Peterson (Eds.), Primate communication. Cambridge, MA: Cambridge University Press.

Clair, R. P. (1986). An examination of escapism within the organizational environment. Unpublished master's thesis. Cleveland State University, Cleveland, OH.

Clair, R. P. (1991). The use of framing devices to sequester organizational narratives: Hegemony and harassment. Paper presented at the annual meeting of the Speech Communication Association, Atlanta, GA.

Clair, R. P. (1993a). The use of framing devices to sequester organizational narratives: Hegemony and harassment. Communication Monographs, 60, 113–136.

Clair, R. P. (1993b). Four facets of hegemony with implications for sexual harassment. Paper presented at the annual meeting of the Speech Communication Association, Miami, FL.

Clair, R. P. (1993c). The bureaucratization, commodification, and privatization of sexual harassment through institutional discourse: A study of the "Big Ten" universities. Management Communication Quarterly, 7, 123–157.

Clair, R. P. (1994a). Hegemony as a simultaneous opposite: An organizational communication analysis of one man's story of sexual harassment. Paper accepted for presentation at the annual meeting of the International Communication Association, Sydney, Australia.

Clair, R. P. (1994b). Hegemony and harassment: A discursive practice. In S. Bingham (Ed.), Conceptualizing sexual harassment as a discursive practice. Westport, CT: Praeger.

Clair, R. P. (1996a). The political nature of the colloquialism, "a real job": Implications for organizational socialization. Communication Monographs, 63, 249–267.

Clair, R. P. (1996b). Discourse and disenfranchisement: Targets, victims, and survivors of sexual harassment. In E. Berlin Ray (Ed.), Communication and the disenfranchised: Social health issues and implications (pp. 313–327). Hillsdale, NJ: Lawrence Erlbaum.

Clair, R. P. (1996c, May). Methodologies for organizational communication researchers in the 21st century. Paper presented at the annual meeting of the International Communication Association, Chicago, IL.

Clair, R. P. (1997). Organizing silence: Silence as voice and voice as silence in the narrative exploration of the treaty of New Echota. Western Journal of Communication, 61, 315–337.

Clair, R. P., Chapman, P. A., & Kunkel, A. W. (1996). Narrative approaches to raising consciousness about sexual harassment: From research to pedagogy and back again. Journal of Applied Communication Research, 24, 241–259.

Clair, R. P., & Kunkel, A. W. (in press). "Unrealistic realities": Child abuse and the aesthetic resolution. Communication Monographs.

Clair, R. P., McGoun, M. J., & Spirek, M. M. (1993). Sexual harassment responses of working women: An assessment of current communication oriented typologies and perceived effectiveness of the response. In G. L. Kreps (Ed.), *Communication and sexual harassment in the workplace* (pp. 209–233). Creskill, NJ: Hampton.

Clair, R. P., & Thompson, K. (1996). Pay discrimination as a discursive and material practice: A case concerning extended housework. *Journal of Applied Communication Research, 24*, 1–20.

Clarke, L. (Ed.). (1982). *The atlas of mankind*. Chicago: Rand McNally.

Clegg, S. (1994a). Weber and Foucault: Social theory for the study of organizations. *Organization Articles, 1*, pp. 149–178.

Clegg, S. (1994b). Power relations and the constitution of the resistant subject. In J. M. Jermier, D. Knights, & W. R. Nord (Eds.), *Resistance and power in organizations*. London and New York: Routledge.

Clegg, S. R. (1989). *Frameworks of power*. London: Sage.

Clegg, S. R., & Dunkerley, D. (1980). *Organization, class and control*. London: Routledge & Kegan Paul.

Clifford, J., & Marcus, G. E. (1986). *Writing culture: The poetics and politics of ethnography*. Berkley: University of California Press.

Clode, D. (1988). *Sexual harassment in the federal government: An update*. Washington, DC: U.S. Government Printing Office.

Coburn, M. F. (1993, January 31). Bra-burning and other myths. *Chicago Tribune*, sec. 36, p. 6.

Cockburn, C. (1991). *In the way of women: Men's resistance to sex equality in organizations*. Ithaca, NY: ILR Press.

Cocks, J. (1989). *The oppositional imagination*. London and New York: Routledge.

Cohen, E. N., & Eames, E. (1982). *Cultural anthropology*. Boston, MA: Little, Brown, & Company.

Collins, E. G. C., & Blodgett, T. B. (1981). Sexual harassment: Some see it, some won't. *Harvard Business Review, 59*(2), 77–95.

Collinson, D. (1994). Strategies of resistance: Power, knowledge and subjectivity in the workplace. In J. M. Jermier, D. Knights, & W. R. Nord (Eds.), *Resistance and power in organizations*. London and New York: Routledge.

Collinson, D. L., & Collinson, M. (1989). Sexuality in the workplace: The domination of men's sexuality. In J. Hearn, D. L. Sheppard, P. T. Sheriff, & G. Burrell (Eds.), *The sexuality of organization* (pp. 91–109). London: Sage.

Communication Studies 298 (forthcoming). Fragments of self at the postmodern bar. *Journal of Contemporary Ethnography*.

Condit, C. M. (1994). Hegemony in a mass-mediated society: Concordance about reproductive technologies. *Critical Studies in Mass Communication, 11*(3), 205–230.

Connell, R. W. (1987). *Gender and power: Society, the person, and sexual politics*. Stanford, CA: Stanford University Press.

Conquergood, D. (1991). Rethinking ethnography: Towards a critical cultural politics. *Communication Monographs, 58*, 179–194.

Conquergood, D. (1994). Homeboys and hoods: Gang communication and cultural space. In L. R. Frey (Ed.), *Group communication in context: Studies of natural groups* (pp. 23–55). Hillsdale, NJ: Lawrence Erlbaum.

Conrad, C. (1983). Organizational power: Faces and symbolic forms. In L. L. Putnam & M. E. Pacanowsky (Eds.), *Communication and organizations: An interpretive approach* (pp. 173–194). Beverly Hills, CA: Sage.

Conrad, C. (1988). Work, hegemony, and self in country work music. *Critical Studies in Mass Communication, 3*, 179–201.

Conrad, C., & Taylor, B. (1994). The context(s) of sexual harassment: Power, silences, and academe. In S. Bingham (Ed.), *Conceptualizing sexual harassment as discursive practice*. Westport, CT: Praeger.

Consalvo, M. (1996, May). *Hegemony, domestic violence and cops: A critique of concordance.* Paper presented at the International Communication Association Conference, Chicago, IL.

Conti, D. B. (1997). The rhetoric of "new feminism": Searching for a cultural backlash. In L. A. M. Perry & P. Geist (Eds.), *Courage of conviction: Women's words, women's wisdom* (pp. 321–337). Mountain View, CA: Mayfield.

Cooper, D. (1995). *Power in struggle: Feminism, sexuality and the state.* New York: New York University Press.

Cooper, R. (1989). Modernism, post-modernism and organizational analysis (3): The contribution of Jacques Derrida. *Organization Studies, 10*(4), 479–502.

Coser, R. (1981). Where have all the women gone? Like the sediment of a good wine, they have sunk to the bottom. In C. F. Epstein & R. L. Coser (Eds.), *Access to power* (pp. 16–36). London: Allen and Unwin.

Courtenay, C. (1916). *The empire of silence.* New York: Sturgis and Walton.

Cox, S., & James, B. (1987). The theoretical background. In S. Cox (Ed.), *Public & private worlds* (pp. 1–22). Sydney, Australia: Allen and Unwin.

Crang, P. (1994). It's showtime: On the workplace geographies of display in a restaurant in southeast England. *Environment and Planning: Society and Space, 12*, 675–704.

Crenshaw, C. (1997). Resisting whiteness' rhetorical silence. *Western Journal of Communication, 61*, 253–278.

Crocker, P. L. (1983). An analysis of university definitions of sexual harassment. *Signs, 8*, 696–707.

Crowdog, M. E., with Erdoes, R. (1990). *Lakota woman.* New York: Grove Weidenfeld.

Crull, P. (1980). The impact of sexual harassment on the job: A profile of the experiences of 92 women. In D. A. Neugarten & J. M. Shafritz (Eds.), *Sexuality in organizations: Romantic and coercive behaviors at work.* Oak Park, IL: Moore Publishing. (Originally published in 1979 as Research Series Report No. 3 under the Working Women's Institute)

Culler, J. (1982). *On deconstruction: Theory and criticism after structuralism.* Ithaca, NY: Cornell University Press.

Daly, M. (1973). *Beyond God the Father: Toward a philosophy of women's liberation.* Boston: Beacon Press.

Daly, M. (1975). The qualitative leap beyond patriarchal religion. *Quest, 1,* 20–40.

Daly, M. (1984). *Pure lust: Elemental feminist philosophy.* Boston: Beacon Press.

Danto, A. (1989). The artistic enfranchisement of real objects: The artworld. In G. Dickie, R. Sclafani, & R. Roblin (Eds.), *Aesthetics: A critical anthology.* New York: St. Martin's Press.

Dauenhauer, B. P. (1980). *Silence: The phenomenon and its ontological significance.* Bloomington: Indiana University Press.

Davidson, J. O. C. (1994). The sources and limits of resistance in a privatized utility. In J. M. Jermier, D. Knights, & W. R. Nord (Eds.), *Resistance and power in organizations.* London and New York: Routledge.

de Beauvoir, S. (1961). *The second sex* (H. M. Parshley, Trans. & Ed). New York: Bantam. (Original work published 1949)

de Certeau, M. (1984). *The practice of everyday life.* Berkeley: University of California Press.

de Certeau, M. (1986). *Heterologies: Discourse on the other.* Minneapolis: University of Minnesota Press.

Deetz, S. A. (1982). Critical interpretive research in organizational communication. *Western Journal of Speech Communication, 46,* 131–149.

Deetz, S. A. (1992). *Democracy in an age of corporate colonization: Developments in communication and the politics of everyday life.* Albany: State University of New York Press.

Deetz, S. A., & Mumby, D. K. (1985). Metaphors, information, and power. *Information and Behavior, 1,* 369–386.

de Laguna, G. A. (1963). *Speech: Its function and development.* Bloomington: Indiana University Press. (Original work published 1927)

Derrida, J. (1973). *Speech and phenomena and other essays on Husserl's theory of signs* (D. B. Allison, Trans.). Evanston, IL: Northwestern University Press. (Original work published 1967)

Derrida, J. (1976). *Of grammatology* (G. Chakavorty, Trans.). Baltimore, MD: John Hopkins University Press. (Original work published 1967)

Dervin, B. (1993). Verbing communication: Mandate for disciplinary invention. *Journal of Communication, 43*(3), 45–54.

Development Alternatives with Women for a New Era (DAWN) written by Gita Sen with Caren Grown (1985). Development, crisis, and alternative visions: Third world women's perspective. New Delhi, India: Deen Dayal Upadhyay Mary.

Devore, I. (1963). Mother-infant relations in free-ranging baboons. In H. L. Rheingold (Ed.), *Maternal behavior in mammals* (pp. 305–335). New York: Wiley.

Dickie, G. (1989). The new institutional theory of art. In G. Dickie, R. Sclafani, R. Roblin (Eds.), *Aesthetics: A critical anthology* (pp. 171–182). New York: St. Martin's Press.

Dickie, G., Sclafani, R., & Roblin, R. (Eds.). (1989). *Aesthetics: A critical anthology* (2nd ed.). New York: St. Martin's Press.

Dinnerstein, D. (1976). *The mermaid and the minotaur: Sexual arrangements and human malaise.* New York: Harper.

DiTomaso, N. (1989). Sexuality in the workplace: Discrimination and harassment. In J. Hearn, D. L. Sheppard, P. T. Sheriff, & G. Burrell (Eds.), *The sexuality of organization* (pp. 77–90). London: Sage.

Dolan, F. M. (1991). Deconstruction's object. *Text and Performance Quarterly, 11,* 190–206.

Douglas, M. (1966). *Purity and danger: An analysis of the concepts of pollution and taboo.* New York: Pantheon.

Duncan, W. J., Smeltzer, L. R., & Leap, T. L. (1990). Humor and work: Applications of joking behavior. *Journal of Management, 16,* 255–278.

Dziech, B. W., & Weiner, L. (1990). *The lecherous professor: Sexual harassment on campus.* Urbana: University of Illinois Press.

Economics and Statistics Administration, Bureau of Census, U.S. Department of Commerce. (1993). *National Data Book.* Washington, DC: U.S. Government Printing Office.

Eisenberg, E. M. (1984). Ambiguity as strategy in organizational communication. *Communication Monographs, 51,* 227–242.

Eisenberg, E. M. (1990). Jamming: Transcedence through organizing. *Communication Research, 17,* 139–164.

Ellis, C., & Flaherty M. G. (1992). *Investigating subjectivity: Research on lived experience.* Newbury Park, CA: Sage.

Engel, W. V. R. (1988). The synchronous development of language and kinesics: Further evidence. In M. E. Landsberg (Ed.), *The genesis of language: A different judgment of evidence* (pp. 227–246). Berlin: Mouton de Gruyter.

Engels, F. (1983). Origin of the family. In M. B. Mahowald (Ed.), *Philosophy of woman* (pp. 101–116). Indianapolis, IN: Hackett. (Excerpted from *Origin of the Family: Private Property and the State,* originally published 1884).

Epstein, C. F. (1988). *Deceptive distinctions: Sex, gender, and the social order.* New Haven, CT: Yale University Press.

Ettinger, G. (1977). Interactions between sensory modalities in nonhuman primates. In A. M. Schrier (Ed.), *Behavioral primatology* (Vol. 1, pp. 71–104). Hillsdale, NJ: Lawrence Erlbaum.

Eulau, H. (1986). *Politics, self, and society.* Cambridge, MA: Harvard University Press.

Ewing, D. W. (1983). *"Do it my way or you're fired!" Employee rights and the changing role of management prerogatives.* New York: Wiley.

Fain, C. T., & Anderton, D. L. (1987). Sexual harassment: Organizational context and diffuse status. *Sex Roles, 5–6,* 291–311.

Fairhurst, G. T. (1986). Male-female communication on the job: Literature review and commentary. In M. L. McLaughlin (Ed.), *Communication Yearbook 9* (pp. 83–116). Beverly Hills, CA: Sage.

Fairhurst, G. T., & Chandler, T. A. (1989). Social structure in leader-member interaction. *Communication Monographs, 56,* 215–232.

Farley, L. (1978). *Sexual shakedown: The sexual harassment of women on the job.* New York: McGraw-Hill.

Faulkner, S. (1995, July 28–30). Storming the citadel. *USA Weekend*, 4–5.

Fedigan, L. M. (1982). *Primate paradigms: Sex roles and social bonds*. Montreal, Quebec: Edan.

Feldman, S. P. (1990). Stories as cultural creativity: On the relation between symbolism and politics in organizational change. *Human Relations, 43*, 809–828.

Ferguson, K. E. (1984). *The feminist case against bureaucracy*. Philadelphia: Temple University Press.

Ferguson, K. E. (1994). On bringing more theory, more voices and more politics to the study of organization. *Organization, 1*, 81–99

Figes, E. (1987). *The seven ages*. London: Flamingo (Original work published 1986)

Fine, M. (1994). Working the hyphens: Reinventing self and other in qualitative research. In N. K. Denzin, & Y. S. Lincoln (Eds.), *Handbook of qualitative research* (pp. 70–82). Thousand Oaks, CA: Sage

Fine, M. G. (1992). *Disruptive voices: The possibilities of feminist research*. Ann Arbor, MI: University of Michigan Press.

Fine, M. G. (1993). New voices in organizational communication: A feminist commentary and critique. In N. Wyatt & S. P. Bowen (Eds.), *Transforming visions: Feminist critiques in communication studies* (pp. 125–166). Creskill, NJ: Hampton.

Fisher, W. (1984). Narration as a human communication paradigm: The case of public moral argument. *Communication Monographs, 51*, 1–22.

Foss, S. K. (1988). Judy Chicago's *The Dinner Party*: Empowering of women's voice in visual art. In B. Bate & A. Taylor (Eds.), *Women communicating: Studies of women's talk* (pp. 9–26). Norwood, NJ: Ablex.

Foss, K. A., & Rogers, R. A. (1994). Particularities and possibilities: Reconceptualizing knowledge and power in sexual harassment research. In S. G. Bingham (Ed.), *Conceptualizing sexual harassment as discursive practice*. Westport, CT: Praeger.

Fottler, M. D. (1976). Attitudes of female nurses toward the male nurse: A study of occupational segregation. *Health and Social Behavior, 17*, 99–111.

Foucault, M. (1972). *The archeology of knowledge* (A. Sheridan Smith, Trans.). New York: Pantheon.

Foucault, M. (1973a). *Madness and civilization: A history of insanity in the age of reason* (R. Howard, Trans.). New York: Pantheon. (Original work published 1961)

Foucault, M. (1973b). *The order of things: An archeology of the human sciences*. New York: Vintage Books. (Original work published 1966)

Foucault, M. (1979). *Discipline and punish: The birth of the prison* (A. Sheridan, Trans.). New York: Vintage Books.

Foucault, M. (1982). Afterword: The subject and power. In H. L. Dreyfus & P. Rabinow (Eds.), *Michel Foucault: Beyond structuralism and hermeneutics* (pp. 208–226). Brighton, UK: Harvester Press.

Foucault, M. (1990). *The history of sexuality: An introduction* (Vol. 1; R. Hurley, Trans.). New York: Vintage (Original work published 1976, English translation 1978)

Foucault, M. (1991). *Remarks on Marx: Conversations with Duccio Trombadori* (R. J. Goldstein & J. Cascaito, Trans.). New York: Semiotext(e). (Original work published 1981)

Fox, M. (1994). *The reinvention of work.* San Francisco: HarperCollins.

Franke, R. H., & Kaul, J. D. (1978). The Hawthorne experiments: First statistical reinterpretation. *American Sociological Review, 43,* 623–643.

Fraser, N. (1989). *Unruly practices: Power, discourse, and gender in contemporary social theory.* Minneapolis: University of Minnesota Press.

Friedan, B. (1963). *The feminine mystique.* New York: Norton.

Frodi, A. (1985). Variations in parental and nonparental response to early infant communication. In M. Reite & T. Field (Eds.), *The psychobiology of attachment and separation* (pp. 351–367). New York: Academic Press.

Frost, P. J. (1987). Power, politics, and influence. In F. M. Jablin, L. L. Putnam, K. H. Roberts, & L. W. Porter (Eds.), *Handbook of organizational communication: An interdisciplinary approach* (pp. 503–548). Newbury Park, CA: Sage.

Frost, P. J., Moore, L. F., Louis, M. R., Lundberg, C. C., & Martin, J. (1985). *Organizational culture.* Newbury Park, CA: Sage.

Frost, P. J., Moore, L. F., Louis, M. R., Lundberg, C. C., & Martin, J. (1991). *Reframing organizational culture.* Newbury Park, CA: Sage.

Gaard, G., (Ed.) (1993). *Ecofeminism: Women, animals, nature.* Philadelphia: Temple University Press.

Gagliardi, P. (1996). Exploring the aesthetic side of organizational life. In S. Clegg, C. Hardy & W. Nord, (Eds.), *Handbook of organizational studies* (pp. 565–580). London: Sage.

Gans, E. (1981). *The origin of language: A formal theory of representation.* Berkeley: University of California Press.

Gans, J. E. (1984). *The mobile minority: Men's success in a woman's profession.* Unpublished Ph.D. dissertation, University of Massachusetts, Amherst.

Gardner, R. A., & Gardner, B. (1969). Teaching sign language to a chimpanzee. *Science, 165,* 664–672.

Gathercoal, R. (1997). *Toward classificatory reflexivity in organizational communication.* Unpublished doctoral dissertation, Purdue University, West Lafayette, IN.

Gershwind, N. (1970). Intermodal equivalence of stimuli in apes. *Science, 168,* 1249.

Gest, T., Saltzman, A., Carpenter, B., & Friedman, D. (October 21, 1991). Harassment: Men on trial. *U.S. News & World Report, 111*(17), 38–40.

Giddens, A. (1979). *Central problems in social theory.* Berkeley: University of California Press.

Giddens, A. (1984). *The constitution of society: Outline of the theory of structuration.* Berkeley: University of California Press.

Giffin, K. (1970). Social alienation by communication denial. *Quarterly Journal of Speech, 56,* 347–457.

Gilmore, P. (1985). Silence and sulking: Emotional displays in the classroom. In D. Tannen & M. Saville-Troike (Eds.), *Perspectives on silence* (pp. 139–162). Norwood, NJ: Ablex.

Girard, R. (1977). *Violence and the sacred* (P. Gregory, Trans.). Baltimore, MD: John Hopkins University Press. (Original work published 1972)

Gitlin, T. (1980). *The whole world is watching: Mass media in the making & unmaking of the new left.* Berkeley: University of California Press.

Glennon, L. M. (1983). Synthesism: A case of feminist methodology. In G. Morgan (Ed.), *Beyond method: Strategies for social research* (pp. 260–271). Beverly Hills, CA: Sage.

Goffman, E. (1956). Embarassment and social organization. *American Journal of Sociology, 62,* 264–274.

Goffman, E. (1959). *Presentation of self in everyday life.* New York: Doubleday Anchor.

Goffman, E. (1963). *Behavior in public places: Notes on the social organization of gatherings.* Glencoe, IL: Free Press.

Goffman, E. (1974). *Frame analysis: An essay on the organization of experience.* Cambridge, MA: Harvard University Press.

González, A., Houston, M., & Chen, V. (Eds.) (1994). *Our voices: Essays in culture, ethnicity, and communication.* Los Angeles: Roxbury.

Goodall, H. L. (1991). *Living in the rock 'n' roll mystery.* Carbondale, IL: Southern Illinois University Press.

Goodall, J. (1971). *In the shadow of man.* Boston: Houghton Mifflin.

Goozner, M. (1993, January 31). Japan discovers sex harassment: Inklings of change in culture that subordinates women. *Chicago Tribune,* sec. 1, p. 21.

Gorden, W. I., & Infante, D. A. (1987). An employee rights scale from a communication perspective. In C. A. B. Osigweh (Ed.), *Communicating employees' responsibilities and rights* (pp. 209–220). New York: Quorum.

Gottfried, H. (1994). Learning the score: The duality of control and everyday resistance in the temporary-help service industry. In J. M. Jermier, D. Knights, & W. R. Nord (Eds.), *Resistance and power in organizations.* London and New York: Routledge.

Gramsci, A. (1971). *Selections from the prison notebooks* (Q. Hoare & G. N. Smith, Eds. & Trans.). New York: International Publishers.

Grauerholz, E., & Koralewski, M. (Eds.). (1991). *Sexual coercion: A sourcebook on its nature, causes, and prevention.* Lexington, MA: Lexington Books.

Griffin, S. (1978). *Woman and nature: The roaring inside her.* New York: Harper & Row.

Grossberg, L. (1986). Is there rock after punk? *Critical Studies in Mass Communication, 3,* 50–74.

Grossberg, L. (1987). Critical theory and the politics of empirical research. In M. Gurevitch & M. Levy (Eds.), *Mass Communication Yearbook 6* (pp. 86–106). Newbury Park, CA: Sage.

Gruber, J. E. (1989). How women handle sexual harassment: A literature review. *Sociology and Social Research, 74,* 3–7.

Gruening, M. (1971). Two suffrage movements. In J. Sochen (Ed.), *The new feminism in twentieth-century America* (pp. 10–14). Lexington, MA: D. C. Heath.

Gutek, B. A. (August 1981). *Experiences of sexual harassment: Results from a representative sample*. Symposium conducted at the convention of the American Psychological Association, Los Angeles.

Gutek, B. A. (1985). *Sex and the workplace: Impact of sexual behavior and harassment on women, men, and organizations*. San Francisco: Jossey-Bass.

Gutek, B. A. (1989). Sexuality in the workplace: Key issues in social research and organizational practice. In J. Hearn, D. L. Sheppard, P. T. Sheriff, & G. Burrell (Eds.), *The sexuality of organization*. London: Sage.

Gutek, B. A., & Cohen, A. G. (1987). Sex ratios, sex role spillover, and sex at work: A comparison of men's and women's experiences. *Human Relations, 40*, 97–115.

Haas, M. R. (1969). *The prehistory of languages*. The Hague, Netherlands: Mouton de Gruyter.

Habermas, J. (1979). *Communication and the evolution of society* (T. McCarthy, Trans.). Boston: Beacon Press.

Habermas, J. (1984). *The theory of communication action: Reason and the rationalization of society* (T. McCarthy, Trans.; Vol. 1). Boston: Beacon Press.

Hall, M. (1989). Private experiences in the public domain: Lesbians in organizations. In J. Hearn, D. L. Sheppard, P. T. Sheriff, & G. Burrell (Eds.), *The sexuality of organizations*. London: Sage.

Hall, S. (1985). Signification, representation, ideology: Althusser and the poststructuralist debates. *Critical Studies in Mass Communication, 2*, 91–114.

Hall, S. (1989). Ideology and communication theory. In B. Dervin, L. Grossberg, B. J. O'Keefe, & E. Wartella (Eds.), *Rethinking communication: Paradigm issues* (Vol. 1, pp. 40–52). Newbury Park, CA: Sage.

Harding, S. G. (1986). *The science question in feminism*. Ithaca, NY: Cornell University Press.

Hearn, J. (1994). The organization(s) of violence: Men, gender relations, organizations, and violences. *Human Relations, 47*, 731–754.

Hearn, J., & Parkin, P. W. (1987). *'Sex' at 'work': The power and paradox of organisation sexuality*. Brighton, UK: St. Martin's Press.

Hearn, J., Sheppard, D. L., Sheriff, P. T., & Burrell, G. (Eds.). (1989). *The sexuality of organization*. London: Sage.

Heckman, S. J. (1990). *Gender and knowledge: Elements of postmodern feminism*. Boston: Northeastern University Press.

Hedges, E., & Fishkin, S. F. (1994). *Listening to silences: New essays in feminist criticism*. New York: Oxford University Press.

Heidegger, M. (1962). *Being and time*. New York: Harper & Row. (Original work published 1926)

Hein, H. (1993). Refining feminist theory: Lessons from aesthetics. In H. Hein & C. Korsmeyer (Eds.), *Aesthetics in feminist perspective* (pp. 3–18). Bloomington and Indianapolis: Indiana University Press.

Hein, H. & Korsmeyer, C. (Eds.). (1993). *Aesthetics in feminist theory*. Bloomington and Indianapolis: Indiana University Press.

Hewes, G. W. (1973). Primate communication and the gestural origin of language. *Current Anthropology, 14*, 5–24.

Hewes, G. W. (1977). Language origin theories. In D. M. Rumbaugh (Ed.), *Language learning by a chimpanzee: The Lana project* (pp. 43–83). New York: Academic Press.

Hickson, M., Grierson, R. D., & Linder, B. C. (1991). A communication perspective on sexual harassment: Affiliative nonverbal behaviors in asynchronous relationships. *Communication Quarterly, 39*, 111–118.

Hill, A. O. (1986). *Mother tongue, Father time: A decade of linguistic revolt.* Bloomington and Indianapolis: Indiana University.

Hill, W. C. O. (1972). *Evolutionary biology of the primates.* New York: Academic Press.

Hinde, R. A. (1982). *Ethology: Its nature and relation with other sciences.* New York: Oxford University Press.

Hockett, C. F. (1960). The origin of speech. *Scientific American, 203*, 3–11.

Hollingdale, R. J. (1973). *Nietzsche.* London and Boston: Routledge & Kegan Paul.

hooks, b. (1984). *Feminist theory: From the margin to the center.* Boston: South End Press.

hooks, b. (1992). *Black looks: Race and representation.* Boston: South End Press.

hooks, b. (1996). Lecture presented at Purdue University, West Lafayette, IN.

Howey, R. L. (1973). *Heidegger and Jaspers on Nietzsche: A critical examination of Heidegger's and Jasper's interpretations of Nietzsche.* The Hague, Netherlands: Martinus Nijhoff.

Hyde, M. J. (1992). Medicine, rhetoric, and euthanasia: A case study in the workings of a postmodern discourse. *Quarterly Journal of Speech, 79*, 201–224.

Jacobson, M. (1996). Art and business in a brave new world. *Organization, 3*, 243–248.

Jamieson, K. H. (1988). *Eloquence in an electronic age: The transforming of political speechmaking.* New York: Oxford University Press.

Jampel, B. (1984). *Among the wild chimpanzees* [Transcript of Documentary]. Washington, DC: National Geographic Society.

Jaworski, A. (1993). *The power of silence: Social and pragmatic perspectives.* Newbury Park, CA: Sage.

Jay, P. (1965). *Field studies.* New York: Academic Press.

Jermier, J. M., Knights, D., & Nord, W. R. (Eds.). (1994). *Resistance and power in organizations.* London and New York: Routledge.

Kahn, C. H. (1979). *The art and thought of Heraclitus: An edition of the fragments with translation and commentary.* Cambridge, UK: Cambridge University Press.

Kanter, R. M. (1977). *Men and women of the corporation.* New York: Basic Books.

Kerr, A. (1986). *The common market and how it works* (3rd ed.). Oxford: Pergamon.

Kipnis, A. R., & Hingston, E. (1993, January/February). Ending the war between the sexes. *Utne Reader, 55*, 69–76.

Kneller, J. (1993). Discipline and silence: Women and imagination in Kant's theory of taste. In H. Hein & C. Korsmeyer (Eds.), *Aesthetics in feminist perspective* (pp. 179–192). Bloomington and Indianapolis: Indiana University Press.

Konrad, A. M., & Gutek, B. A. (1986). Impact of work experiences on attitudes toward harassment. *Administrative Science Quarterly, 31,* 422–438.

Konsky, C., Kang, J., & Woods, A. M. (1992, November). *Communication strategies in instances of workplace sexual harassment.* Paper presented at the annual meeting of the Speech Communication Association, Chicago, IL.

Korsmeyer, C. (1993). Introduction: Philosophy, aesthetics, and feminist scholarship. In H. Hein & C. Korsmeyer (Eds.), *Aesthetics in feminist perspective* (pp. vii–xv). Bloomington and Indianapolis: Indiana University Press.

Kramarae, C. (1981). *Women and men speaking.* Rowley, MA: Newbury House.

Kreps, G. L. (1993). *Sexual harassment: Communication implications.* Cresskill, NJ: Hampton Press.

Kristeva, J. (1989). *Language: The unknown* (A. M. Menke, Trans.). New York: Columbia University Press. (Original work published 1981)

Krizek, B. (1992). Goodbye old friend: A son's farewell to Comiskey Park. *Omega: Journal of Death and Dying, 25,* 87–93.

Laclau, E., & Mouffe, C. (1985). *Hegemony and socialist strategy.* London: Verso.

Lafontaine, E., & Tredeau, L. (1986). The frequency, sources, and correlates of sexual harassment among women in traditional male occupations. *Sex Roles, 15,* 433–442.

Lakoff, R. T. (1975). *Language and woman's place.* New York: Harper & Row.

Lakoff, R. T. (1990). *Talking power: The politics of language in our lives.* New York: Basic Books.

Langer, S. (1951). *Philosophy in a new key.* Cambridge, MA: Harvard University Press.

Lee, C. (1992). Sexual harassment: After the headlines. *Training, 29,* 23–31.

Lerner, G. (1986). *The creation of patriarchy.* New York: Oxford University Press.

Lieberman, P. (1975). *On the origins of language.* New York: Macmillan.

Lieberman, P., Crelin, E. S., & Klatt, D. H. (1972). Phonetic ability and related anatomy of the newborn and adult human, Neanderthal man, and the chimpanzee. *American Anthropologist, 74,* 287–307.

Linell, P. (1991). Accommodation on trial: Processes of communicative accommodation in courtroom interaction. In H. G. J. Coupland & N. Coupland (Eds.), *Contexts of accommodation: Developments in applied sociolinguistics.* Cambridge: Cambridge University Press.

Liska, J. (1984). *Symbols: The missing link?* Paper presented at the 10th Congress of the International Primatological Society, Nairobi, Kenya.

Livingston, J. A. (1982). Responses to sexual harassment on the job: Legal, organizational, and individual actions. *Journal of Social Issues, 38*(4), 5–22.

Lloyd, G. E. R. (1966). *Polarity and analogy.* Cambridge, UK: Cambridge University Press.

Lorde, A. (1984). *Sister outsider.* Trumansburg, NY: Crossing Press.

Loy, P. H., & Stewart, L. P. (1984). The extent and effects of the sexual harassment of working women. *Sociological Focus, 17,* 31–43.

Lukacs, G. (1971). *History and class consciousness* (R. Livingston, Trans.). Cambridge, MA: MIT Press.

Lyotard, J.-F. (1984). *The postmodern condition: A report on knowledge* (G. Bennington & B. Massumi, Trans.). Minneapolis: University of Minnesota Press. (Original work published 1979)

MacKinnon, C. A. (1979). *Sexual harassment of working women.* New Haven, CT: Yale University Press.

MacKinnon, C. A. (1982). Feminism, marxism, method, and the state: An agenda for theory. *Signs, 7*(3), 515–544.

MacKinnon, C. A. (1989). *Toward a feminist theory of the state.* Cambridge, MA: Harvard University Press.

MacKinnon, C. A. (1991). Does sexuality have a history? *Michigan Quarterly Review, 30,* 1–11.

MacKinnon, C. A. (1993). *Only words.* Cambridge, MA: Harvard University Press.

Mahowald, M. B. (Ed.), (1983). *Philosophy of woman: An anthology of classic and current concepts* (2nd ed.). Indianapolis, IN: Hackett.

Marcovich, M. (1967). *Heraclitus: Greek text with a short commentary.* Merida, Venezuela: Los Andes University Press.

Marshall, J. (1958). Man as a hunter. *Natural History, 67,* 293–309.

Martin, B. (1982). Feminism, criticism, and Foucault. *New German Critique, 27,* 3–30.

Martin, J. (1990). Deconstructing organizational taboos: The suppression of gender conflict in organizations. *Organization Science, 1,* 339–359.

Martin, J., Feldman, M. S., Hatch, J. M., & Sitkin, S. B. (1983). The uniqueness paradox in organizational stories. *Administrative Science Quarterly, 28,* 438–453.

Martin, J., & Meyerson, D. E. (1988). Organizational culture and the denial, channeling, and acknowledgment of ambiguity. In M. Moch, L. Pondy, & H. Thomas (Eds.), *Managing ambiguity and change.* New York: Wiley.

Marx, K. (1983). "Alienated Labor" from economico-philosophical manuscripts of 1844. In E. Kamenka (Ed. & Trans.), *The portable Karl Marx (pp. 131–146).* New York: Penguin Books. (Original published 1844)

Maslow, A., & Mintz, N. (1956). Effects of esthetic surroundings: I. Initial effects of three esthetic conditions upon perceiving 'energy' and well-being in faces. *Journal of Psychology, 41,* 247–254.

Matsumoto, V. (1984). Japanese American women during World War II. *Frontiers, 8*(1).

Mayo, E. (1947). *The human problems of an industrial civilization.* Boston: Harvard Business School.

McDermott, R. P., & Roth, D. R. (1978). The social organization of behavior: Interactional approaches. *Annual Review of Anthropology, 7,* 321–345.

McFetters, A. (1991, December 22). Pearls that could only have come from Bush's well-read lips. *Chicago Tribune,* sec. 4, p. 3.

McGuire, P. C. (1985). *Speechless dialect: Shakespeare's open silences*. Berkeley: University of California Press.

McKinney, K., & Maroules, N. (1991). Sexual harassment. In E. Grauerholz & M. Koralewski (Eds.), *Sexual coercion: A sourcebook on its nature, causes, and prevention* (pp. 29–44). Lexington, MA: Lexington Books.

McRobbie, A. (1981). Settling accounts with subcultures: A feminist critique. In T. Bennett, G. Martin, C. Mercer, & J. Woolcott (Eds.), *Culture, ideology and social process* (pp. 111–124). London: Routledge & Kegan Paul.

Metts, S., Haefner, M., & Konsky, C. (1987). *The role of the communication environment in perceptions of organizational satisfaction and commitment/alienation among women in the Catholic church*. Paper presented at the annual meeting of the Speech Communication Association, Boston.

Meyerson, D. E. (1991a). "Normal" ambiguity? A glimpse of an occupational culture. In P. J. Frost, L. F. Moore, M. R. Louis, C. C. Lundberg, & J. Martin (Eds.), *Reframing organizational culture* (pp. 131–144). Newbury Park, CA: Sage.

Meyerson, D. E. (1991b). *Nested blindspots: A feminist critique and re-vision of stress talk [Draft]*. Ann Arbor, MI: University of Michigan School of Business Administration.

Meyerson, D. E., & Martin, J. (1987). Cultural change: An integration of three different views. *Journal of Management Studies, 24*, 623–647.

Mills, A. J. (1989). Gender, sexuality and organization theory. In J. Hearn, D. L. Sheppard, P. T. Sheriff, & G. Burrell (Eds.), *The sexuality of organization* (pp. 29–44). London: Sage.

Mintz, N. (1956). Effects of esthetic surroundings: II. Prolonged and repeated experience in a "beautiful" room and "ugly" room. *Journal of Psychology, 41*, 459–466.

Mitroff, I. (1987). *Business NOT as usual*. San Francisco: Jossey-Bass.

Mooney, J. (1992). *James Mooney's history, myths, and sacred formulas of the Cherokee*. Asheville, NC: Historical Images. (Original works published in 1900 and 1891)

Moraga, C. (1983). *Loving in the war years: Lo Que Nunca Pasó Sus Labios*. Boston: South End Press.

Morgan, R. (1993). *The word of a woman: Feminist dispatches 1968–1992*. New York: Norton.

Morris, R., & Wander, P. (1990). Native American rhetoric: Dancing in the shadows of the Ghost Dance. *Quarterly Journal of Speech, 76*, 164–191.

Morrison, L. (1990). Committee meeting. In S. Martz (Ed.), *If I had a hammer: Women's work in poetry, fiction, and photographs* (p. 65). Watsonville, CA: Papier-Maché Press.

Mortensen, C. D. (1991). Communication, conflict, and culture. *Communication Theory, 1*, 273–293.

Mouffe, C. (1979). Hegemony and ideology in Gramsci. In C. Mouffe (Ed.), *Gramsci and Marxist theory* (pp. 168–204). London: Routledge & Kegan Paul.

Mumby, D. K. (1987). The political functions of narrative in organizations. *Communication Monographs, 54*, 113–127.

Mumby, D. K. (1988). *Communication and power in organizations: Discourse, ideology and domination.* Norwood, NJ: Ablex.

Mumby, D. K. (1993). Critical organizational studies: The next 10 years. *Communication Monographs, 60,* 18–25.

Mumby, D. K., & Putnam, L. L. (1992). The politics of emotion: A feminist reading of bounded rationality. *Academy of Management Review, 17,* 465–486.

Murray, V., & Gandz, J. (1980, December). Games executives play: Politics at work. *Business Horizons,* pp. 11–23.

Neugarten, D. A., & Shafritz, J. M. (1980). *Sexuality in organizations: Romantic and coercive behaviors at work.* Oak Park, IL: Moore.

Neumann, M. (1992). The trail through experience: Finding self in the recollection of travel. In C. Ellis & M.G. Flaherty (Ed.), *Investigating subjectivity* (pp. 176–201). Newbury Park, CA: Sage.

Nietzsche, F. (1954). *The birth of tragedy from the spirit of music* (Trans. P. Fadiman). In *The Philosophy of Nietzsche* (pp. 947–1088). New York: Random House. (Original work published 1872)

Nietzsche, F. (1968). *The will to power—1870–1888* (Trans. W. Kaufmann & R. J. Hollingdale). New York and London: Vintage Books. (Original work published 1901)

Nietzsche, F. (1974). *The twilight of the idols.* In O. Levy (Ed.) & A. M. Ludovici (Trans.), *The complete works of Friedrich Nietzsche.* New York: Gorden Press. (Original work published 1888)

Nietzsche, F. (1989). On truth and lying in an extra-moral sense. In S. Gilman, C. Blair, & D. Parent (Eds. & Trans.), *Friedrich Nietzsche on rhetoric and language.* New York: Oxford University Press. (Original work published 1873)

O'Barr, W. (1982). *Linguistic evidence: Language, power and strategy in the courtroom.* New York: Academic Press.

Olsen, T. (1989). *Silences.* New York: Delta/Seymour Lawrence. (Original work published 1978)

O'Neil, W. L. (1986). The fight for suffrage. *Wilson Quarterly, 10,* 99–109.

Orr, W. F., & Cappannari, S. C. (1964). The emergence of language. *American Anthropologist, 66,* 318–324.

Osigweh, C. A. B. (1987). Communication, responsibilities, and pro-rights revolution in the industrial workplace. In C. A. B. Osigweh (Ed.), *Communicating employee responsibilities and rights* (pp. 1–40). New York: Quorum.

Ottensmeyer, E. J. (1996). Too strong to stop, too sweet to lose: Aesthetics as a way to know organizations. *Organization, 3,* 189–194.

Our stories: Communication professionals' narratives of sexual harassment. (1992). *Journal of Applied Communication Research, 20,* 363–390.

Paetzold, R. L., & O'Leary-Kelly, A. M. (1993). Organizational communication and the legal dimensions of hostile work environment sexual harassment. In G. L. Kreps (Ed.), *Communication and sexual harassment in the workplace* (pp. 63–77). Creskill, NJ: Hampton.

Paludi, M. A. (Ed.). (1990). *Ivory power: Sexual harassment on campus.* Albany: State University of New York Press.

Papanek, H. (1973). Men, women, and work: Reflections on the two person career. *American Journal of Sociology, 78*, 852–872.

Parkin, W. (1989). Private experiences in the public domain: Sexuality and residential care organizations. In J. Hearn, D. L. Sheppard, P. T. Sheriff, & G. Burrell (Eds.), *The sexuality of organization* (pp. 110–124). London: Sage.

Peaden, C. H. (1993). Condillac and the history of rhetoric. *Rhetorica, 11*, 135–156.

Penelope, J. (1990). *Speaking freely: Unlearning the lies of the father's tongue.* New York: Pergamon.

Perelman, C., & Tyteca, L. O. (1969). *The new rhetoric* (J. Wilkinson & P. Weaver, Trans.). Notre Dame, IN: University of Notre Dame Press. (Original work published 1958)

Perry, A. M. & Geist, P. (Eds.) (1997). *Courage of conviction: Women's words, women's wisdom.* Mountain View, CA: Mayfield.

Personal Narrative Group (Ed.). (1989). *Interpreting women's lives: Feminist theories and personal narratives.* Bloomington: Indiana University Press.

Petronio, S. (Ed.) (1994). Special issue: The dialogue of evidence: A topic revisited. *Western Journal of Communication, 58.*

Phelan, S. (1990). Foucault and feminism. *American Journal of Political Science, 34*, 421–439.

Picard, M. (1952). *The world of silence* (S. Godman, Trans.). South Bend, IN: Regnery/Gateway. (Original work published 1948)

Piven, F. F., & Cloward, R. A. (1971). *Regulating the poor: The functions of public welfare.* New York: Pantheon.

Piven, F. F., & Cloward, R. A. (1979). *Poor people's movement.* New York: Vintage Books.

Polanyi, M. (1958). *Personal knowledge.* Chicago: University of Chicago Press.

Polanyi, M. (1969). *Knowing and being.* Chicago: University of Chicago Press.

Pollock, D. (1994). (Un)Becoming "voices": Representing sexual harassment in performance. In S. G. Bingham (Ed.), *Conceptualizing sexual harassment as discursive practice.* Westport, CT: Praeger.

Pondy, L., Morgan, G., Frost, P., & Dandridge, T. (1983). *Organizational symbolism.* Greenwich, CT: JAI Press.

Pringle, R. (1989). Bureaucracy, rationality and sexuality: The case of the secretaries. In J. Hearn, D. L. Sheppard, P. T. Sheriff, & G. Burrell (Eds.), *The sexuality of organization* (pp. 158–177). London: Sage.

Putnam, L. L. (1982, Spring). In search of gender: A critique of communication and sex-roles research. *Women's Studies in Communication, 5*, 1–9.

Putnam, L. L., & Holmer, M. (1992). Framing, reframing, and issue development. In L. L. Putnam & E. Roloff (Eds.), *Communication and negotiation* (pp. 128–155). Beverly Hills, CA: Sage.

Putnam, L. L., & Mumby, D. K. (1993). Organizations, emotion, and the myth of rationality. In S. Fineman (Ed.), *Emotion in organizations* (pp. 36–57). London: Sage.

Putnam, L. L., & Pacanowsky, M. E. (1983). *Communication and organizations: An interpretive approach.* Beverly Hills, CA: Sage.

Putnam, L. L., & Sorenson, R. L. (1982). Equivocal messages in organizations. *Human Communication Research, 8,* 114–132.

Rains, P. M. (1971). *Becoming an unwed mother: A sociological account.* Chicago: Aldine/Atherton.

Ramazanoglu, C. (1993). *Up against Foucault: Explorations of some tensions between Foucault and feminism.* London and New York: Routledge.

Ramirez, R. (1966). Wrapping form and organizational beauty. *Organization, 3,* 233–242.

Rawlins, W. K. (1987). Gregory Bateson and the composition of human communication. *Research on Language and Social Interaction, 20,* 53–77.

Rawlins, W. K. (1998). From ethnographic occupations to ethnographic stances. In J. S. Trent (Ed.), *In communication: Views from the helm for the 21st century.* Boston: Allyn and Bacon.

Ray, E. B. (1996). *Communication and disenfranchisement: Social health issues and implications.* Mahway, NJ: Lawrence Erlbaum.

Redding, W. C. (1979). Organizational communication theory and ideology: An overview. In D. Nimmo (Ed.), *Communication Yearbook 3* (pp. 309–341). New Brunswick, NJ: Transaction Books.

Revesz, G. (1956). *The origins and prehistory of language* (J. Butler, Trans.). New York: Philosophical Library. (Original work published 1946)

Rich, A. (1978). *The dream of a common language: Poems 1974–1977.* New York: Norton.

Rich, A. (1984). *On lies, secrets, and silence: Selected prose 1966–1978.* London: Virago. (Original work published 1979)

Richards, M. C. (1962). *Centering.* Middletown, CT: Wesleyan University Press.

Richardson, L. (1992). The consequences of poetic representation: Writing the other rewriting the self. In C. Ellis & M. G. Flaherty (Eds.), *Investigating subjectivity* (pp. 125–137). Newbury Park, CA: Sage.

Richardson, L. (1995). Narrative and sociology. In J. Van Maanen (Ed.), *Representation in ethnography* (pp. 198–221). Thousand Oaks, CA: Sage.

Ritchie, L. D., & Price, V. (1991). Matters micro and macro: Special issues for communication research. *Communication Research, 18*(2), 133–139.

Roethlisberger, F. L., & Dickson, W. (1939). *Management and the worker.* New York: Wiley.

Ronai, C. R. (1992). The reflexive self through narrative: A night in the life of an erotic dancer/researcher. In C. Ellis & M. G. Flaherty (Eds.), *Investigating subjectivity* (pp. 102–124). Newbury Park, CA: Sage.

Rosen, M. (1985). Breakfast at Spiro's: Dramaturgy and dominance. *Journal of Management Studies, 25*(5), 463–480.

Rosen, M. (1988). You asked for it: Christmas at the bosses' expense. *Journal of Management Studies, 25,* 463–480.

Rothschild, J., & Miethe, T. D. (1994). Whistleblowing as resistance in modern work organizations: The politics of revealing organizational deception and abuse. In J. M. Jermier, D. Knights, & W. R. Nord (Eds.), *Resistance and power in organizations.* London and New York: Routledge.

Rumbaugh, D. M. (1977). Language behavior of apes. In A. M. Schrier (Ed.), *Behavioral primatology* (Vol. 1, pp. 105–138). Hillsdale, NJ: Lawrence Erlbaum.

Sanders, W. (1987). Freedom of speech and private sector at-will employment: Implications for society, the individual, and management. In C. A. B. Osigweh (Ed.), *Communicating employee responsibilities and rights* (pp. 63–72). New York: Quorum.

Sandler, B. (1988). *Sexual harassment: A new issue for institutions, or these are the times that try men's souls.* Paper presented at the Cornell Conference on Sexual Harassment on Campus, New York.

Sandler, B. R. (1992, November). *Confronting sexual harassment on campus.* An interactive teleconference sponsored by the National Association of Student Personnel Administration (NASPA), Washington, DC.

Saville-Troike, M. (1985). The place of silence in an integrated theory of communication. In D. Tannen & M. Saville-Troike (Eds.), *Perspectives on silence* (pp. 3–18). Norwood, NJ: Ablex.

Schaper, E. (1989). Plato and Aristotle on the arts: From prelude to aesthetics. In G. Dickie, R. Sclafana, & R. Roblin (Eds.), *Aesthetics: A critical anthology* (2nd ed.). New York: St. Martin's Press.

Scheibel, D. (1996). Appropriating bodies: Organ(izing) ideology and cultural practice in medical school. *Journal of Applied Communication Research, 24,* 310–331.

Schiappa, E. (1989). The rhetoric of nukespeak. *Communication Monographs, 56,* 253–272.

Schiappa, E. (1991). Defining reality: The politics of meaning. Unpublished manuscript, Purdue University, West Lafayette, IN.

Schiappa, E. (1991). *Protagoras and logos: A study in Greek philosophy and rhetoric.* Columbia: University of South Carolina Press.

Schiappa, E. (1993). Arguing about definitions. *Argumentation, 7,* 403–417.

Scott, J. C. (1991). The evidence of experience. *Critical Inquiry, 17,* 773–797.

Scott, R. L. (1993). Dialectical tensions of speaking and silence. Quarterly Journal of Speech, 79, 1–18.

Sennett, R. (1977). *The fall of public man.* New York: Knopf.

"Sexual harassment: Survey results in Hong Kong." (1992, July 11). *The World Journal,* Hong Kong. (Original Chinese version of the article provided by T. Y. Lau and translated by G. Q. Zhang)

Sexual harassment: Walking the corporate line. (1991) [Film]. Santa Monica, CA: Salinger Films.

Showalter, E. (1985). *The new feminist criticism: Essays on women, literature, and theory.* New York: Pantheon.

Silko, L. M. (1981). *Storyteller.* New York: Seaver Books.

Silvers, A. (1989). Once upon a time in the artworld. In G. Dickie, R. Sclafani, & R. Roblin (Eds.), *Aesthetics: A critical anthology.* New York: St. Martin's Press.

Skolnikoff, S. C. (1982). A cognitive analysis of facial behavior in Old World monkeys, apes, and human beings. In C. T. Snowdon, C. H. Brown, & R. Peterson (Eds.), *Primate communication* (pp. 303–367). Cambridge, UK: Cambridge University Press.

Smart, B. (1986). The politics of truth and the problem of hegemony. In D. Hoy (Ed.), *Foucault: A critical reader* (pp. 157–173). Oxford, UK & New York: Basil Blackwell.

Smircich, L. (1983). Concepts of culture and organizational analysis. *Administrative Science Quarterly, 28,* 339–358.

Smith, A. (1937). *The wealth of nations.* New York: Modern Library/Random House. (Orginal work published 1776)

Smith, B. (1996, June 29). Citadel opens its door after all-male policy ruled unconstitutional. *Journal & Courier,* p. A3.

Smith, D. E. (1987). *The everyday world as problematic.* Milton Keynes, UK: Open University Press.

Smith, R. C. (1990/1993). *In pursuit of synthesis: Activity as a primary framework for organizational communication.* Unpublished dissertation, University of Southern California. Los Angeles, CA. (The 1993 version is an unpublished summary of the dissertation.)

Smith, R. C. (1992). *Images of organizational communication.* Unpublished manuscript, Purdue University.

Smith, R. C. (1993, May). Images of organizational communication: Root-metaphors of the organization-communication relation. Paper presented at the annual meeting of the International Communication Association, Washington, DC.

Smith, R. C., & Eisenberg, E. M. (1987). Conflict at Disneyland: A root-metaphor analysis. *Communication Monographs, 54,* 368–380.

Snavely, B. K., & Fairhurst, G. T. (1984). The male nursing student as a token. *Research in Nursing and Health, 7,* 287–293.

Snowdon, C. T., Brown, C. H., & Peterson, M. R. (1982). Linguistic and psycholinguistic approaches to primate communication. In C. T. Snowden, C. H. Brown, & M. R. Peterson (Eds.), *Primate communication.* Cambridge: Cambridge University Press.

Solomon, C. M. (1990). Careers under glass. *Personnel Journal, 69,* 99–105.

Spender, D. (1980). *Man made language* (2nd ed.). London: Routledge & Kegan Paul.

Spender, D. (Ed.). (1983). *Feminist theories.* New York: Pantheon.

Spender, D. (1984). Defining reality: A powerful tool. In C. Kramarae, M. Schulz, & W. M. O'Barr (Eds.), *Language and power* (pp. 194–205). Beverly Hills, CA: Sage.

Stack, C. B. (1974). *All our kin: Strategies for survival in a black community.* New York: Harper & Row.

Stahl, S. D. (1989). *Literary folklores and the personal narrative.* Bloomington: Indiana University Press.

Stecker, R. (1989). The end of an institutional definition of art. In G. Dickie, R. Sclafani, & R. Roblin (Eds.), *Aesthetics: A critical analogy* (2nd ed.; pp. 206–213). New York: St. Martin's Press.

Steinem, G. (1992). *Revolution from within: A book of self-esteem.* Boston: Little, Brown.

Stewart, L. P. (1981). Whistleblowing: Implications for organizational communication. *Journal of Communication, 30*(4), 90–101.

Stienstra, D. (1994). *Women's movements and international organizations.* New York: St. Martin's Press.

238   REFERENCES

Stolnitz, J. (1989). The aesthetic attitude: From aesthetics and philosophy of art criticism. In G. Dickie, R. Sclafani, & R. Roblin (Eds.), *Aesthetics: A critical anthology* (pp. 334–341). New York: St. Martin's Press.

Strati, A. (1996). Organizations viewed through the lens of aesthetics. *Organization, 3*, 209–218.

Strine, M. S. (1992). Understanding "how things work": Sexual harassment and academic culture. *Journal of Applied Communication, 20*, 391–400.

Stross, B. (1976). *The origin and evolution of language.* Dubuque, IA: Wm. C. Brown.

Swadesh, M. (1951). Diffusional cummulation and archaic residue as historical explanations. *Southwestern Journal of Anthropology, 7*, 1–21.

Tancred-Sheriff, P. (1985). Women's experience, women's knowledge and the power of knowledge. *Atlantis, 10*, 106–117.

Tancred-Sheriff, P. (1989). Gender, sexuality, and organization theory. In J. Hearn, D. L. Sheppard, P. T. Sheriff, & G. Burrell (Eds.), *The sexuality of organization* (pp. 45–55). London: Sage.

Tangri, S. S., Burt, M. R., & Johnson, L. B. (1982). Sexual harassment at work: Three explanatory models. *Journal of Social Issues, 38*(4), 33–54.

Tannen, D., & Saville-Troike, M. (1985). *Perspectives on silence.* Norwood, NJ: Ablex.

Tanner, N. M. (1981). *On becoming human.* Cambridge: Cambridge University Press.

Tanner, N. M., & Zihlman, A. (1976). Discussion paper: The evolution of human communication: What can primates tell us? *Annals New York Academy of Sciences, 279–280*, 467–480.

Taylor, B. C. (1996). Make bomb, save world: Reflections on dialogic nuclear ethnography. *Journal of Contemporary Ethnography, 25*, 120–143.

Taylor, B., & Conrad, C. R. (1992). Narratives of sexual harassment: Organizational dimensions. *Journal of Applied Communication, 20*, 401–418.

Terpstra, D. E., & Baker, D. D. (1988). Outcomes of sexual harassment charges. *Academy of Management Journal, 31*, 185–194.

Thomas, C. S. (1982). *Sex discrimination in a nutshell.* St. Paul, MN: West Publishing.

Tilghman, B. R. (1989). Reflections on aesthetic theory. In G. Dickie, R. Sclafani, & R. Roblin (Eds.), *Aesthetics: A critical anthology.* New York: St. Martin's Press.

Tolstoy, L. (1960). *What is Art?* (A. Maude, Trans.). Indianapolis, IN: Hackett. (Original work published 1896)

Tong, R. (1989). *Feminist thought.* Boulder, CO: Westview.

Trethewey, A. (1992). *Power, discourse, and the confessing subject: A poststructuralist feminist analysis of a human service organization.* Paper presented at the annual meeting of the Central States Speech Association, Cincinnati, OH.

Trigger, B. G. (1990). *The Huron: Farmers of the north* (2nd ed.). Fort Worth: Harcourt Brace Jovanovich.

Trujillo, N. (1992). Interpreting (the work and the talk of) baseball: Perspectives on ballpark culture. *Western Journal of Communication, 56*, 350–371.

Trujillo, N. (1993). Interpreting November 22: A critical ethnography of an assassination site. *Quarterly Journal of Speech, 79,* 447–466.

Trujillo, N., & Dionisopoulos, G. (1987). Cop talk, police stories, and the social construction of organizational drama. *Central States Speech Journal, 38*(3 & 4), 196–209.

Ukens, C. (1991). Sexual harassment: A fact of pharmacy life. *Drug Topics, 135,* 16–18.

United States Merit Systems Protection Board. (1981). *Sexual harassment in the federal workplace: Is it a problem?* (MS 1.2: Se9). Washington, DC: Government Printing Office.

United States Merit Systems Protection Board. (1988). *Sexual harassment in the federal government: An update.* Washington, DC: Government Printing Office.

van Dijk, T. (Ed.) (1997a). *Discourse as structure and process: A multidisciplinary introduction* (Vol. 1). London: Sage.

van Dijk, T. (Ed.) (1997b). *Discourse as social interaction. Discourse studies: A multidisciplinary introduction* (Vol. 2). London: Sage.

Van Maanen, J. (Ed.). (1995). *Representation in ethnography.* Thousand Oaks, CA: Sage.

van Manen, M. (1990). *Researching lived experience: Human science for an action sensitive pedagogy.* Albany: State University of New York Press.

Violanti, M. T. (1996). Hooked on expectations: An analysis of influence and relationships in the tailhook reports. *Journal of Applied Communication Research, 24,* 67–82.

Waggoner, C. E. (1997). The emancipatory potential of feminine masquerade in Mary Kay cosmetics. *Text and Performance Quarterly, 17,* 256–272.

Wagner, E. J. (1992). *Sexual harassment in the workplace: How to prevent, investigate and resolve problems in your organization.* New York: Amacom Books.

Wander, P. (1983). The aesthetics of fascism. *Journal of Communication, 33,* 70–78.

Warren, C. (1996). *Subject shifting and shape changing: The sexually abusive female therapist as media scapegoat.* Paper presented at the annual meeting of International Communication Association, Chicago.

Watzlawick, P. (1978). *The language of change: Elements of therapeutic communication.* New York: Basic Books.

Watzlawick, P., Beavin, J. B., & Jackson, D. (1967). *Pragmatics of human communication.* New York: Norton.

Weber, M. (1947). *The theory of social and economic organizations* (T. Parsons, Trans.). New York: Oxford University Press.

Weedon, C. (1987). *Feminist practice and poststructuralist theory.* New York: Basil Blackwell.

Weick, K. E. (1979). *The social psychology of organizing* (2nd ed.). New York: Random House.

Weitz, M. (1989). Art as an open concept: From the opening mind. In G. Dickie, R. Sclafani, & R. Roblin (Eds.), *Aesthetics: A critical anthology.* New York: St. Martin's Press.

Werhane, P. H. (1987). Defining and communicating employee and employer rights in an institutional context. In C. A. B. Osigweh (Ed.), *Communication employee responsibilities and rights* (pp. 41–52). New York: Quorum.

West, C. (1993). *Race matters*. Boston: Beacon Press.

White, D. A. (1996). "It's working beautifully!" Philosophical reflections on aesthetics and organization theory. *Organization, 3*, 195–208.

Whitson, S., & Poulakos, J. (1993). Nietzsche and the aesthetics of rhetoric. *Quarterly Journal of Speech, 79*, 131–145.

Williams, C. L. (1989). *Gender differences at work: Women and men in nontraditional occupations*. Berkeley: University of California Press.

Williams, D. S. (1995). *The discursive politics of sexual harassment: A feminist poststructuralist reading of the Hill-Thomas hearings*. Unpublished doctoral dissertation, Purdue University, West Lafayette, IN.

Willis, P. E. (1977). *Learning to labour: How working class kids get working class jobs*. Farnborough, UK: Saxon House.

Wolf, M. (1992). *A thrice told tale: Feminism, postmodernism & ethnographic responsibility*. Stanford, CA: Stanford University Press.

Woman-beater is to wed. (1995, July 15). *Chicago Tribune*, sec. 1, p. 7.

Women's Action Coalition (WAC). (1993). *WAC Stats: The facts about women*. New York: The New Press.

Wood, J. T. (1992). Telling our stories: Narratives as a basis for theorizing sexual harassment. *Journal of Applied Communication Research, 20*, 349–362.

Wood, J. T. (1994). Saying it makes it so: The discursive construction of sexual harassment. In S. Bingham (Ed.), *Conceptualizing sexual harassment as discursive practice* (pp. 17–30). Westport, CT: Praeger.

Wood, J. T., & Conrad, C. (1983). Paradox in the experiences of professional women. *Western Journal of Speech Communication, 47*, 305–322.

Wood, J. T., & Cox, J. R. (1993). Rethinking critical voice: Materiality and situated knowledges. *Western Journal of Communication, 57*, 278–287.

Wuthnow, R., Hunter, J. D., Bergesen, A., & Kurzweil, E. (1984). *Cultural analysis: The work of Peter L. Berger, Mary Douglas, Michel Foucault, and Jurgen Habermas*. London: Routledge & Kegan Paul.

APPENDIX A

Men Suffer, Too: A Story of Sexual Harassment by Michael Gray

Sexual harassment is finally being talked about everywhere today, thanks to a few well-publicized cases. Even though some of the talk is derisive, this could be the best chance I'll get to tell my story. It may seem an unusual twist to an already complex subject. It may just be that I'm the first to speak up about it.

In November of 1989 I began employment at a medical facility in the [city where I live] area. I was one of quite a number of male nursing assistants employed there. After a month-long orientation, professionally conducted and seemingly helpful, I went to work on my assigned floor, where all I learned in orientation became superfluous. There were many times when I volunteered for duties on the floor but was effectively stopped from doing my job by my co-workers. They rejected my enthusiasm by saying, "That doesn't need to be done," or, "I want to do that later." I often worked alone for the first three hours of our third-shift work day so that my co-workers could sleep in a lounge (something they were not supposed to do). I thought I was being a willing worker and a nice guy.

Within weeks, an incident occurred that told me something was going on and that it was aimed in my direction.

I was sitting at a table with my fellow nursing assistants, all female, when I suddenly became the object of an inquisition. They demanded to know if I was a virgin, if I had ever had oral sex, if I had ever been with a black woman, and so on. I found this line of questioning inappropriate, since it had nothing to do with our work responsibilities. I asked that the subject be dropped. Eventually it was, when the women decided to get up and do some work.

I am no goodie-two-shoes prude. It is important for all of us to maintain a sense of humor. However, this sort of hostile baiting is in no way humorous, especially from co-workers of the opposite sex who have more seniority.

I reported this incident to the head nurse (also a man) on the floor soon afterward. Our shift supervisor was present at the time it occurred, but said nothing; she even seemed amused by it. The head nurse indicated that I should get used to such things, because they happen all the time in such institutions. I accepted this because I felt I had no choice.

After the first of the year, I was summoned to a meeting with several administrative officers of the facility, given my first job evaluation, and summarily fired. I was in shock. The things said about me were nearly all exaggerations. Some had no basis in fact at all.

I was offered the opportunity to quit. I preferred being fired. This would give me the opportunity to fight for my unemployment benefits. I did so, and to my amazement, I won. It was ruled that the distrustful working relationship was not particularly my fault and that I was often not communicated with properly. I then filed a charge of sexual harassment with the Equal Employment Opportunity Commission.

About two weeks later, the most astonishing thing about this entire incident came to light for me, almost by accident. I was having lunch in a local restaurant when I spotted someone I knew and worked with briefly at the facility. The individual walked over and sat down beside me.

"I told myself that if I ever saw you again, I would tell you what they did to you," began the story I was finally told. This person revealed to me that while I was still employed at the facility, the head nurse came in on a night I was off-duty and held a floor meeting with all my co-workers. He passed out copies of magazine articles about schizophrenia and multiple personality. He stated that I fit the descriptions to a T, and indicated that he wanted input on just what to do with me.

The very idea of such a slanderous, amateur diagnosis from an unqualified person is enough to take one's breath away. But from a trusted health-care professional? And to deliberately publicize it! My work environment needed no additional poisoning. I added this information to my initial charge with the E.E.O.C.

In my case, the harassment was so inescapably obvious that no one even attempted to deny it. However, the Commission ruled that my co-workers were counseled about their abusive behavior and the harassment stopped at that time; ignoring the vicious and retaliatory floor meeting in which I was labeled for the rest of my life. The Commission ruled that poor work performance was the reason for dismissal, even though I and my work were affected by the hostile environment.

The most frightening aspect of this story is the fact that the administration of the facility probably knew all along what was happening to me and allowed it to continue, virtually approving of it as some sort of practical business measure. It is truly difficult to sue the State of [state in which I reside] or a facility that accepts state funds. Most attorneys shy away from defamation suits because they are not profitable, even though it's plain to see I've been wronged. The state demands that actual damage or loss, usually monetary, be incurred before reparations are in order. In essence, it seems the state is saying that if you don't have a fortune, a business, or a stellar reputation to lose, you don't have anything to lose. Not even the state ACLU would express interest in my case.

My character was assassinated. I couldn't work for over a year. I still have fears about jumping into the job market in this area. I feel I'm left with little to look forward to and entirely too much to explain. All I expected were my human and civil rights. What I received was inhuman. Worst of all, my relationships with women were damaged and clouded in ways too deep to speak of.

My tax dollars and yours are sometimes used to support the health care industry. I think portions of it are out of control. We should consider what might happen to [the state's] precious business climate should the rest of the world discover how backward this state is. Perhaps that's an asset in someone's eyes. There's nothing like an easily exploited workforce in these times.

I have awfully little faith left in state and federal agencies, especially the Equal Employment Opportunity Commission. Can you blame me? It almost sounds as though some of our bureaucrats are too busy harassing and intimidating others to investigate charges of harassment and intimidation.

APPENDIX B

Schedule of Interview Questions

1. Was your story edited (minor or major revisions)?
2. What was your title at work?
3. Have you stayed in the medical field?
4. What are your future plans?
5. Could you detail the harassment experience? For example, what do you think prompted the nurses to act in a sexually harassing manner toward you? How many women harassed you? Were there any other incidents of sexual harassment, other than what you mentioned in your article?
6. Do you know if they, the female nurses, did this to any other men or women?
7. In your story you say that you reported this to the head nurse, who was a man, and that you found out later that he had concocted stories about your being a schizophrenic, but first he told you to get used to it, that these things happen all the time. Can you recall if these were his exact words and if he gave you any other advice about the situation (good or bad)? Why do you think the head nurse made up these stories about you? What purpose would it serve?
8. What prompted you to report this to the EEOC? Did you receive encouragement from friends, relatives, or your coworkers?
9. Would you describe your visit to the EEOC? Would you describe their follow-up on the matter?
10. Did you ever witness the female nurses being harassed, perhaps by doctors?
11. Did anyone suggest in any way that you may have misunderstood the intentions or the behavior of the nurses who harassed you?
12. Did anyone suggest that you drop the matter for the sake of the organization or morale or any other reason?
13. You said the head nurse told you to get used to it because "it happens all the time." Did anyone else suggest this to you?
14. Did anyone make a joke or trivialize what you were experiencing?

15. Did you actually label it as harassment at the time of the occurrence?

16. How did other people suggest you handle the situation? Did anyone suggest that this should be handled at the personal level?

17. How did you respond to the nurses' comments at first? Did you ever tell these nurses that you had a girlfriend whether you do or not, just to get them to stop? Did you ignore their comments at first? You said that you asked that the subject be dropped, can you remember exactly how you asked them?

18. What was the most frustrating aspect of this whole experience for you?

19. What would you tell other men or women who find themselves in similar situations?

20. How has this experience with sexual harassment affected your life?

21. Would you tell me about writing the article that appeared in the newspaper?

NAME INDEX

SUBJECT INDEX